TEXAS MUSEUMS: A GUIDEBOOK

Sponsored by the Texas Association of Museums

TEXAS MUSEUMS

A GUIDEBOOK *by Paula Eyrich Tyler and Ron Tyler*

UNIVERSITY OF TEXAS PRESS, AUSTIN

International Standard Book Number
0-292-78062-1 (cloth); 0-292-78063-X (paper)
Library of Congress Catalog Card Number
83-80350
Copyright © 1983 by the University of Texas
Press
First edition, 1983
Requests for permission to reproduce material
from this work should be sent to Permissions,
University of Texas Press, Box 7819, Austin,
Texas 78712.

For reasons of economy and speed, this volume has been printed from computer-generated
tapes furnished by the authors, who assume full
responsibility for its contents.

ACKNOWLEDGMENTS

As inveterate museum-goers, we have visited and revisited dozens of museums throughout the state. In many instances, we have obtained our information firsthand, although in most cases we have had to rely on the employees and volunteers of the institutions themselves to provide accurate information. We would like to thank everyone who kindly and promptly responded to our frequent questionnaires. It is impossible, in the amount of space that we have been provided, even to list the names of those without whom this project would have been impossible, but for whatever measure of success we have achieved, we are indebted to their generous cooperation as well as to the assistance of the staff of the Museum Services Division of the Texas Historical Commission and Phil Martin of the Texas Association of Museums. We would especially like to thank John Crain of the Dallas Historical Society and James C. Martin of the San Jacinto Museum of History for reading the introduction and offering helpful suggestions and corrections. Cindy Leo of the Texas Historical Commission read the introduction and offered valuable suggestions and made the project feasible in the beginning by supplying names and addresses for many of the institutions.

Finally, we would like to thank John McFarlen, president of Software Publishers, Inc., of Arlington, whose friendship and talent with computers made the project possible.

INTRODUCTION

The time has long passed when museums could be considered awesome, stuffy, depopulated buildings preserving a few esoteric objects. For the past several years the leading public attraction in the nation has not been a football or baseball team but the Metropolitan Museum of Art. The same desire to see the curious, beautiful, or historic has led to increased attendance in Texas museums as well. This book is intended as an introduction to the diversity and wealth of the state's museums. We do not offer it as a definitive study, or even a complete listing, of Texas museums, but rather as a guide to the more than 540 institutions that exhibit art, history, natural history, science and technology, or archaeology to the public.

Museums are a relatively recent development, even in the history of America. When Charles Willson Peale opened his exhibition of art, natural history, and science as the first public museum in the United States in 1786, he followed the debut of the British Museum, the first modern government-sponsored museum, by only thirty-three years. Perhaps the first museum in Texas was nothing more than the exhibition in a local hotel room of an itinerant limner's portrait samples, but in 1879 Sam Houston Normal Institute (now State University) established a museum to preserve materials relating to Sam Houston, president of the Republic and senator and governor of the state, and in 1881 Albert Fredrich began the collection of horns that became the Buckhorn Hall of Horns in San Antonio. By the turn of the century the Museum of Human Anatomy at the Medical Branch of the University of Texas (1890), the Strecker Museum at Baylor University in Waco (1893), and the teaching museum at Our Lady of the Lake College in San Antonio (1896) were in operation, and art associations throughout the state had given birth to fledgling art galleries in Houston, Dallas, San Antonio, Fort Worth, and several other cities.

A few museums, such as the Texas Confederate Museum (1904), were established during the early twentieth century to honor the state's heroes and war dead, and the Witte Museum in San Antonio dates from 1926. But the 1936 Centennial celebration of Texas independence was the major impetus to museum-building in the state. Several buildings were constructed in Fair Park in Dallas, which was the official headquarters for the celebration, and museums were also built in El Paso, Houston, Austin, Huntsville, and other cities. The Museum of Art, Hall of State, Museum of Natural History, Aquarium, Garden Center, and Health and Science Museum in Dallas, the San Jacinto Museum of History in Houston, the Texas Memorial Museum in Austin, the Sam Houston Memorial Museum in Huntsville, and the El Paso Centennial Museum all date from this cultural and building boom during the 1930s.

The 1976 National Bicentennial inspired even more effort as local historical societies throughout Texas established museums in old jails, courthouses, railroad depots, and other historic buildings, and museums already in existence added to their space and installed new exhibitions. Museums have been established in the remains of Spanish missions and old forts and in the homes of such famous men and women as the writer O. Henry, the sculptor Elisabet Ney, and Presidents Dwight D. Eisenhower and Lyndon Johnson. Exhibitions have been set up at the sites of battlegrounds and Indian settlements and on board the first battleship to carry the state's name.

Museum growth since World War II has been phenomenal. Long famous for its philanthropists, Texas is fortunate that a number of them chose to establish museums. Perhaps the Kimbell Art Museum and the Amon Carter Museum in Fort Worth are the most obvious examples, but the McNay Art Museum in San Antonio, the Stark Museum of Art in Orange, Bayou Bend in Houston, the Sid Richardson Collection of Western Art in Fort Worth, and the Diamond M Museum in Snyder also owe their existence to the inspiration of a single collector or family.

The McNay Art Museum opened to the public in 1954, housed in Marion Koogler McNay's Mexican-Mediterranean style mansion and exhibiting her sensitive mix of French paintings, with masterpieces by Cézanne, Gauguin, Redon, and Picasso, as well as a stunning group of nineteenth- and twentieth-century American watercolors. The Amon Carter Museum followed in 1961, presenting the unexcelled collection of paintings and sculpture by Frederic Remington and Charles M. Russell that Amon G. Carter, Sr., had accumulated in his pursuit of art of the American West. In 1966 the Houston Museum of Fine Arts opened Bayou Bend, the mansion that John F. Staub had designed for Miss Ima Hogg and her brothers, with their encyclopedic collection of American furniture, paintings, silver, and china. The Kimbell Art Museum, based on the collection of European and British paintings that Kay Kimbell had acquired during his lifetime, opened in 1972, and in 1978 the Stark Museum of Art, containing H. J. Lutcher Stark's vast assortment of American paintings and sculpture, rare books, letters, manuscripts, prints, American Indian artifacts, Steuben glass, and porcelains, opened its doors. The Sid Richardson Collection of Western Art in Fort Worth, the latest of these galleries, opened in 1982.

Other museums not named for individual donors have benefited from generous gifts. The El Paso Museum of Art received fifty-seven old master paintings and two sculptures from the Samuel H. Kress Foundation in 1961, and the museums of the University of Texas at Austin have been given a large group of Texas artist Frank Reaugh's paintings, novelist James Michener's collection of twentieth-century American art, C. R. Smith's collection of American western art, and many more. The Hogg Brothers' collection of paintings by Frederic Remington is a perennial attraction at the Museum of Fine Arts, Houston, as is the huge nineteenth-century scene by Frederic Edwin Church entitled *The Icebergs*, given anonymously to the Dallas Museum of Art.

Nor have outstanding acquisitions by Texas museums been limited to gifts. The nation perhaps first became aware of Texas museums' serious commitment to quality in 1965 when the Fort Worth Art Museum acquired a major painting by Picasso during a nationally televised benefit auction, with the money going to assist in the restoration of flood-damaged art treasures in northern Italy. With its recent purchases of paintings by Georges de la Tour, Chardin, Velázquez, and Picasso, the Kimbell Art Museum in Fort Worth has become internationally recognized as a leader in the quest for masterpieces. The Museum of Fine Arts, Houston, won much publicity for its recent acquisition of a well-known Picasso, while the Amon Carter Museum in Fort Worth continues to enlarge upon the holdings of its original donor in the field of nineteenth- and early twentieth-century American art with purchases of stunning works by American masters, such as William Michael

Harnett, Martin Johnson Heade, and William Merritt Chase.

Significant exhibitions have also brought Texas museums into the spotlight. The recent El Greco exhibition at the Dallas Museum of Art is perhaps the best example, in terms of both scholarly reception and public response, but the era of "blockbuster" exhibits in Texas dates at least from the 1973 Kimbell exhibition of the French Impressionists from the Hermitage Museum in the Soviet Union. The Museum of Fine Arts, Houston, followed in 1974 with an exhibition of Old Masters from Russia, and the more recent and much-heralded exhibition of paintings by Cézanne drew record crowds. The Dallas Museum of Art subsequently played host to "Pompeii A.D. 79" and "Shakespeare and the Globe," while the Kimbell exhibited "The Bronze Age of China," which drew more than 280,000 in attendance. History and natural science museums have joined in the contest for the public eye, as the Fort Worth Museum of Science and History recently exhibited a huge show entitled "Creativity," and the Houston Museum of Natural Science displayed the exhibition of gold objects and artifacts from Peru.

Large and important exhibitions have almost become routine today, but there is a further development that demonstrates significant growth and maturity among the state's museums. Texas museums have long shown exhibitions organized by other institutions, but recently they have begun to research and organize some of their own shows. One of the most outstanding Bicentennial exhibitions in the nation was organized by the Amon Carter Museum, which has a twenty-year record of producing its own shows. "The Face of Liberty" included the famous Gilbert Stuart portraits of George and Martha Washington as well as portraits of Benjamin Franklin, Thomas Jefferson, and other well-known Revolutionary figures. The exhibition of Gustave Caillebotte's paintings at the Museum of Fine Arts, Houston, established his scholarly reputation, Frank Stella reemerged in an exhibit at the Fort Worth Art Museum, and the more recent series of exhibitions organized by the Kimbell—Vigée Le Brun, Japanese Buddhist sculpture from the sixth through the thirteenth centuries, and Ribera—have all won national critical acclaim.

Not all the attention has been devoted to exhibitions. Over the years museum trustees have become aware of the role of the museum itself as a work of art. The first bold stroke occurred in 1954 when the Houston Museum of Fine Arts commissioned Ludwig Mies van der Rohe, one of the great twentieth-century architects, to design its new wing. Cullinan Hall opened in 1954, and the master plan was finished with the addition of the Brown Pavilion in 1974. Philip Johnson, one of Mies's followers, designed the Amon Carter Museum (1961) and the Art Museum of South Texas (1972) in Corpus Christi, and Louis I. Kahn of Philadelphia designed one of the great museums in the country in the Kimbell Art Museum (1972). Recently the Cambridge Seven, a Connecticut design group, won plaudits for its striking renovation of the old Lone Star brewery for the San Antonio Museum of Art, and the Dallas Museum of Art commissioned Edward Larrabee Barnes, the architect of the very successful Walker Art Center in Minneapolis, to design its new building in the downtown cultural district.

The most numerous group of museums in the state is the history museums, which range from tiny collections of artifacts exhibited in an old log cabin to the massive Panhandle-Plains Historical Museum in Canyon, the largest state-owned museum as well as the oldest, founded in 1929. Like the Panhandle-Plains Museum, the Dallas Historical Society was the beneficiary of the Works Progress Administration program whereby talented artists painted murals in state-owned buildings. The Historical Society, which occupies the Hall of State in Fair Park, boasts handsome murals in which famous characters and various events in the history of the state are depicted.

A vital appreciation of the state's history can be seen in those cities-as-museums, San Antonio and Galveston. San Antonio has refurbished its downtown section and riverwalk to the point that it is one of the most charming in the nation. Within easy walking distance of the winding San Antonio River are several museums, unique either in themselves, such as the Alamo, the "shrine of Texas liberty," or in their approach to the history of the state, such as the Institute of Texan Cultures in San Antonio, which is organized according to the ethnic groups that settled the state. Other museums that elaborate on San Antonio's heritage and the Hispanic contribution to Texas are located in the same area.

Galveston, equally as enticing and representative of a totally different era and culture, offers the museums and shops lining The Strand, the "Wall Street of the Gulf," that recall the glory days of Texas's major port before the 1900 devastation of the city by hurricane, a tall ship, the *Elissa*, and a new and innovative Center for Transportation.

As one might expect, oil, which has played an overwhelming role in the history and economy of the state, is also represented among the museums. At least three are devoted exclusively to telling the story of oil and energy development: the East Texas Oil Museum in Kilgore, the Permian Basin Petroleum Museum in Midland, and the Western Company Museum in Fort Worth. Several of the state's large history and natural history museums, such as the Houston Museum of Natural Science, also have large exhibitions devoted to the history of oil and its technology.

Transportation also claims its share of interest, with the San Antonio Museum of Transportation and the Pate Museum of Transportation outside Fort Worth steadily enlarging their collections. The Panhandle-Plains Historical Museum has a large display devoted to transportation, from the buggies and wagons of pioneer West Texas to the automobile, and perhaps the greatest homage to trains in the state is Galveston's new Center for Transportation and Commerce.

The most unusual museum in the state is probably the Confederate Air Force Flying Museum, a large collection of World War II airplanes that are all in working condition. Located in Harlingen, the Confederate Air Force puts its more than 100 vintage aircrafts through their paces each October, with a few enemy planes thrown in to heighten the drama, but the Spitfires, Mustangs, and Flying Fortresses are on exhibit year-round.

Even in a state as historically rich as Texas, however, museums are not mired in the past. The Fort Worth Museum of Science and History, with its new Omni Theater and laser shows, gives a taste of the future as well as of the aesthetics of science and technology. Two other sites provide a look into ongoing research as well as a sense of the past: the National Aeronautics and Space Administration's headquarters in Houston and the University of Texas McDonald Observatory just outside Fort Davis. Tours and exhibitions are available at both facilities, even though they are both involved in the forefront of research in their respective fields.

While it is apparent that the quality and variety of museums in the state are great, the staggering reality is that the number of museums has increased almost geometrically in the past decade. In 1952 the editors of the *Handbook of Texas* set out to list the most important museums in the state in a four-paragraph-long article; in 1976 they estimated the number of museums at more than 200. Only two years later, the Texas Historical Commission published a directory of 410 museums, which the commission defined as "organized and permanent nonprofit institutions, essentially educational or aesthetic in purpose, which exhibit objects with intrinsic value to science, history, art, or culture, and which are open to the public."

We have been more relaxed in our definition, seeking instead institutions that have exhibitions open to the public—hence our inclusion of state parks, zoos, and other institutions which feature instructional displays and programs. Perhaps this partially explains the increased number of listings—over 500—in this guide, but, in fact, the number of museums in the state has continued its rapid increase. The latest figures from the Texas Historical Commission list a total of more than 600 institutions either open to the public or in one phase or another of being built, staffed in most instances by volunteers. Hoping to make this guide as current as possible, we have not included museums that are not yet open.

Ten regional maps of the state have been provided to assist you in planning your visits. Each entry contains addresses, instructions on how to find the museum when we thought it necessary, and telephone numbers. We have described what you might expect to see at the museum, have called attention to any outstanding displays or collections that might be of particular interest, and have listed the hours that the museum is open as well as the admission charge, if any. Symbols provide additional information that might be of practical value, such as whether there is a bookstore, gift shop, or restaurant, whether a person in a wheelchair would have access to the exhibitions, and the designated status of certain historical structures or sites. The symbols are:

*	Accredited by the American Association of Museums
H	Adequate access for the handicapped
R	Restaurant or snackbar
B	Bookstore or gift shop
T	Historical marker placed by the Texas Historical Commission or other state agency
N	National Register
HABS	Historic American Buildings Survey

Abilene Fine Arts Museum

801 S. Mockingbird   Abilene 79605
915/673-4587   H, B

Located in Oscar Rose Park, the Abilene Fine Arts Museum features twelve to sixteen different exhibitions each year, which range from recent work by Texas artists to works of the masters such as Picasso and Goya, as well as exhibitions from its small permanent collection of paintings, sculpture, prints, artists' books, and decorative arts. The museum also sponsors an annual competition for the best work by regional artists.

Open Tuesday through Friday from 9 A.M. to 5 P.M., Saturday and Sunday, 1 to 5 P.M. Admission, free.

The gallery of the Abilene Fine Arts Museum.

Abilene Zoological Gardens

U.S. 36 at Loop 322   Abilene 79604
914/672-9771

The Abilene Zoological Gardens is a small zoo containing mammals, birds, reptiles, and amphibians.

Open from Memorial Day through Labor Day, Monday through Friday from 10 A.M. to 5 P.M., Saturday and Sunday from 10 A.M. to 7 P.M. After Labor Day and to Memorial Day, daily from 10 A.M. to 5 P.M. Closed New Year's Day, Thanksgiving, and Christmas. Admission, adults $1; seniors over 59 and children, $.50. Group rates are available. No charge for members.

ACU Museum

1602 Campus Court   Abilene 79601
915/677-1911, Ext. 2266   B

The ACU Museum was established in 1976 and is dedicated to the history of Abilene Christian University, which was founded in 1906. Housed in the former G. L. Jennings residence built in 1929, the museum collection contains a wall hanging featuring various scenes from the history of the university in fabric art-stitchery, embroidery, and appliqué as well as a number of other items relating to ACU.

Open on Sunday afternoons and special occasions. Admission, free.

ALBANY
Map 10

Fort Griffin State Historical Park

15 miles north of Albany on U.S. 283
Albany 76430
915/762-3592   H, T, N, HABS

Federal troops established Fort Griffin on the Clear Fork of the Brazos River in 1867 as part of the post–Civil War defense of the Texas frontier. Abandoned in 1881, the fort site presently includes a restored bakery, two replicas of enlisted men's huts, and ruins of various stone buildings. The visitor center contains a small exhibit outlining the military, civilian, and Indian activities associated with the fort.

Open daily from 8 A.M. to 5 P.M. Admission, $2 for car park entrance fee.

Ledbetter Picket House

700 Railroad Street   Albany 76430
915/762-3087   T

The W. H. Ledbetter House, a restored frontier ranch home with period furnishing, is one of the few remaining picket houses in which the rough hewn boards are placed upright on a log sill to form the walls. Spaces between the boards are then filled with clay, mud, or stucco. The house contains the relics of the Ledbetter Salt Works, founded in 1860.

Open daily from 8 A.M. to 5 P.M. Admission, free.

The Old Jail Foundation, Inc.

Route 1, Box 1   Albany 76430
915/762-2269   T, N

Built in 1878 to contain such desperados as "Hurricane Bill" and John Selman, the old Albany Jail has now been restored and turned into an Art Research Center that is both an exhibition hall and an expanding art reference library. The permanent collection includes drawings,

The Ledbetter Pickett House, Albany. Photograph by Todd Webb. Courtesy Amon Carter Museum, Fort Worth.

prints, and paintings by well-known European and American artists. The gallery of Oriental art includes terra-cotta tomb figures from the Han, Wei, Sui, and T'ang dynasties, art of later dynasties, and Japanese, Cambodian, and Indian art. Works by American, West German, Belgian, and Italian sculptors are exhibited in the Marshall R. Young Courtyard.

The jail was designed by Texas architect John S. Thomas of Thomas and Woerner, who was also the designer of the Tarrant County Courthouse in Fort Worth.

Open Thursday, Friday, and Saturday from 10 A.M. to 5 P.M., Sunday from 2 to 6 P.M. Admission, free.

ALICE
Map 5

South Texas Museum

66 S. Wright (one block south of South Main)
Alice 78332
512/668-8891

The old McGill Brothers ranching headquarters, which is patterned after the architecture of the Alamo in San Antonio, provides a home for the South Texas Museum, which displays material related to agriculture and ranching in South Texas. Farming equipment, ranching tools such as branding irons and barbed wire, carpenter tools, sewing machines, and old irons are among the many items on exhibit. A recent addition is a photographic exhibit of railroad locomotives with artifacts such as railroad ties, watches, lan-

South Texas Museum, Alice.

terns, and other items reminiscent of early day railroading.

Open Tuesday through Friday from 1 to 5 P.M., Saturday from 10 A.M. to 5 P.M. Closed Sunday and Monday. Admission, free, but a donation is appreciated.

ALPINE
Map 8

Museum of the Big Bend
Sul Ross State University
U.S. 90 Entrance   Alpine 79830
915/837-8143   B

The Museum of the Big Bend presents exhibitions that relate primarily to the Big Bend region, including historical material from prehistoric times to the twentieth century. Prime ranch land today, the Big Bend country was the last stronghold of the Apaches as they resisted being placed on reservations. Ranchers began to move into the area at the close of the Mexican War in 1848, and settlement increased, particularly after the railroad was completed through the Trans-Pecos in 1882. Of special interest are photographs and other historical material relating to the Mexican Revolution, ranching, and settlement in the Big Bend.

Open Tuesday through Saturday, 9 A.M. to 5 P.M., Sunday 1 to 5 P.M. Closed on Monday. Admission, free.

ALTO
Map 2

Caddoan Mounds State Historic Site

Six miles southwest on S.H. 21   Alto 75925
409/858-3218   H, T, N

Also known as the George C. Davis site, Caddoan Mounds includes two ceremonial mounds, a burial mound, and much of a village site of the prehistoric Caddo Indians of East Texas. An interpretive exhibit in the visitor center presents information on the mound builders. A full-scale reconstruction of a Caddoan house and wayside exhibits are included on the self-guided tour through the site. A program of experimental archaeology is planned to use the house for special study purposes.

Open daily from 8 A.M. to 5 P.M. Day use fee, adults, $.50; children, 6 to 12, $.25.

ALVIN
Map 4

Alvin Museum

Science Building
Alvin Community College   Alvin 77511
713/331-6458   H

The Alvin Museum, which contains various artifacts and photographs relating to the southeast Texas area, is devoted to local history. The city, located in northeastern Brazoria County, was incorporated in 1893, after the Houston Tap and Brazoria Railroad connected Richmond with Galveston in 1876.

Open by appointment. Admission, free.

Museum of the Big Bend, Sul Ross State University, Alpine.

*Amarillo Art Center

2200 Van Buren Street   Amarillo 79109
806/372-8356   H, B

Housed in a building designed by Edward Durell Stone, a nationally known architect, and located on the campus of Amarillo College, the Amarillo Art Center specializes in American art since 1900. More than sixteen exhibits a year are presented in the four main galleries of the handsome structure, most of which are accompanied by the publication of catalogues, posters, and gallery brochures. The permanent collection features a good collection of photographs taken by members of the Farm Security Administration during the 1930s and 1940s and original drawings and paintings by contemporary Texas artists.

Open Tuesday through Friday 10 A.M. to 5 P.M., Wednesday from 7 to 9:30 P.M., and Saturday and Sunday from 1 to 5 P.M. Closed on Monday and during August. Admission, free.

Don Harrington Discovery Center

1200 Streit Drive   Amarillo 79106
806/355-9547   H, B

The Discovery Center features exhibits on medical and physical science, a solar telescope, and a planetarium.

Exhibits are open September through May, Monday through Friday from 8 A.M. to 5 P.M., Saturday from 10 A.M. to 5 P.M. and from 7 to 9 P.M., and Sunday from 1 to 5 P.M. Planetarium shows are at 11 A.M., 2, 3:30, and 8 P.M. on Saturday and at 2 and 3:30 P.M. on Sunday. June through August, Tuesday and Wednesday from 10 A.M. to 5 P.M., Thursday through Saturday from 10 A.M. to 5 P.M. and 7 to 9 P.M., and Sunday from 1 to 5 P.M. Planetarium shows are at 11 A.M., 1, and 2 P.M. Tuesday through Saturday, 7:30 P.M. Thursday through Saturday, and 2 and 3:30 P.M. on Sunday.

Admission to the exhibits is free, except for some special shows. Admission to the planetarium, $1.50 adults, $1 for students and senior citizens.

Chambers County Historical Museum

Courthouse Annex   Anahuac 77514
409/267-3543 or 267-3452   H

The Chambers County Historical Museum contains Indian relics, period costumes, old ledgers, letters, farm equipment, quilts, pictures, and other items from the history of the Texas

Amarillo Art Center, Amarillo College. Photograph by Tom Livesay.

Don Harrington Discovery Center, Amarillo.

Gulf Coast. The first permanent settlement in Anahuac occurred in 1821, when a Spanish fortress was established there and made a port of entry for American colonists. Genealogical records and archaeological reports are also displayed.

Open Monday through Friday from 8 A.M. to 5 P.M., Saturday and Sunday by appointment. Admission, free.

Dr. Nicholas T. Schilling's Medical Office Museum

Washington Avenue and Cummings Street
Anahuac 77514
409/267-3452   H, T

Dr. Nicholas T. Schilling, who came to Chambers County in 1874, practiced surgery, dentistry, and general medicine and fitted eyeglasses in the Anahuac area until his death in 1919. His daughter kept his office intact until it was given to the County Historical Commission. It is now a museum in which you can see his medical supplies and paraphernalia, his accounts and ledgers, and his worn saddlebags, which he used as he made his rounds.

Open by appointment. Admission, free.

ANGLETON
Map 4

Brazoria County Historical Museum

Brazoria County Courthouse   Angleton 77515
409/849-5711, Ext. 455   N

Angleton became the county seat of Brazoria County south of Houston in 1897, and the courthouse was constructed soon after that. Now three rooms have been devoted to exhibiting the history of the region, arranged by pre-statehood, the plantation era, and post-1900. On display are old newspapers and various kinds of exhibits. Traveling exhibits are also on display from time to time.

Open Thursday, Friday, and Saturday from 1 to 5 P.M. Admission, free.

ARCHER CITY
Map 10

Archer County Historical Museum

Old Jail, one block northeast of the
Courthouse   Archer City 76351
817/423-6426   H, B

The Archer County Historical Museum contains pioneer household items that relate to school, business, and social and ethnic groups and that trace the history of Archer County from prehistory through the nineteenth century into the twentieth. Also on exhibit are artifacts, saddles, books, maps, tools, oilfield equipment, and the jail's original hanging gallows.

Open Saturday from 9 A.M. to 6 P.M., Sunday from 1 to 6 P.M. Also open on some holidays. Admission, free.

ARLINGTON
Map 1

Fielder Museum

1616 W. Abram at Fielder Road
Arlington 76013
817/460-4001   H, T

Housed in the 1914 Fielder "Home on the Hill," the museum features exhibits on the history of the region, including old photographs of Arlington, which grew out of an 1842 settlement, and reconstructions of a country store, a barber shop, and a bedroom. Exhibitions change monthly.

Open Tuesday through Friday from 9:30 A.M. to 2:30 P.M., Sunday 1:30 to 4:30 P.M. Closed Monday and Saturday. Admission, free.

University of Texas at Arlington
Special Collections Department
Library
Arlington 76019
817/273-3391   H

Rotating exhibitions, primarily from the Special Collections Department, are presented on the sixth floor of the Library. Prominent among the collections are the Jenkins Garrett Library, which contains rare books, newspapers, manuscripts, and other primary sources, and The Cartographic History Library, which includes rare and unusual maps and atlases which concentrate on the New World, Texas, the Gulf of Mexico, and the American West.

Open Monday through Friday from 8 A.M. to 5 P.M., Saturday from 10 A.M. to 2 P.M. Admission, free.

University of Texas at Arlington
University Art Gallery
Fine Arts Building
601 Monroe Street   Arlington 76019
817/273-2891   H

Established in 1975 when the Fine Arts Complex was completed, the Gallery features annual exhibitions by faculty and students as well as one-man and group shows and loan exhibitions. The collection consists of a small group of paintings, sculpture, and prints, mainly by nineteenth-century and contemporary American artists.

Open Monday through Friday from 9 A.M. to 4 P.M., Sunday from 1 to 4 P.M. Closed on Saturday. Admission, free.

ARP
Map 2

Arboretum Inc.
McDonald Farms and Campground
Route 1 (13 miles southeast of Tyler on S.H. 64)   Arp 75750
214/859-7574

The Arboretum, located on eighty-three acres surrounding Swan Bay on Lake Tyler East, contains more than 220 species of plants that are labeled by both their common and botanical

Art Gallery, University of Texas at Arlington.

names. Some plants of historical importance included.

Open daily at 10 A.M. Admission is free, but you must register at the McDonald Farms and Campground office. Groups should call ahead for an appointment.

AUSTIN
Map 6

Archer M. Huntington Art Gallery
See University of Texas at Austin

Barker Texas History Center
See University of Texas at Austin

Daughters of the Republic of Texas Museum
See State Capitol Complex

Elisabet Ney Studio
304 East 44th Street   Austin 78751
512/458-2255   H, T, N, HABS

The Elisabet Ney Studio contains examples of the working techniques as well as the completed sculptures of this German-born artist in an authentic period working environment. Born in Germany in 1833, Ney studied sculpture in Munich before immigrating with her husband, Dr. Edmund Montgomery, to Texas in 1872. She lived at Liendo Plantation in Waller County and concentrated on raising her children, while her husband, a scientist and philosopher, continued his research and experiments. Wanting to resume her sculpture, however, Miss Ney won the commission to execute the statues of Stephen F. Austin and Sam Houston for the Texas Exhibit at the Chicago World's Fair in 1893. The pair now represents Texas in the Hall of Sculpture in

Elisabet Ney Museum, Austin.

Elisabet Ney in her studio, c. 1895. Her sculpture of Stephen F. Austin that is now in the Na-
tional Hall of Sculpture in the U.S. Capitol can be seen behind her to her left. Photograph by
Ernst Wilhelm Raba.

the National Capitol. The commission motivated her to construct this studio, where she worked until her death in 1907. Said to be one of four surviving nineteenth-century sculptor's studios, the house, which contains Ney's memorial collection, has just been restored to its original state.

Open Tuesday through Friday from 11 A.M. to 4:30 P.M., Saturday and Sunday from 2 to 4:30 P.M. Admission, free.

French Legation Museum
802 San Marcos Street   Austin 78702
512/472-8180   T, HABS

Built in 1840 for Jean Pierre Isidore Alphonse Dubois de Saligny, the French chargé d'affaires of King Louis Philippe of France, the legation was constructed with handcut lumber from Bastrop and doors, windows, and hardware from France. It served as the residence of the French king's representative to the Republic of Texas. It was purchased by the state legislature in 1945 with money left over from a federal appropriation for the celebration of the 1936 Centennial of Texas Independence.

Now restored, the house features period Creole furnishings and an authentic early French kitchen. Dubois occupied the house until April, 1841, when he left Austin, perhaps because of the so-called "Pig War," in which his landlord, Richard Bullock, refused to keep his pigs out of Dubois's yard. Although he continued as the

The French Legation Museum, Austin.

French envoy to Texas, he never again visited Austin or occupied the house. It is the only building of the foreign governments that recognized Texas which still exists.

Open Tuesday through Sunday from 1 to 5 P.M. Admission, adults $1; children under 12 $.50. Scheduled tours, $.50 per person.

George Washington Carver Museum

1165 Angelina   Austin 78702
512/472-8954   H, T

Located in the old Carver Library building, the George Washington Carver Museum features the local, regional, and national history of blacks. Opened in 1979, the museum collects and preserves books, photographs, manuscripts, city/county records, maps, and other information that relates to the history of blacks.

Open Tuesday and Wednesday from 10 A.M. to 6 P.M., Thursday from noon to 8 P.M., Friday and Saturday from noon to 5 P.M. Admission, free.

The Governor's Mansion.

See State Capitol Complex

Humanities Research Center

See University of Texas at Austin, Leeds Gallery

Jourdan Bachman Pioneer Farm

11418 Sprinkle Cut-Off Road   Austin 78754
512/837-1215   H

The Jourdan Bachman farm is a reconstruction of an 1850s Central Texas farm consisting of twenty buildings on eighty acres. Visitors may experience pioneer and Indian life-styles through a series of "hands-on" exhibits.

Open Monday through Friday from 9 A.M. to 1 P.M., and by reservation. Call for information on admission.

Laguna Gloria Art Museum

3809 West 35th Street   Austin 78763
512/458-8191   H (partially), B, HABS

The Laguna Gloria Art Museum, located in an Italianate villa on twenty-nine acres on the shores of Lake Austin, features various twentieth-century American art forms in exhibitions, films, lectures, tours, and performances. The museum is a showcase for regional as well as modern masters of painting, sculpture, photography, dance, film, and architecture.

The house itself has quite a history. Constructed in 1916 at the foot of Mount Bonnell, it

Laguna Gloria Art Museum, Austin. Photograph by Ron Tyler.

is located on the site that Stephen F. Austin, known as the "father of Texas" for his role in colonizing the state, had selected for his home-site shortly before his death in 1836. It was constructed by Clara Driscoll Sevier, famous as the savior of the Alamo, and her husband, H. H. Sevier. They gave the home to the Texas Fine Arts Association in 1943, and Laguna Gloria Art Museum assumed its operation in 1961.

Open Tuesday through Saturday from 10 A.M. to 5 P.M., Sunday from 1 to 5 P.M. Open Thursday evening until 9 P.M. Closed Monday. Admission, free.

Leeds Gallery
See University of Texas at Austin

Lyndon Baines Johnson Library and Museum
See University of Texas at Austin

Mabel Davis Rose Garden
2220 Barton Springs Road
Zilker Park   Austin 78746
512/477-8672   H

Located in the Austin Garden Center on the shores of the Colorado River, the Mabel Davis Rose Garden was dedicated in 1973. The labeled shrub and climbing roses are at their height of beauty in May. There are occasional garden club flower exhibitions.

Open 9 A.M. to dark. Admission, free.

Moody Hall Atrium Gallery
St. Edwards University
3001 South Congress Avenue   Austin 78704
512/444-2621, Ext. 327

Art exhibits by local or area artists are presented in this 60 by 80 feet open atrium with skylights.

Open weekdays from 8 A.M. to 8 P.M., weekends from 8 A.M. to 5 P.M. There is an admission charge.

Museo del Barrio de Austin
1619 E. 1st Street   Austin 78702
512/477-5770

Devoted to the development, documentation, and encouragement of Chicano arts, the Museo del Barrio de Austin presents exhibitions of Chicano and Latino art. As a part of the National Network of Chicano Art Galleries, the museum also collects and is currently cataloguing books, periodicals, posters, and photographs of material pertaining to Chicano arts and literature.

Open Monday through Friday from 9 A.M. to 5 P.M. Admission, free.

Natural Science Center
401 Deep Eddy Avenue   Austin 78703
512/472-4523

Exhibitions, displays, and live animals focus on the natural science of the Austin and Central Texas area. The Natural Science Center is a part of Outdoor Nature Programs, a citywide system of outdoor recreation programs and facilities.

Open Monday through Friday from 8 A.M. to 5 P.M., Saturday from 9 A.M. to 5 P.M., Sunday from 1 to 5 P.M. Admission fees vary.

Neill-Cochran House
2310 San Gabriel   Austin 78705
512/478-2335   T, B, HABS

The Neill-Cochran House was built c. 1853 by Abner Cook, also architect of the Governor's Mansion and Woodlawn (the former home of Governor Elisha M. Pease). It is a good example of Greek Revival architecture as it appeared in Texas, with the local limestone providing a handsome contrast for the six white Doric columns which form the two-story gallery across the front of the house. Built for Washington Hill, the house now bears the name of two prominent

The Neill-Cochran House, Austin.

families who later owned it, Andrew Neill and Judge T. B. Cochran. It has been refurnished authentically.

Tours Wednesday through Sunday at 2, 3, 4, and 5 P.M. Groups by appointment only. Closed holidays. Admission, $1.

O. Henry Home Museum

409 E. Fifth Street   Austin 78701
512/472-1903   T, HABS

Featuring a collection of personal memorabilia, the museum was the home of William Sidney Porter—O. Henry, the famous short story author—and his wife, Austinite Athol Estes, and daughter, from 1892 until 1895 when it was located at 308 E. 4th Street. Porter worked in a drug store, sold real estate, served as a draftsman in the Old Land Office, was a teller in the First National Bank, and published a newspaper called *Rolling Stone* while he was in Austin. He moved to Houston in 1895 to accept a job with the *Houston Post.* Special events include holiday festivities on Christmas and Valentine's Day as well as an annual Pun-off.

Open Monday through Saturday from 11 A.M. to 4:30 P.M., Sunday from 2 to 4:30 P.M. Admission, free.

State Capitol Complex
Daughters of the Republic of Texas Museum

112 E. Eleventh Street   Austin 78701
512/477-1822   T

Housed in the Old Land Office Building, constructed in 1856–1857, the Daughters of the Republic of Texas Museum exhibits Indian artifacts and paintings, sculpture, and other materials related to the history of early Texas. Numismatic and philatelic collections make up a part of the exhibit. The museum shares the Old Land Office Building with the Texas Confederate Museum.

Open Monday through Friday from 9 A.M. to noon and 1 to 5 P.M. Admission, free. Closed on state and national holidays.

State Capitol Complex
The Governor's Mansion

11th and Colorado   Austin 78711
512/475-2121   T, N, HABS

The oldest building in the Capitol complex, the Governor's Mansion was built in 1853–1855 by Abner Cook. Elisha M. Pease was the first governor to occupy it. Having just undergone a multi-million-dollar restoration, the mansion is a splendid reminder of nineteenth-century grandeur. Historical paintings and antique furniture are on display in the public rooms, including Robert Onderdonk's well-known painting *The Fall of the Alamo*. Stephen F. Austin's desk, Governor Pease's sofa and hammered sheet metal clock, and early portable bookcases are also exhibited. Even the nails that Governor James S. Hogg pounded in the banister of the stairway nearly 100 years ago to keep his children from sliding down are still in place. Carpets have been pulled up to reveal the wide-planked pine floors, and the "Green Room" has been returned to its original use as a library.

Public tours are available from 10 A.M. to noon on Monday, Wednesday, and Friday. Admission, free.

The Governor's Mansion, Austin. Photograph by Richard Tyler.

State Capitol Complex
State Capitol Building
Austin 78711

512/475-3070   H, T, N, HABS

Constructed in 1882–88 from Texas red granite quarried from Granite Mountain near Marble Falls, the Texas State Capitol soars to a height of 309 feet, 8 inches, and is topped by a 17 feet high statue of the Goddess of Liberty. Designed by Detroit architect E. E. Myers, who also designed the state capitols of Michigan and Colorado, the building was constructed with the aid of convict labor at the quarry and Scottish stone masons at the site.

An excellent brochure describing the Capitol is available at the Texas Highway Department Tourist Information Center, which is located in the rotunda and is open seven days a week. When the Legislature is not in session, both the House and the Senate chambers are open for viewing. There are a number of historical paintings in the Capitol, including Henry McArdle's famous *Battle of San Jacinto* and *Dawn at the Alamo* located in the Senate Chamber. The Capitol is now undergoing restoration to repair the near-disastrous effects of an early-1983 fire that threatened to consume the entire building.

Tours are available from 9 A.M. to 4:30 P.M., and the dome is open 24 hours. Admission, free.

William H. Huddle's **The Surrender of Santa Anna,** *1886 (oil on canvas 71½ × 114 in.), is on view in the State Capitol Building, Austin. Photograph courtesy Texas Highway Department.*

State Capitol Complex
Texas Confederate Museum
112 E. 11th Street   Austin 78701
512/472-2596   T, HABS

Founded in 1904 in the Texas State Capitol, the Texas Confederate Museum moved in 1919 to the Old Land Office Building, which was constructed in 1857 and once housed the patents, deeds of title, and land documents of the Republic of Texas and later those of the state. Exhibitions pertain to Confederate history and include regimental flags, uniforms, paintings, and relics.

Open Monday through Friday 9 A.M. to noon, 1 to 5 P.M. Closed Saturday, Sunday, and holidays. Admission, free.

State Capitol Complex
Texas State Library
Lorenzo de Zavala State Archives and Library Building
State Capitol Grounds
12th and Brazos   Austin 78711
512/475-2445   H, B

The Texas State Library is primarily the depository for the state library and archives (including the private manuscript collections for such prominent Texans as Sam Houston, Mirabeau B. Lamar, and John H. Reagan), but the lobby exhibition area is open to the public. It is dominated by a 45-foot Peter Rogers mural that depicts several significant Texas motifs. Fourteen small exhibit cases contain original documents, maps, and artifacts from several periods of Texas history, including examples of the archaeological treasures recovered from a seventeenth-century Spanish shipwreck off the coast of Texas (on long-term loan from the Texas Historical Commission), some of the furniture belonging to Governor Elisha M. Pease and his family, and one of the laminated glass windows from the State Capitol Building (the only colored glass in the original structure).

The exhibition area is open Monday through Saturday from 8 A.M. to 5 P.M. Admission, free. The Library and Archives divisions are open to the public Monday through Friday from 8 A.M. to 5 P.M. on a slightly more restrictive basis.

Texas Confederate Museum
See State Capitol Complex
Texas Memorial Museum
See University of Texas at Austin

Texas State Library
See State Capitol Complex

University of Texas at Austin
Archer M. Huntington Art Gallery
Art Building, 23rd & San Jacinto
Harry Ransom Center, 21st & Guadalupe
Austin 78712
512/471-7324   H (Call ahead), B

In two display areas, the Archer M. Huntington Art Gallery features exhibitions from its collection, including Greek and Roman art, nineteenth- and twentieth-century American art, contemporary Latin American art, and a large print and drawings collection from all periods. The permanent collection also includes more than 300 twentieth-century American paintings given by the novelist James A. Michener and his wife as well as the Barbara Duncan Collection of Latin American paintings, given by Mr. and Mrs. John C. Duncan. Temporary exhibitions are presented on a monthly basis in both display areas.

Open Monday through Saturday 9 A.M. to 5 P.M., Sunday from 1 to 5 P.M. Admission, free.

Archer M. Huntington Art Gallery, Harry Ransom Center, University of Texas at Austin.

University of Texas at Austin
Barker Texas History Center
Sid Richardson Hall, Unit 2
Austin 78712
512/471-5961   H

The Barker Texas History Center is the most extensive repository in existence for the study of the historical development of the state of Texas. Its collections include manuscripts, photographs, and visual materials as well as published materials. Display cases in the reading room as well as in a nearby gallery feature changing exhibits that reflect the material in the Center as well as various aspects of research on Texas, the South, the Southwest, and the West.

Open Monday through Saturday from 8 A.M. to 5 P.M. Closed Sunday and on official university holidays. Admission, free.

University of Texas at Austin
Leeds Gallery
Humanities Research Center
Fourth Floor, Harry Ransom Center
West Mall from Guadalupe Street
Austin 78712
512/471-4664   H

The Leeds Gallery is the public exhibition area for materials from the Humanities Research Center, which was established by Dr. Harry Ransom, president and chancellor of the University, to contain the University's acquisitions of fine arts materials, rare books and manuscripts, theater arts, and photography accumulated since its opening in 1883. Literary research materials emphasize the importance of the creative process, from the earliest rough drafts and sketches to the finished first edition book or painting. The collection emphasizes materials from the last three centuries, specializing in American, British, and French materials.

The Humanities Research Center Art Collection, housed on the fourth floor of the Academic Center, features a strong collection of portraiture, graphics from the sixteenth-century to the twentieth-century European, book illustration, typography, and watercolor. Special Collections Rooms surround Leeds Gallery and are open for study every weekday: The Alfred A. and Blanche Knopf Library (twentieth-century literature, 1920 to the present), The J. Frank Dobie Library and Art Collection (Western and Texas folklore and history), The Edward Larocque Tinker Collection (the American cowboy, Mexican *va-*

John Singer Sargeant, Lady Cynthia Asquith, *1909. From the Collection of the Leeds Gallery, Humanities Research Center, University of Texas at Austin.*

21

quero, and Argentinian *gaucho*), The Esther Hoblitzelle Memorial Room, and the Erle Stanley Gardner Study.

The outdoor walkway around the building affords the visitor a view of the State Capitol Building and the river and hill country.

Open from 8 A.M. to 4:45 P.M. Admission, free. Tours are available on request.

University of Texas at Austin
The Lyndon Baines Johnson Library and Museum
One block west of I-35   Austin 78705
512/482-5137   H, B

The LBJ Library houses the papers of Lyndon Baines Johnson, 36th President of the United States. On exhibit are mementoes and memorabilia of Johnson's lengthy and illustrious career in politics, from New Deal Congressman during President Franklin D. Roosevelt's term to Senator from Texas to Vice President to President in 1963. A multimedia production on Johnson's life is shown regularly in the new Orientation Theater.

There are exhibits on International Affairs, Heads of State Gifts, and Presidential History. New exhibitions on the Great Society and the war in Vietnam have been added recently during a $2.3 millions renovation. The Library features a reproduction of the Oval Office as it appeared during President Johnson's administration and also presents special exhibitions relating to the Presidency and to American history.

The University of Texas Visitors Center is located in the nearby Sid Richardson Building.

Open daily from 9 A.M. to 5 P.M. Closed Christmas. Admission, free.

University of Texas at Austin
Texas Memorial Museum
2400 Trinity   Austin 78705
512/471-1604   H, B

One of the museums built during the 1936 celebration of the Texas Centennial, the Texas Memorial Museum opened its doors in 1939. It is a renowned research institution with exhibitions crowded into the only one of three planned units that was constructed: the geology and paleontology of Texas on the first floor, including fossils and casts of pre-historic animals; the notable events of Texas history, including a large collection of firearms, in the Memorial Hall on the entrance level; botany and zoology of Texas

The Lyndon Baines Johnson Library and Museum, Austin. Photograph by Richard Tyler.

This ceremonial stool is a part of the "New Guinea" exhibit on the fourth floor of the Texas Memorial Museum, Austin. Courtesy Texas Memorial Museum, Austin.

on the third floor; and anthropology of Texas on the fourth floor. Notable holdings include the photographs of cowboy photographer Erwin E. Smith of Bonham and Henry C. Pratt's large painting entitled *View of Smith's West Texas Ranch*. Special exhibits are also presented on the second floor.

The sculpture of the group of mustangs, located in front of the museum, is Texas' first major monument to its wildlife. The well-known American sculptor A. Phiminster Proctor was chosen by J. Frank Dobie, Texas folklorist and author, to do the work. A stallion, five mares, and a colt are included in the grouping. Proctor visited Texas ranches and observed more than 100 mustangs before he finally chose the models for the monument, which was delayed by World War II and finally unveiled in Austin May 31, 1948.

Open Monday through Friday from 9 A.M. to 5 P.M., Saturday and Sunday from 1 to 5 P.M. Admission, adults $1; students $.50.

Azle Historical Museum

124 W. Main   Azle 76020
No telephone

Constructed in 1936 as the Jim Nation Building, the Azle Historical Museum now houses objects and artifacts relating to the history of the area. Included in the exhibit are a spinning wheel, doctor's saddle bag equipped with bottles and pills, apothecary scales from the first drug store in the community, early toys, and books.

Open Tuesday through Thursday from 12 to 4 P.M. and by appointment. Admission, free.

Callahan County Pioneer Museum

4th and Market Streets   Baird 79504
915/854-1718   H (through the north door)

The Callahan County Pioneer Museum was founded in 1939 and is located in the basement of the county courthouse. It houses displays pertaining to the early history of the county. Special programs include an open house each November and tours for school children.

Open Monday through Friday, 9 A.M. to noon, 1 P.M. to 5 P.M. Admission, free.

Frontier Times Museum

506 13th Street   Bandera 78003
512/796-3864   H, B, T

Founded in 1921 by J. Marvin Hunter, author, printer, and publisher of *Frontier Times* magazine, the Frontier Times Museum houses more than 30,000 items ranging from a South American shrunken human head to prehistoric Indian relics, to pioneer implements, to a small collection of Western American paintings by such artists as Oscar E. Berninghaus, W. R. Leigh, Olaf Weighorst, and Charles M. Russell.

Open 10 A.M. to noon, 1 to 4:30 P.M. Tuesday through Saturday; 1 to 4:30 P.M. Sunday. Closed Monday. Admission, adults $1; children $.25.

Bastrop County Historical Society Museum

702 Main Street   Bastrop 78602
512/321-6177   T

Situated in a house constructed in the mid-nineteenth century, the Bastrop County Historical Society Museum contains material relating to Indians of the region as well as early pioneers. The brick addition to the house was constructed by German immigrant Joe B. Fehr, who obtained the bricks from the nearby Lottman's brick kilns in the hills east of Bastrop.

Bastrop was known as Mina during the Spanish and Mexican periods and it is located where

El Camino Real, running from Nacogdoches to San Antonio, crossed the Colorado River.

Open Saturday and Sunday afternoon. Admission, adults $.50; children under 12 $.25.

BAY CITY
Map 4

Matagorda County Historical Museum

1824 Sixth Street   Bay City 77414
409/245-7502   H

Devoted to the history of the Matagorda County area, the museum documents the story of the early pioneers through exhibitions and collections, which include documents, photographs, rare books, genealogical materials, and a run of the *Matagorda Gazette,* an early newspaper. The museum is housed in the old city hall–fire station complex.

Open Tuesday through Friday from 3 to 5 P.M., Sunday from 2 to 5 P.M. Admission, free.

BAYTOWN
Map 4

Baytown Historical Museum

Community Building
3430 Market Street   Baytown 77520
713/427-8768   H, B

This historical museum displays exhibits that relate to the history of the area, which was first settled when Nathaniel Lynch set up Lynch's Ferry in 1822 and William Scott built his home near the present town in 1824.

Open Sunday through Friday from 1 to 5 P.M.

BEAUMONT
Map 4

Babe Didrikson Zaharias Memorial

Gulf Street exit off I-10   Beaumont 77703
713/833-4622

Mildred Ella "Babe" Didrikson grew up in Beaumont and went on to become one of the outstanding women athletes of her day. She won two gold medals and a silver one in the 1932 Olympics and, after marrying wrestler George Zaharias in 1938, won every major golf title from 1940 to 1950. She was voted the outstanding woman athlete of the first half of the twentieth century by the Associated Press. In one large room the memorial exhibits her medals, trophies, photographs, and newspaper clippings that Babe and others saved in scrapbooks.

Open daily from 9 A.M. to 5 P.M. Closed Christmas. Admission, free.

Beaumont Art Museum

1111 Ninth Street   Beaumont 77702
409/832-3432   H, B

Located in a Southern Regency style mansion designed by the Houston architect John F. Staub, who also designed Bayou Bend in Houston, the

Beaumont Art Museum presents temporary art exhibitions as well as selections from the permanent collection of primarily Texas artists. Like several other Texas art museums, the Beaumont Art Museum is located in a renovated private residence that also has an interesting history. Completed in 1936 for J. Cooke Wilson, one of the founding partners of Humble Oil Company, and his wife, the house is reminiscent of New Orleans dwellings with its wrought iron trim. The downstairs rooms have been changed into galleries, but the ceiling moldings, oak parquet floors, and terrazzo floored garden room tell of its splendor when it was the first air conditioned private residence in the state. The upstairs rooms have been made into a sales gallery and offices, meeting rooms, and classrooms for the museum. The surrounding five-acre landscape contains many specimens of horticultural interest, because both Wilsons were interested in gardening and selected this small portion of the Big Thicket, a heavily wooded area of Southeast Texas, for their estate. The grounds are now used for museum workshops, performing arts, and Kaleidoscope, an annual arts and crafts festival.

A new museum has been designed by E. Verner Johnson & Associates, Boston, for a beautiful twenty-acre site not far from the present museum, which makes innovative use of the area's alternating heavy rainfall and abundant sunshine. The projected opening date is 1985.

Open Tuesday through Friday 10 A.M. to 5 P.M., Saturday and Sunday 2 to 5 P.M. Admission, free.

Gladys City Boomtown
University Drive and U.S. 69/96/287
Beaumont 77710
409/838-8896 or 835-0823   H, B, T

Gladys City Boomtown, a reconstruction of the original boomtown, is an oil boom village consisting of surveyors' and lawyers' offices, a tank company, a pharmacy and doctor's office, a general store, and other structures modeled after the original Gladys City. Spindletop Museum, which is located on the nearby Lamar University campus, contains exhibits relating to the history of Spindletop, the early oil industry, and the area.

Gladys City Boomtown recalls the economic boom in southeast Texas that followed the Lucas Gusher in 1901. Anthony F. Lucas was an

The great Spindletop Oil Field signaled the beginning of the industrial age for Texas. Courtesy Spindletop Museum, Beaumont.

Austrian-born engineer who leased Spindletop Hill from Pattillo Higgins, who believed that there was oil in the field but had been unsuccessful in finding it. Lucas began drilling in October, 1900. The first Spindletop well blew in on January 10, 1901, at a rate of 80,000 to 100,000 barrels per day until it was capped. Nine days later "boomers," promoters, and fortune seekers poured into Beaumont. The hastily constructed clapboard shacks were called Gladys City (named after a seven-year-old girl in Higgins's Sunday School class). Spindletop quickly played out because of overproduction, but more than 600 oil companies, including Texaco, Mobil, Gulf, and Humble trace their beginnings to the

Gladys City boom. The Lucas Gusher Monument Association has placed a 58-foot granite obelisk at the reconstructed Gladys City, which is located approximately three-quarters of a mile north of the original site because of soil subsidence. It has been designated a National Historic Landmark.

Spindletop Museum is open Monday through Friday 1 to 5 P.M. Gladys City is open Tuesday through Friday and on Sunday from 1 to 5 P.M. and on Saturday from 9 A.M. to 5 P.M. Admission to the museum, free; to Gladys City, adults $.50, children $.25.

John Jay French Trading Post Museum

2995 French Road   Beaumont 77706
409/898-0348   H, B, T, N, HABS

John Jay French was a tanner and merchant who moved from Connecticut and New York to Texas in 1845. Hoping to participate in the booming Gulf Coast trade, he established himself in Brazoria, Liberty, and Jefferson counties as well as Louisiana before settling in Beaumont. The museum consists of the restored two-story house that he constructed in 1845 as well as a semi-detached kitchen and outbuildings including a wash house, a corn crib, a smoke house, and a tannery similar to the one that he would have operated. The pre–Civil War furnishings were made in Texas.

A program of quarterly exhibits featuring decorative arts of the mid-nineteenth century assists in interpreting life on the Texas frontier.

Open Tuesday through Saturday from 10 A.M. to 4 P.M., Sunday from 1 to 4 P.M. Closed Monday and holidays. Admission, adults $1, students $.50.

BELTON
Map 3

Sid Richardson Museum of the University of Mary Hardin-Baylor

Mabee Student Center
Belton 76513
817/939-5811   H

Devoted to the history of the university, the Sid Richardson Museum contains material relating to former students and faculty, including books written by former students and faculty, equipment from the early days of the chemistry department, clothing, jewelry, and china belonging to former students, and former student Oveta Culp Hobby's WAC uniform.

Open by request. Admission, free.

John Jay French Home, Beaumont.

BENJAMIN
Map 10

Knox County Museum
Courthouse
U.S. 82 and S.H. 6   Benjamin 79505
817/454-2191
   Displays related to early Knox County settlers and contain old photographs and ranch gear, such as saddles. The county was organized and Benjamin, located on the Kansas City, Mexico, and Orient Railroad, was made the county seat in 1886.
   Open Monday through Friday from 8 A.M. to 5 P.M.

BIG BEND NATIONAL
PARK
Map 8

Visitor Center
Panther Junction
Big Bend National Park 79834
915/477-2251   H, B
   The Visitor Center at Panther Junction has a small exhibit relating to the history and natural history of the Big Bend Country. There is also a visitor center at Rio Grande Village. At either place you can obtain a map of the national park,

which indicates historic places as well as self-guiding trails. Regular lectures are also presented on the Big Bend region.

The visitor centers are open daily from 8 A.M. to 5 P.M., except during the summer when the Panther Junction center is open until 7 P.M., and Rio Grande Village center is open only on Saturday and Sunday. Admission, free.

BIG SPRING
Map 7

Heritage Museum
510 Scurry   Big Spring 79720
915/267-8255   H, B

The museum, devoted to early and local history of the Big Spring area, was founded in 1971. Exhibitions include displays of Indian and pioneer artifacts, including a nineteenth-century bedroom, saddles, branding irons, and other artifacts of early Howard County. Changing exhibitions focus on various aspects of Big Spring history and art.

Open Tuesday through Friday from 10 A.M. to 5 P.M., Saturday from 1 to 5 P.M. Admission, free, but a donation is requested.

BOERNE
Map 6

Historical House Museum
402 E. Blanco Street (on the hill behind the Public Library)   Boerne 78006
512/249-2469   B

The Kuhlmann-King House was built between 1885 and 1890 and is named for William Kuhlmann, a German immigrant druggist in Boerne who built the house, and Edmund King, an English immigrant, who later lived in it. The house, as well as the separate kitchen, are furnished authentically with quilts, crochet, and children's toys. Barry Anthony DeYoung, noted regional artist, once lived in the house, and some of his paintings are on display.

Open Thursday from 2 to 5 P.M. and by appointment. A donation is requested for admission. For information, write the Boerne Area Historic Preservation Society, P.O. Box 178, Boerne 78006.

Theis House
Corner of Main and Newton   Boerne 78006
No telephone

Built in the late 1850s by Phillip Jacob Theis, a German-born settler and blacksmith who came to Texas in 1855, the museum contains collections and pioneer memorabilia. The homestead of the "chink and daubing" construction was used as an armory during the 1870s when

Phillip's son, August, was an officer in the state militia.

Open for tours by appointment. Write Mr. and Mrs. Edgar Bergmann (owners), P.O. Box 400, Boerne, Texas 78006.

BONHAM

Map 1

Fannin County Museum

Third Floor, Courthouse   Bonham 75418
214/583-8042   T

The Museum Room of the Fannin County Courthouse contains pictures and artifacts relating to early history of the North Texas area, specifically Bonham and Fannin County. The museum was founded in 1965.

Open Monday through Friday from 8 A.M. to noon, 1 to 5 P.M. Admission, free.

Old Fort Inglish Replica

U.S. 82 West   Bonham 75418
214/583-3441   H, B

The original Fort Inglish was built by Bailey Inglish, who led the first small group of eight or ten families to the site of present-day Bonham in 1836. The stockade provided protection to the settlers for the next seven or eight years—until the Indians were driven from the North Texas area.

The original fort rotted down, and Congressman Sam Rayburn served as chairman of a committee to build the first replica for the Texas Centennial in 1936. The second replica was built for the Bicentennial. Nineteenth-century tools, household items, and rough furniture are displayed inside the stockade. A cabin and two small barns are located in the surrounding park.

Open April through September daily from 9 A.M. to 5 P.M., weekends from 1 to 5 P.M. Admission, free, but a donation is requested.

Sam Rayburn House

One and one-half miles west on U.S. 82
Bonham 75418
214/583-5558   B, T, N

This white, clapboard house was home to Sam Rayburn, the youngest man to become Speaker of the Texas House and the Speaker of the U.S. House of Representatives longer than any other man, from 1940 to 1961 (except for the 80th and 83rd Congresses when he was minority leader). "Mr. Sam" built the "Homeplace" for his family in 1916, and it remained in the family until it opened to the public, restored and furnished to its 1961 state, when Rayburn died.

The Sam Rayburn House, Bonham.

Open Tuesday through Friday from 10 A.M. to 5 P.M., Saturday from 1 to 5 P.M., and Sunday from 2 to 5 P.M. Closed Thanksgiving and Christmas. Admission, free.

Sam Rayburn Library

West Sam Rayburn Drive   Bonham 75418
214/583-2455   B

The Rayburn Library, dedicated in 1957, contains the books and papers of Sam Rayburn. On display are many of the historic mementos collected by the Speaker during his more than half a century of service, including his gavel, the white marble rostrum which was moved from the House of Representatives when it was redecorated in 1955, a 2,500-year-old Grecian urn presented to the Speaker by the Athens Palace Guard, and an exact replica of the Speaker's Capitol office. Also on display are many historic photographs, cartoons, and documents from the Rayburn years.

The library is open Monday through Friday from 10 A.M. to 5 P.M., Saturday from 1 to 5 P.M., and Sunday from 2 to 5 P.M. Closed Thanksgiving and Christmas. Admission, free.

Hutchinson County Historical Museum

618 N. Main   Borger 79007
806/273-6121   B, T

Exhibitions relate to local history, from "Coronado in Borger" to the Battle of Adobe Walls, one of the last Indian-white battles on the Plains, to the 1926 oil boom, during which Borger was placed under martial law. The Adobe Walls battle is commemorated by a large painting of the Comanche Chief Quanah Parker, who led the Kiowas and Comanches against a small group of buffalo hunters.

Open Sunday 2 to 4 P.M.; Monday 11 A.M. to 4:30 P.M.; Wednesday through Saturday 11 A.M. to 4:30 P.M. Closed Tuesday. Admission, free.

Heart of Texas Historical Museum

117 High Street   Brady 76858
No telephone

Housed in the McCulloch County Jail (from 1910–1973), the Heart of Texas Historical Museum presents exhibits relating to the early history of the area. On display are turn-of-the-century costumes as well as books, World War I artifacts, and the furnishings of a 1920 law office.

Open Saturday through Monday from 1 to 5 P.M.

Heart of Texas Historical Museum, Brady.

Brazosport Museum of Natural Science

400 College Drive   Brazosport 77566
409/265-7831   H, B

Located between Lake Jackson and Clute, the museum specializes in the interpretation of the Texas Gulf coast. Exhibitions include the largest shell collection on display in the Southern United States, a large carved ivory collection, and an Allosaurus replica, which is approximately 10 by 25 feet. The Hall of Archaeology features Indian artifacts found on the Dow-Cleaver site in Freeport, including pottery which has been reassembled from pieces found at the site. Minerals, fossils, wildlife and shorebird exhibits, and aquariums and an underwater diorama are also a part of the exhibit.

Open Tuesday through Saturday from 10 A.M. to 5 P.M., Sunday from 2 to 5 P.M. Closed on Monday. Admission, free. Special tours may be arranged by calling in advance.

Breckenridge Aviation Museum

Stephens County Airport   Breckenridge 76024
817/559-3201

The Breckenridge Aviation Museum is a flying museum of World War II aircraft, such as a Chance Vought F4U-4 and F4U-5N Corsair.

Open daily. Admission, free.

Swenson Memorial Museum of Stephens County

116 W. Walker   Breckenridge 76024
817/559-8471   H, B

The Swenson Memorial Museum houses a collection of artifacts dealing with ranching, farming, town life, and oil from the 1850s through 1945. Of particular interest is the 1920–1930 era dentist office and the music room, which contains an 1890 pump organ as well as other instruments.

The Museum also presents temporary exhibits relating to the history of Stephens County and the area.

Open Tuesday through Saturday from 10 A.M. to noon, 1 to 4 P.M. and by special appointment. Admission, free.

Waller County Historical Museum

906 Cooper Street   Brookshire 77423
713/934-2826   H, B

Located in the historic Donigan House, which was constructed in 1913 by Dr. Paul Donigan, a young Armenian-American, the Waller County Historical Museum features changing exhibitions of history and art that relate to the area. In addition, antique furniture, assorted crystal, china, and silver are on exhibit. An interesting feature of the house is Dr. Donigan's cellar, which he could not put underground because of water seepage. He built his cellar above ground and covered the outside walls with pressed tin.

Open weekdays from 10 A.M. to 2 P.M. and weekends by appointment. Closed Thursday. Admission, free.

BROWNFIELD
Map 9

Terry County Heritage Museum

602 E. Cardwell Street   Brownfield 79316
806/637-2467   H (two steps at the entrance),
B, T (site of the original Terry County jail)

The old A. M. Brownfield home is the site of the Terry County Heritage Museum, which features an old-fashioned kitchen, parlor, and newly completed exhibit room, which houses material on local heritage. Exhibits relate to the history of the area, including Indians, early pioneers, and ranching.

Open Wednesday and Sunday from 2 to 4 P.M. and by appointment. Admission, $.25.

BROWNSVILLE
Map 5

Brownsville Art League Museum

Neale Drive   Brownsville 78520
512/542-0941   T

Located within old Fort Brown, near the Texas Southmost College campus, the Brownsville Art League is dedicated primarily to the instruction and exhibition of art. It is housed, however, in a historic structure, the Neale House, which is generally considered to be the oldest structure in the city. The permanent collection includes works by N. C. Wyeth and others who conducted workshops for the members of the League.

Open Monday, Wednesday, Thursday, and Friday from 9:30 A.M. to 3 P.M., and Tuesday from 1 to 4 P.M. Admission, free.

Gladys Porter Zoo

500 Ringgold Street   Brownsville 78520
512/546-2177   H, B, R

Concern for the vanishing wildlife of the world prompted the construction of the Gladys Porter Zoo in 1971. The Zoo is laid out in five major areas: Africa, Asia, Indo-Australia, Tropical America, and a non-geographic area where the animals are housed together for the convenience of caring for them. The Zoo specializes in breeding rare and endangered species and has two species of antelope found at no other zoo in the world.

Open daily from 10 A.M. to dusk. Admission, adults $3.00; students $2.00; children $1.00.

Stillman House Museum
13th Street and Washington
Brownsville 78520
512/542-3929   B, T, N, HABS

Built in 1850, the Stillman House was the residence of Charles Stillman, the founder of Brownsville. Today it contains family memorabilia and period furnishings, and presents displays on early Brownsville history. Coming from Connecticut in 1829, Stillman settled in Matamoros and pursued his living as a ship owner, land developer, and merchant. Following the war between the United States and Mexico, he moved to the northern shore of the river and established Brownsville, named for Major Jacob Brown, who was killed during the war with Mexico. Stillman built his Greek Revival house within the tradition of Mexican architecture along the Rio Grande, the gable walls above the roof being the primary characteristic.

Open Monday through Friday from 10 A.M. to noon, 2 to 5 P.M., Sunday, 2 to 5 P.M. Admission, $1 for adults; student groups free.

BRYAN
Map 3

Brazos Valley Museum of Natural Science
Brazos Center
3232 Briarcrest Drive   Bryan 77801
409/779-2195   H, B

Founded by the American Association of University Women in 1961, the Brazos Valley Museum of Natural Science is located in the Brazos Center. Approximately 30 acres of the Brazos County Park remain in a natural state and serve as a laboratory and nature trail for the museum. Exhibitions are presented on local natural and cultural history. A Discovery Room, including live animals, is open year around.

Open Thursday through Saturday from 9 A.M. to 5 P.M., Sunday from 1 to 5 P.M. Admission, free.

BURNET
Map 6

Fort Croghan Museum
About three miles south of Burnet on Hamilton Creek   Burnet 78611
No telephone

Founded in 1849 as a part of the chain of forts across the Texas frontier, Fort Croghan guarded the northwestern approaches to Austin until the last of the troops was moved out in 1855. Many

Stillman House Museum, Brownsville. Photograph by Todd Webb. Courtesy Amon Carter Museum, Fort Worth.

early Burnet residents lived in the fort buildings until they could move onto their own land. Today the Burnet County Historical Society has restored the 1.7 acres of the old fort grounds, including the only stone building, the Powder House, and a small portion of the drill grounds. Since all of the original buildings of the fort had been destroyed, several area buildings that had been built at the time of the fort were moved onto the property and furnished with period items.

Open April through September Monday through Wednesday and Saturday from 8 A.M. to 5 P.M., Sunday from 10 A.M. to 4 P.M.

Longhorn Cavern Museum
Longhorn Cavern State Park
10 miles southwest of Burnet off U.S. 281
Burnet 78611
512/756-4680   B, T, N

Containing exhibitions on mineralogy and local history, Longhorn Cavern Museum is a part of Longhorn Cavern State Park, of which the major attraction is the cave itself. The museum is housed in the former administration building, which was constructed by the Civilian Conservation Corps during the 1930s. Currently on exhibit are photographs of the construction of the building, the old dance hall that used to be in the cavern, and several features of the cave. Also on exhibit are native rocks, a complete map of the known cave, and a geological profile of the area.

Open daily from 9 A.M. to 5 P.M. (March 1 through October 1); Wednesday through Sunday from 9 A.M. to 3 P.M. (October 1 through March 1). Admission to the museum is free.

CALDWELL
Map 3

Burleson County Historical Museum

County Courthouse   Caldwell 77836
No telephone   H

The Burleson County Historical Museum features exhibitions of Indian artifacts and other archaeological materials, artifacts from the Mexican Fort Tenoxtitlan, and from the pioneer and colonial history of Burleson County, and some nineteenth-century period furniture in a Victorian bedroom and a pioneer kitchen setting.

Open Friday from 2 to 5 P.M. and by appointment. Admission, free.

CAMERON
Map 3

Milam County Historical Museum

Main and Fannin   Cameron 76520
817/697-9223   H, B, T, N

Located in the old Milam County Jail, the museum presents exhibitions relating to humans and nature in Milam County and Texas. The building, recorded as a Texas historic landmark and on the national register for historic buildings, was constructed by the Pauly Jail Manufacturing Company of St. Louis in 1895. The exterior is brick trimmed with unique sandstone carvings. The cast iron tub in the bathroom, the built-in cabinet in the kitchen, and the wood-burning heater in the stairwell recall the days when the sheriff and his family lived in the jail.

Open Tuesday through Saturday 9 A.M. to noon, 1 to 5 P.M. Admission, free, but a voluntary contribution is requested.

CANYON
Map 9

Palo Duro Canyon State Park

12 miles east of Canyon on S.H. 217
Canyon 79015
806/488-2227   H, T, N

This scenic canyon on the Prairie Dog Town Fork of the Red River has exposed deposits spanning about 200 million years of geologic time. It was the scene of a decisive battle in 1874 between Comanche and Kiowa Indians and the U.S. Army troops under Colonel Ranald Mackenzie. Two years later Charles Goodnight be-

Burleson County Historical Museum, Caldwell. Photograph by Richard Tyler.

gan his cattle ranching enterprise in the canyon. The history of Palo Duro is presented in an interpretive exhibit in the park's visitor center. The symphonic drama *Texas*, by Paul Green, is performed in the outdoor amphitheater during the summer. Write or call for information.

The Visitor Center is open 8 A.M. to 5 P.M. daily June through August, from 8 A.M. to 5 P.M. Friday through Sunday during May, Saturday and Sunday September through April. Admission, $2 for car park and entrance fee.

*Panhandle-Plains Historical Museum

2401 Fourth Avenue   Canyon 79016
806/655-7191 or 655-7194   H, B

The oldest state-supported museum in Texas, the Panhandle-Plains Historical Museum is also one of the largest. Located in a beautiful 1930s structure decorated with murals by Texas artists Ben Carlton Mead and Harold Bugbee, the museum contains more than a quarter-million square feet of exhibit, storage, workroom, and office space. Exhibitions include the pre-history

The Panhandle-Plains Historical Museum, Canyon.

Entrance Hall of the Panhandle-Plains Historical Museum, Canyon. Photograph by Ron Tyler.

of the Panhandle as well as early pioneers, the Southern Plains Indians, ranching, and transportation; the Hall of Texas History, the Hall of the Southern Plains Indians, the Hall of the Cattlemen, a Pioneer Village, historic fashions, and an art gallery. Collections total more than 1,500,000 items, with major holdings in anthropology, paleontology, natural history, art, furniture and decorative arts, and history. The library, which is open weekdays, contains more than 10,000 volumes, 16,000 photographs, and 100 major manuscript collections.

On the museum grounds is the old T-Anchor Ranch Headquarters, the oldest intact structure in the Panhandle. This typical West Texas ranch building was constructed in 1877 and, along with its outbuildings, is open in the summer during regular museum hours or by appointment.

Open weekdays from 9 A.M. to 5 P.M., Sunday 2 to 5 P.M. Closed New Year's Day, Thanksgiving, and Christmas. Admission, free.

CARROLLTON
Map 1

A. W. Perry Homestead Museum

1509 North Perry   Carrollton 75006
214/323-5019

Located in a ten-acre park that is part of the original 640-acre homestead tract, the A. W. Perry home was completed in 1909 using lumber from the first Perry home. Perry was one of the founders of Carrollton. In this one-and-a-half-story house the tools and furnishings that made the Perry family comfortable during its more than half-a-century residence are still on display. Many of the native trees remain, and the spring-fed well has provided water for more than 100 years.

Open Tuesday and Thursday from 1 to 4 P.M., Sunday from 1:30 to 4 P.M. Admission, free.

CASTROVILLE
Map 6

Landmark Inn State Historic Site

U.S. 90 at Medina River Bridge
Castroville 78009
512/538-2133   H, T, N, HABS

Construction at the Landmark Inn site began in 1849 with a house for a member of Henri Castro's European colonists. The original building was soon expanded to become a well-known resting point on the San Antonio–El Paso road. The site gained additional importance for its store, gristmill, and cotton gin. The inn has now been restored and offers eight rooms where overnight guests can sample 1940s-style hospitality. A small exhibit in the building outlines the history of this Castroville site. The grounds, including the stabilized gristmill and dam, are accessible by a self-guided tour. Call for more information.

Open daily from 8 A.M. to 8 P.M. Admission, adults $.50, children age 6 to 12 $.25 day use fee.

CENTER
Map 2

Shelby County Museum

Shelbyville and Riggs Street   Center 75935
409/598-5470

Center was founded as the county seat of Shelby County in 1866 and was incorporated in 1893. Permanent exhibits in the museum, which

41

Interior, Landmark Inn, Castroville. Photograph by Todd Webb. Courtesy Amon Carter Museum, Fort Worth.

was founded in 1962, pertain to local history and county research material.

Open by appointment. Admission, free.

CHAPPELL HILL
Map 3

Chappell Hill Historical Society Museum

College Street   Chappell Hill 77426
409/836-9127   H

Changing exhibitions relating to the history of the Chappell Hill area are presented regularly. Displays include farming equipment, a blacksmith shop, a nineteenth-century kitchen, and a Confederate Room, which contains manuscripts, documents, and photographs. The museum is located in an old school building, constructed on the site of the Chappell Hill Male and Female Institute.

Open Sunday from 1:30 to 5 P.M. Admission, free, but a donation is requested. Group tours by appointment.

CHILDRESS
Map 9

Childress County Heritage Museum

Corner of Main and Avenue F, N.W.
Childress 79201
817/937-2261

Located on the courthouse square, the museum emphasizes the history of Childress County from prehistory through the Childress Army Air Field days of World War II. Exhibits include material relating to the early Indian cultures, ranching, farming, railroads, and turn-of-the-century interiors.

Open Monday through Friday, 9 A.M. to 5 P.M., Saturday, 9 A.M. to 1 P.M. Admission, free.

CLEBURNE
Map 1

Layland Museum

201 N. Caddo Street   Cleburne 76031
817/641-3321, Ext. 375   H, B, T, N

The Layland Museum collection consists primarily of material gathered by W. J. Layland, who was a plumber nine months of the year and a collector, archaeologist, and story teller the other three. There are literally hundreds of items relating to the Indians of the Southwest, the Plains, and the Northwest. Layland also collected Civil War material, including a number of rifles.

The museum, which is housed in the first building in Cleburne to be designed by a professional architect, the old Carnegie Library, also contains other exhibits relating to the history of Johnson County, such as a two-way radio built by J. Frank Thompson that enabled the Cleburne Police Department to have radio communication before some of the larger cities.

Open Monday through Friday from 10 A.M. to noon, 1 to 5 P.M., Saturday from 9 A.M. to 1 P.M. Admission, free.

CLEVELAND
Map 4

Austin Memorial Center

220 S. Bonham   Cleveland 77327
713/592-3920   H

Both a library and a museum, the Austin Memorial Center displays various antique and hobby collections as well as a small collection of etchings, glassware, and paintings of local historic buildings. In the Austin Memorial Room, a bedroom suite that once belonged to Potter Palmer of the Palmer House in Chicago is on display, as are other items of furniture and bric-a-brac, all donated by the late Charles and Bessie Sims Austin, benefactors of the Center. The Center also presents changing art and history exhibitions.

Open Monday through Friday from 9:30 A.M. to 5 P.M., except for Tuesday, noon to 8 P.M., and Saturday, 9:30 A.M. to 12:30 P.M. Admission, free.

CLIFTON
Map 1

Bosque Memorial Museum

Avenue Q, West of S.H. 6   Clifton 76634
817/675-3845

Related primarily to the history of Bosque County, the museum contains collections of

Texas rock and fossils, and pioneer clothing and memorabilia, including household items from the homes of Norwegian immigrants.

Open Friday and Saturday 10 A.M. to 5 P.M., Sunday from 2 to 5 P.M. Admission, adults $1; children and students $.50. Tours are available by appointment. Call 817/675-8733.

COLEMAN
Map 10

Coleman Museum
City Park   Coleman 76834
915/625-4128   H

Devoted to the history of Coleman County, the museum is housed in a replica of a Camp Colorado building built in 1936. Exhibits include farm machinery, an old windmill, and a blacksmith shop.

Open Saturday and Sunday from 1 to 6 P.M. in April, May, and September; daily except Thursday from 1 to 6 P.M. in June, July, and August. Admission, free.

COLLEGE STATION
Map 3

Texas A&M University
J. E. Rudder Exhibit Hall
College Station 77844
409/845-8501   H

Various art exhibitions are presented in the University Art Exhibit, in the Rudder Exhibit Hall.

Open from 8 A.M. to 11 P.M. daily. Admission, free.

Texas A&M University
Memorial Student Center Gallery
College Station 77844
713/845-1515   H

Various art exhibitions are presented in the Memorial Student Center Gallery (Room 104), while paintings of Texas A&M former student E. M. ("Buck") Schiwetz and the Carl Metzger Gun Collection, which has some especially famous Colts, can be seen in the Memorial Student Center Schiwetz Lounge and on the third floor, respectively.

Open from 8 A.M. to 8 P.M. daily. Admission, free.

COLORADO CITY
Map 7

Colorado City Museum
183 West Third Street   Colorado City 79512
915/728-8285

Founded in 1960, the museum features exhibitions on local paleontology and pioneer settlement, including a permanent exhibition of photographs of early settlement in Mitchell County, which was organized out of Bexar County in 1876.

Coleman Museum, Coleman.

Alley Log Cabin, Columbus.

Open Tuesday through Sunday from 2 to 5 P.M., closed on Monday. Admission, free, but donations are accepted.

COLUMBUS
Map 4

Alley Log Cabin

1200 Bowie Street   Columbus 78934
No telephone   H

Abraham Alley, one of Stephen F. Austin's "Old Three Hundred" colonists, built this square-notch oak log cabin in 1836, immediately after the Runaway Scrape when all the houses in the Columbus area had been burned to prevent aiding the oncoming Mexican army. The cabin remained on its original site until 1976, when it was moved to its present location. The house is furnished in period furnishings.

Open during the annual homes tour the third weekend in May and by appointment. Write Magnolia Homes Tour, Inc., P.O. Box 817, Columbus, Texas 78934. There is an admission charge.

Koliba Home Museum

1124 Front Street   Columbus 78934
409/732-2913

Constructed during the Republic of Texas (1836–1845), the Koliba Home was originally occupied by Stephen Townsend, the first sheriff of Colorado County. The Court Oak, where Judge R. M. (Three-Legged Willie) Williamson presided over Texas' first district court in 1837, is directly behind the house. Former State Representative Homer Koliba and his wife now live in the house, which came to them through her family. The museum portion of the home contains early household items and tools as well as pioneer memorabilia.

The museum is open from 10 A.M. to 6 P.M. each day, and Mr. and Mrs. Koliba give guided tours. There is a small charge for admission.

Senftenberg-Brandon House

616 Walnut Street   Columbus 78934
No telephone   H, B, T

Originally a four-room Greek Revival house constructed by Phoecian Tate in the 1860s, the Senftenberg-Brandon House went through several families as well as architectural changes. The Senftenberg family added the second floor, the ornate stairway, and the verandas in the 1880s. The Brandon family purchased the house in the 1890s and made a few additional changes. The rooms have been done in period furnishings, many of which were made in the Columbus area.

Today the house has been restored by Magnolia Homes Tour, Inc., and is open as a museum during the third weekend in May and by appointment. A group of thirty or more can schedule tours of the historic homes as well as lunch. Write Magnolia Homes Tour, Inc., P.O. Box 817, Columbus, Texas 78934. An admission fee is charged.

Koliba Home Museum, Columbus.

The Senftenberg-Brandon House, Columbus.

United Daughters of the Confederacy Museum

County Courthouse Square   Columbus 78934
No telephone   N

The United Daughters of the Confederacy Museum is housed in a building that was originally built for a water tower. The U.D.C. met in the building beginning in 1926 and it was made a museum, emphasizing the history of Colorado County, in 1961.

Open the third weekend in May and on special occasions. Admission, free.

COMANCHE
Map 10

Comanche County Historical Museum

W. Moorman Road   Comanche 76442
No telephone

Devoted to the history of the Comanche County area, which, although it was a part of the Mexican government's grant to Stephen F. Austin and Samuel May Williams, was not settled until 1854. The county was organized in 1856, and the town was established in 1858.

Open Sunday from 2 to 4:30 P.M. and by appointment. Admission, free.

COMSTOCK
Map 7

Seminole Canyon State Historical Park

9 miles west of Comstock on U.S. 90
Comstock 78837
915/292-4464   H (exhibits only), N

For more than 12,000 years humans have occupied this region near the mouth of the Pecos River. Ancient pictographs, some thought to be 8,500 years old, decorate the walls of many rock-shelters in this rugged canyon area. This human presence is the subject of a large interpretive exhibit in the Seminole Canyon visitor center which concludes with modern ranching activities in the region. Guided tours at 10 A.M. and 3 P.M. daily take visitors down into Seminole Canyon to see the fine examples of rock art found in the Fate Bell Shelter. Because some moderately strenuous hiking is involved, persons planning to take the tour should be in good physical condition.

Open daily from 8 A.M. to 5 P.M. Admission, $2 per car park entrance fee.

COOPER
Map 1

Patterson Memorial County Library and Museum

700 West Dallas Avenue   Cooper 75432
214/395-2934

Founded in 1968, the museum is located in the old Texas Midland Railway Station, which was constructed in 1913. It contains exhibitions and material relating to the history of Delta County, which was organized in 1870. Cooper was laid out in 1874 and incorporated in 1881.

Open Monday through Friday from 8 A.M. to 4 P.M. Admission, free.

CORPUS CHRISTI
Map 5

*Art Museum of South Texas

1902 N. Shoreline Drive   Corpus Christi 78403
512/883-3844   H, B

Housed in a beautiful building designed by Philip Johnson and John Burgee of New York, the Art Museum of South Texas is a bronze-trimmed, concrete monolith built on the Gulf of Mexico. Vast expanses of glass offer natural daylight for the works of art and at the same time provide a breathtaking view of the bay. Of this second museum that he designed in Texas (the Amon Carter Museum in Fort Worth being the other), Johnson said, "I tried to design a space that in itself without any pictures, without any reason for being, would be exciting." The first floor is a sweep of pure white, an unimpeded area including the two-story main gallery, the center of the museum's activity. Off the main gallery are more intimate exhibition areas and the museum shop and auditorium. A sixty-foot second-story walkway highlights the attractive second floor, which provides a view of the main gallery below and access to the outdoor sculpture court.

The museum's program consists of changing art exhibitions, lectures, films, and cultural events.

Open Tuesday through Saturday from 10 A.M. to 5 P.M., Sunday from 1 to 5 P.M. Admission, free.

*Corpus Christi Museum

1900 North Chaparral Street
Corpus Christi 78401
512/883-2862   H, B

While emphasizing national award-winning exhibitions on earth sciences, anthropology, natural history, archeology, history, and marine science, the Corpus Christi Museum also includes a gallery for local art exhibits, a 10,000 volume reference library, and a study collection for South Texas natural history. Exhibits include ancient Egyptian artifacts, fossils, minerals, shells, and arts and crafts of all humankind. There are various dioramas, murals, and period rooms featuring antique furniture. A special feature of the weekend is "Front Porch," where anyone who

Corpus Christi Museum.

wants to perform may do so on the museum stage.

Open Tuesday through Saturday 10 A.M. to 5 P.M., Sunday from 2 to 5 P.M. Closed on Monday. Admission, free.

Malaquite Beach Visitor Center
Padre Island National Seashore
9405 South Padre Island Drive
Corpus Christi 78418
512/933-8068   H, B

The exhibits at the Malaquite Beach Visitor Center deal with the formation of the barrier island, Padre Island, and the forces affecting it, things to do and see at the National Seashore, and small seasonal displays of the various types of shells and beachcombing items that wash onto the beach.

Open daily from 9 A.M. to 4 P.M. Admission, free.

Museum of Oriental Cultures
426 S. Staples Street   Corpus Christi 78401
512/883-1303   H, B

The exhibitions consist of Hakata dolls, masks, architectural scale models of shrines and temples, and reproductions of classic Oriental works as well as Oriental decorative artifacts. The museum was founded in 1973 by Mrs. Billie

T. Chandler, who had been a teacher of the children of the American military forces in Japan for fifteen years, to assist in cultural understanding between the Japanese and American people.

Open Monday through Friday from 10 A.M. to noon and 1 to 4 P.M., Sunday from 2 to 5 P.M. Closed Saturday. Admission, adults $1; students $.35; children under 12 $.25; museum members, free.

CORSICANA
Map 1

Pioneer Village

912 West Park Avenue   Corsicana 75110
214/872-1468   T

The seven log buildings of Pioneer Village show different facets of early life in Texas. The structures include an Indian trading post, a barn, a slave cabin, a blacksmith shop, and a general store. Various items, including archaeological specimens, clothing, tools, and antique furniture are on display in the structures.

Open Monday through Saturday 9 A.M. to 5 P.M., Sunday 1 to 5 P.M. Admission, adults $.50; children $.25.

Kabuki actor, from the collection of the Museum of Oriental Cultures, Corpus Christi.

Coupland Museum

Coupland 78615
512/856-2484   B

Housed in the old Coupland Depot, the museum includes mementoes and artifacts from early railroad days in central Texas, including the original railroad office and pictures of early train wrecks in Coupland. A Rock Island Railroad caboose with a wooden cupola has been added recently.

Open Friday, Saturday, and Sunday, and by special request. A donation is requested for admission.

Sturdy's Prairie Box House Museum

3 blocks east of U.S. 377   Cresson 76035
817/283-3640 or 396-4371   T

Richard Bruce, a stock raiser and member of a pioneer Johnson County family, purchased the land and built this modest frame house in 1889. The current owners have restored it and filled it with more than 2,000 antiques, including an ice cream cone maker, an 1898 toaster, an 1876 potato chip slicer, and a hand pump vacuum cleaner.

Open during June, July, and August Wednesday through Sunday from 1 to 5 P.M. Group tours by appointment year around. Nominal admissions charge.

Crosby County Pioneer Memorial Museum

101 Main Street (corner of U.S. 82 and F.R. 651)   Crosbyton 79322
806/675-2331   T

The front facade of the Crosby County Pioneer Memorial Museum is a replica of Hank Smith's rock house, the first home on the Plains of West Texas. The museum depicts the chrono-

Crosby County Pioneer Memorial Museum, Crosbyton.

logical development of the Crosby County Land District. The home life of settlers, from 1877 to 1930, is featured in the east wing of the museum. There are also early agricultural implements on exhibit. A reconstructed half dugout house gives a good idea of how many of the early arrivals in West Texas lived.

Open Tuesday through Saturday from 9 A.M. to noon, 2 to 5 P.M., Sunday from 2 to 4 P.M. May through September. Admission, free.

CROWELL
Map 10

Fire Hall Museum

116 N. Main Street   Crowell 79227
No telephone   H, B

The museum contains historical exhibits, but specializes in "living history" classes for school children.

Open Monday through Saturday from 10 A.M. to 5 P.M., Sunday from 1 to 5 P.M. Admission, free.

Foard County Courthouse Museum

County Courthouse   Crowell 79227
817/474-2581

The museum contains early documents and photographs as well as artifacts pertaining to the settlement of Foard County, which was organized in 1891. Perhaps the most interesting historical event that took place in the county was the recapture of Cynthia Ann Parker by a company of Texas Rangers under the command of Captain Lawrence Sullivan ("Sul") Ross in 1860.

Open daily from 9 A.M. to 5 P.M. Admission, free.

Foard County Museum

McAdams Ranch
15 1/2 miles west of Crowell on F.R. 654
Crowell 79227
817/655-3395   B

The Foard County Museum, located on a private ranch, contains material on early ranching families in the area as well as various works of art and household furnishings. Various antiques such as animal traps, corn grinders, a loom, and old furniture and clothes are on display. In addition, there are exhibits of dolls, quilts, books, cut glass, silver, and china as well as ranching gear such as saddles, fencing tools, a chuckwagon box and cooking utensils.

Open from June through September by appointment only. Admission, free.

DeWitt County Historical Museum, Cuero. Photograph by Phil Martin.

DeWitt County Historical Museum

312 E. Broadway   Cuero 77954
512/275-6322   B

The F. W. Bates–H. D. Sheppard home is maintained by the DeWitt County Historical Commission as a historical house museum. Except for special exhibits, which are arranged approximately four times a year, three rooms of the house are furnished in the style of the late Victorian era. The house was constructed in 1886 partially with lumber salvaged from the ruins of the family home in Indianola, which was destroyed by the hurricane of August, 1886.

Open Thursday and Friday from 9 A.M. to 5 P.M., Sunday from 2 to 5 P.M. Admission, free.

Morris County Historical Museum

Route 1, Box 280   Daingerfield 75638
No telephone   T

The first settlers arrived in the Daingerfield area in 1840, but it was not made the county seat of Morris County until 1876. The museum relates to the history of the area.

Open Sunday from 2 to 5 P.M.

XIT Museum

108 East 5th Street   Dalhart 79022
806/249-5390   H, B

Located across the street from the Dallam County Courthouse, the XIT Museum is devoted to the history of Dallam and Hartley counties and to the XIT Ranch, which was established in 1895 by a Chicago company on land it had received in return for building the State Capitol in Austin. Period rooms, including a turn-of-the-century parlor, a bedroom and kitchen, and a pioneer chapel help tell the story of the settlement of the Panhandle. Also on exhibit are Indian artifacts and an antique gun collection.

The museum is unusual in that it is sponsored by a historical association made up of two counties, Dallam and Hartley, hence the name of the city, Dalhart, which is actually located in both counties.

Open Tuesday through Saturday from 2 to 5 P.M., and the first Sunday of each month from 2 to 5 P.M. Admission, free, but a contribution is accepted.

The XIT Museum, across the street from the courthouse, Dalhart.

DALLAS
Map 1

African-American Cultural Heritage Center
Nolan Estes Educational Plaza
3434 South R. L. Thornton Freeway
Dallas 75224
214/375-1600   H

One of four cultural heritage centers sponsored by the Dallas Independent School District, the African-American Heritage Center emphasizes the contributions of Afro-American culture. Among the displays are wood carvings from Mali, fertility dolls from Ghana, a Bamun chief's stool from Cameroon, and a Mingani dancer from Pende. Also on exhibit are decorative quilts, baskets, textiles, pottery, jewelry, and paintings that reflect a broad range of African and African-American traditions. In addition, there is a collection of documents and photographs that reflect the black experience in Texas and Dallas.

Open from 10 A.M. to 4 P.M. on school days. Admission, free.

Age of Steam Museum
See Fair Park

Asian-American Cultural Heritage Center
Tom Gooch Early Childhood Center
4030 Calculus Road   Dallas 75234
214/241-6111   H

Established in an effort to further the understanding of Asian arts, philosophies, and customs, the Asian-American Cultural Heritage Center features a display of dolls, including a life-size Boys Day Doll dressed in a samurai warrior costume, a rare set of heirloom dolls representing the Emperor, Empress, and their court in early Japan, and numerous Indian, Chinese, Korean, Filipino, and other Japanese dolls. Also on display are carved temple figures, musical instruments from Thailand and India, decorative porcelain tea sets from China and Japan, Indian jewelry, and an exhibit of children's school supplies from the People's Republic of China. Art objects include Indian *pichvai* paintings on fabric; a thirty-six–inch carved rosewood Ganesha, the elephant-headed god of good luck; Japanese silk screen and wood block prints; Filipino shell paintings; Thai temple rubbings; and a hand painted Chinese Koromandel screen.

Open from 10 A.M. to noon and 1 to 4 P.M. on school days. Admission, free. Call to arrange a tour. DISD tours are usually scheduled during the morning.

Biblical Arts Center
7500 Park Lane (across from NorthPark Center)   Dallas 75225
214/691-4661   H, B

Housed in a building reminiscent of the early Christian era structures in the Holy Land, the Biblical Arts Center exhibits art and artifacts related to the Bible. The East Gallery is an area for changing exhibitions, and the West Gallery is a multi-purpose area for performing arts events. The central feature of the atrium is the replica of the Garden Tomb of Christ in Jerusalem, accurate in detail and scale. The Founders Gallery displays art collected from throughout the world by Mattie Caruth Byrd, founder of the Biblical Arts Center.

The 20 × 124 foot *Miracle at Pentecost* mural by Dallas artist Torger Thompson is presented in its own theater in a dramatic display of light and sound. The Miracle at Pentecost Museum displays the preliminary sketches, photographs, and other research material that Thompson used during the more than four years' work on the mural.

Open Tuesday through Saturday from 10 A.M. to 5 P.M., Sunday from 1 to 5 P.M. Closed Monday, New Year's Day, Thanksgiving, and Christmas Eve and Day. An admission is charged, but there are group rates for 10 or more persons.

Dallas Aquarium
See Fair Park
Dallas Arboretum & Botanical Society
See White Rock Lake Park
Dallas Civic Garden Center
See Fair Park
Dallas Historical Society
See Fair Park
Dallas Museum of Art
See Fair Park
Dallas Museum of Natural History
See Fair Park
DeGolyer Estate
See White Rock Lake Park

Fair Park
Age of Steam Museum
Washington & Parry   Dallas 75226
214/361-6936   H

The Age of Steam Museum features exhibitions relating to railroading: Dallas's oldest depot, the world's largest steam locomotive, and a 1930 passenger train. Furniture, china, and other artifacts and memorabilia from the railroad's heyday are also on display.

Open Sunday from 11 A.M. to 5 P.M. Admission, adults $1; children under 16, $.50.

Fair Park
Dallas Aquarium
First and Martin Luther King   Dallas 75226
214/428-3587   H

Over 2,000 different specimens of aquatic animals are on display, including more than 300 species, from native fresh-water species to cold fresh-water species, tropical fresh-water species, marine tropical species, reptiles, and amphibians and aquatic mammals. Feeding times: fresh-water fish Monday and Thursday at 3 P.M.; tropical fish Monday through Friday at 9 A.M.

Open Monday through Saturday, 9 A.M. to 5 P.M., 1 to 5 P.M. Sunday. Admission, free.

Fair Park
Dallas Civic Garden Center
Dallas 75226
214/428-7476   H, B, R,

The Tropical Garden Room of the Dallas Civic Garden Center covers more than 6,000 square feet, houses more than 450 varieties of tropical plants from all over the world, and features a naturalistic waterfall that creates a pool for tropical fish and aquatic plants. In addition, the Garden Center also offers several outdoor gardens, including the Contemporary Gardens, the Callier Garden, the All American Garden, the Herbert Marcus Senior Garden, the Jonsson Garden, and the Shakespeare Garden. Braille markers have been placed in the Herb and Scent Garden for the enjoyment of the blind.

Open Monday through Friday from 10 A.M. to 5 P.M., Saturday from 9 A.M. to 5 P.M., and Sunday from 2 to 5 P.M. Closed Christmas Eve and Day. Admission, free to the outside gardens; to the Tropical Conservatory, adults $.50; children $.25. Free from 9 A.M. to 1 P.M. on Saturday.

Fair Park
Dallas Historical Society
Hall of State   Dallas 75226
214/421-5136   B, H, T

Located in the Hall of State building, which was constructed for the Texas Centennial in 1936, the Dallas Historical Society was founded in 1922. Exhibitions pertain to Dallas, Texas, the Southwest, and American history, and include traveling exhibitions as well as exhibits organized from the extensive museum and archive collections of the Society.

The Hall of State contains handsome murals by Texas artists such as Tom Lea and monumental-size sculptures of six Texas heroes by Pompeo Coppini, Italian-born sculptor who fell in love with the romantic history of Texas and created what J. Frank Dobie, the Austin writer and sage, called "his monstrosities." The Hall of State is one of the finest examples of art deco architecture in the state. The Society also maintains a fine library and archives devoted to Dallas and Texas history.

Open Monday through Saturday from 9 A.M. to 5 P.M., Sunday and holidays from 1 to 5 P.M., and from 10 A.M. to 7 P.M. during the State Fair of Texas. Admission, free.

Fair Park
*Dallas Museum of Art
Dallas 75226
214/421-4187   H, R, B

Like many other museums in Texas, the Dallas Museum of Art began when an art association formed within the public library in 1903 to sponsor art exhibits. In 1936 the museum moved into one of the Centennial buildings in Fair Park, and in 1962 it merged with the Dallas Museum of Contemporary Arts to form the Dallas

Detail of the new Dallas Museum of Art, showing one of the barrel vaults which will house the Museum's Contemporary Galleries. Courtesy Dallas Museum of Art.

The new Dallas Museum of Art in the downtown cultural district. Photograph by Dan Barsotti. Courtesy Dallas Museum of Art.

Edward Hopper, Lighthouse Hill, *1927. 28¼ × 39½ in. Courtesy Dallas Museum of Art, Gift of Mr. and Mrs. Maurice Purnell.*

This Seated Man with Hands on Knees, *from the Veracruz region of Mexico, is a part of the vast pre-Columbian collection at the Dallas Museum of Art. Courtesy Dallas Museum of Art, The Nora and John Wise Collection, Loan.*

Museum of Art. The collection includes superb examples of pre-Columbian and African art and Impressionist, Classical, nineteenth- and twentieth-century American, Japanese, and Baroque art. Highlights are the pre-Columbian gold collection, a superb group of Guatemalan textiles, and an excellent example of Camille Pissarro's Pointillist period, *Apple Pickers,* Edward Hopper's *Lighthouse Hill,* Andrew Wyeth's *That Gentleman,* and the huge landscape, *The Icebergs,* by the American artist Frederic Edwin Church. In addition, the museum is strong in twentieth-century art, including five paintings by Piet Mondrian, and works by Rene Magritte, Mark Rothko, Franz Kline, Tom Wesselmann, and others.

Twelve to fourteen temporary shows on various subjects are presented each year. Recent exhibitions include the international touring exhibiton of El Greco paintings, the Shakespeare collection from the world-famous Folger Library, Pompeii, and photographs by Richard Avedon and Cartier-Bresson.

The museum is soon to move into its newly completed and spacious downtown quarters at

1717 N. Harwood. Designed by Edward Larrabee Barnes, one of the most successful of today's museum architects, it will occupy 8.9 acres in the city's central business district and will offer almost three times more exhibit space than the former facility. There are permanent exhibit areas for Traditional European and American art, Non-Western art, and contemporary art. A 9,500 square feet area has also been set aside for temporary exhibitions, and the excellent Gallery Buffet restaurant has been expanded and placed to overlook the downtown skyline.

Open Tuesday through Saturday, 10 A.M. to 5 P.M., Sunday 1 to 5 P.M. Closed Monday. Admission, free.

Fair Park
*Dallas Museum of Natural History
2nd and Grand   Dallas 75226
214/421-2169   H, B

Also located in a Centennial building in Fair Park, the Dallas Museum of Natural History features exhibits that interpret the plants and animals, rocks, and minerals and fossils of Texas and the Southwest. Fifty dioramas depict Texas wildlife in their natural environments, while the Bird Hall and the Earth Science Hall show scientific specimens for easy identification and interpretation. Traveling exhibitions cover a broad range of world-wide natural history subjects.

Dallas Museum of Natural History, Fair Park.

Open Monday through Saturday from 9 A.M. to 5 P.M., Sundays and holidays from 12 to 5 P.M. Admission, free.

Fair Park
*The Science Place/Southwest Museum of Science and Technology
First and King Avenue   Dallas 75223
214/428-8351   H, B, R

The Science Place is an innovative museum and learning center concerned with both the natural and social sciences. There are more than 115 permanent exhibits in The Science Place, including the Gossamer Penguin, the first solar-powered airplane. The museum is developing new, "hands-on" exhibits on such topics as energy, future human environments, computers, health and anatomy, communications, and engineering.

The museum also presents regularly scheduled traveling exhibitions and has a planetarium, which has regular shows at 2:30 and 3:30 P.M. on Saturdays and Sundays. "Concert Under the Stars" programs are available throughout the year.

Open Tuesday through Saturday from 9 A.M. to 5 P.M., Sunday from 12 to 5 P.M. Closed Monday. Admission, adults $1, children 17 years and under and senior citizens $.50; an additional $.50 is charged for the planetarium shows. Call for information about the planetarium or about changing exhibitions.

Hall of State
See Fair Park, Dallas Historical Society

International Museum of Cultures
7500 W. Camp Wisdom Road   Dallas 75236
214/298-3331   H, B

Opened in May, 1981, the International Museum of Cultures focuses exclusively on contemporary cultures of living people. Exhibitions include "Jungle Potters," which focuses on the present-day pottery-making skills and artistry of the Quichua Indians of Ecuador, and "Nuevo Destino," which tells the life story of a Shipibo Indian in Peru who is taking a leading role in promoting education among his people.

Open Tuesday through Saturday from 10 A.M. to 5 P.M., Sunday 2 to 5 P.M. Admission, free.

McCord Theater Collection
See Southern Methodist University

Meadows Museum
See Southern Methodist University

Mexican-American Cultural Heritage Center
Pinkston Annex (Thomas Edison)
2940 Singleton Boulevard   Dallas 75212
214/630-1680   H

The Mexican-American Cultural Heritage
Center calls attention to the strong Hispanic
influence in Texas history. With exhibits of
pre-Columbian artifacts from central Mexico,
eighteenth-century Spanish colonial *Santos*
(wood carvings of saints), clothing and riding
gear used by the Mexican *charros* and *vaqueros*
(ranchers and cowboys), and a variety of traditional Hispanic folk art and toys, the Center
points out the common heritage of both Texas
and Mexico. Temporary exhibitions are also presented, both in the Center and in various other
locations in Dallas.

Open during school days from 8 A.M. to 5 P.M.
Admission, free.

Museum of African-American Life and Culture
3837 Simpson-Stuart Road (two blocks off
I-45)   Dallas 75241
214/372-8738

Located in Oak Cliff on the Bishop College
campus, the Museum of African-American Life
and Culture displays traditional African sculpture and ceremonial objects as well as African-
American art. There is a regular schedule of exhibitions, which includes traveling shows from
other institutions. An archival program actively
collects and preserves historical documents and
memorabilia of outstanding blacks of the Southwest. The museum sponsors several annual art
exhibitions and symposia on art and history. The
museum plans to move to renovated quarters
soon.

Open Monday through Friday from noon to 4
P.M., and by appointment. Admission, free.

National Broadcast Museum
1701 Market Street   Dallas 75202
214/748-1112   H, B

Objects and memorabilia associated with the
broadcast industry are the specialty of this museum. Items on exhibit include the personal mi-
croscope that Thomas A. Edison used to inspect
diamond phonograph needles, ornate victrolas,
early television sets, rock and roll star Bill
Haley's favorite guitar, Columbia Broadcasting

System newsman Walter Cronkite's microphone, and an example of the most contemporary videotape machines. The broadcast industry, from transmitter (an old water-cooled model that belonged to radio station WRR of Dallas) to studio (control room used by WOAI in San Antonio until recently) to receiver (several elaborate models), is covered in the museum's exhibits. Most of the exhibits are "hands-on," and touching is encouraged.

A "Jot 'Em Down Store," a 1930s general store patterned after the one that Lum and Abner made famous, is filled with antique signs, old 78 rpm records, and a restored radio, and two listening booths permit visitors to listen to the museum's collection of more than 150 original old-time radio shows.

The museum is scheduled to move to The Dallas Communications Complex—The Studios at Las Colinas, 6301 N. O'Connor Boulevard, Irving 75062, two miles west of I-35 and Royal Lane.

Open Wednesday through Friday from 11 A.M. to 4 P.M., Saturday and Sunday from 11 A.M. to 5 P.M. Closed Christmas Day. Admission, adults $2; children $1.

Native American Cultural Heritage Center
Sequoyah Environmental Science Academy
3635 Greenleaf Street   Dallas 75212
214/631-3920   H

Exhibits of tribal artifacts represent the six geographical areas of the United States: Southeast, Southwest, Northwest Coast, North, Great Plains, and Great Basin. All the tribes found in each area are listed, and artifacts of many of them are exhibited. Among the displays are Iroquois moccasins, a Delaware ribbonwork skirt, a Kiowa dress and cradleboard, a Cheyenne rawhide *parfleche* (pouch), multi-colored porcupine quillwork, and Navaho weavings. There are more than 600 American Indian tribes, and the Center heightens awareness of their heritage and their role in American society.

Open during school days from 8 A.M. to 5 P.M. Admission, free.

Neiman-Marcus ArchiveShowcase
Fifth Floor   Main and Ervay streets
Dallas 75201
214/573-5780   H, B, R

Created in 1982 as a part of the seventy-fifth anniversary celebration of the founding of the

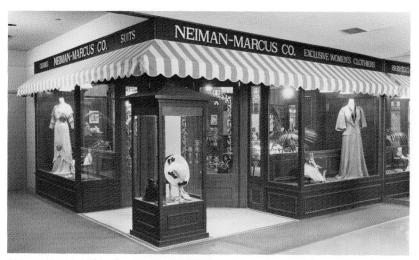

Neiman-Marcus ArchiveShowcase, on the fifth floor of the famous specialty store in Dallas.

Neiman-Marcus specialty store, the Archive-
Showcase presents the store's early history and
personalities through advanced audiovisual techniques, automation, and static displays. The origin of such well-known features as the Christmas Book and the Fortnight celebrations are
highlighted along with certain historic moments
in the famous specialty store's past.

Open during store hours. Admission, free.

*Old City Park

1717 Gano Street   Dallas 75215
214/421-5141   H, R, B, T, HABS

A museum of architectural and cultural history sponsored by the Dallas County Heritage
Society, Old City Park contains structures that
represent North Central Texas from 1840 to
1910. Included are Millermore (1855–1862), the
Gano Log House (1845–1846), barn, print shop,
cellar house, Miller Log House (1847), Depot
(1886), Renner School (1888), hotel, doctor's office, bank, dental office, church, 1876 farmhouse
restaurant, general store, Victorian mansion,
multi-media program, and gift shop. The structures are arranged by theme: Transportation
Complex, Victorian Architecture, Ante-Bellum
Complex, the Education and Religion Complex,
Commercial Arts, and Rural Settlement.

Open Tuesday through Friday from 10 A.M. to
4 P.M., Saturday and Sunday from 1:30 to 4:30

Dog-trot log house (1845–1846), Old City Park, with the Dallas skyline in the background.

P.M. Admission to the park grounds is free, but there is a fee to tour the historic buildings: adults $4, children 6 to 12 $2, senior citizens 65 and older $2. Volunteer guides are available, and Discovery Tours are available for school children.

The Science Place
See Fair Park

Southern Methodist University
McCord Theater Collection
Fondren Library
Dallas 75225
214/692-1002   H

The McCord Theater Collection, founded on the campus of Southern Methodist University in 1933, is an important collection of material from cinema, circus, opera, dance, theater, vaudeville, radio, and television from many cities, but with special emphasis on Texas. Exhibits of pictorial history and artifacts—including photographs, paintings, and engravings—of more than a century of performing arts are on display.

Open during library hours by appointment. Admission, free.

Southern Methodist University
Meadows Museum
Owen Art Center
Dallas 75275
214/692-2516   B (catalogues and a brochure
are available from the guard)

Opened in 1965, the Meadows Museum began
with a gift of mostly-Spanish paintings acquired
by the late Dallas businessman Algur H. Meadows, whose frequent trips to Spain permitted
him to develop an interest in that country's
great museums and art. Today the museum contains one of the finest collections of Spanish art
outside Spain. Included in the more than 100
paintings that cover over 400 years of Spanish
art history are masterpieces by Goya, Velázquez,
Zurbaran, Murillo, and other notable Spanish
artists as well as more than 200 first-edition
prints by Goya, which are exhibited on a rotating basis. The museum has also added Latin
American and twentieth-century Spanish works
by Juan Gris, Joan Miró, and Diego Rivera.

Open Monday through Saturday 10 A.M. to
5 P.M., Sunday 1 to 5 P.M. Tours (in English or
Spanish) are available by calling 214/692-2853.
Admission, free.

Main Gallery, Meadows Museum, Southern Methodist University, Dallas. Photograph by Debora Hunter.

The Southwest Museum of Science and Technology
See Fair Park, The Science Place

White Rock Lake Park
Dallas Arboretum & Botanical Society
8617 Garland Road   Dallas 75218
214/327-8263   H (partially), N (DeGolyer home and gardens)

The Dallas Arboretum & Botanical Society headquarters is located on the old Camp Estate overlooking White Rock Lake. The combined sixty-six acres, including the DeGolyer Estate (see separate listing), are being developed into a new botanical garden. Various plants, historical gardens, and the DeGolyer home can be seen during the tours. There is also a wildflower area and displays of ornamental plants and flowers. Call for further information, especially for tours of the DeGolyer home.

Open Tuesday through Sunday from 9 A.M. to 8 P.M. in the summer, 9 A.M. to 5 P.M. in the winter. Admission, free.

White Rock Lake Park
DeGolyer Estate
8525 Garland Road   Dallas 75218
214/324-1401   H, N

Built in 1939–40, this Spanish Colonial Revival mansion was the home of the noted petroleum geologist, scientist, and book collector Everett Lee DeGolyer and his wife Nell. The library is of particular interest, as is the view of White Rock Lake from the dining room. The house has been partially furnished with antiques belonging to the DeGolyer family and is used as a cultural center for meetings, classes, seminars, and cultural events.

Tours are given Tuesday at 1, 2, and 3 P.M. and Wednesday through Friday from 10 A.M. to 3 P.M. on the hour. Closed Monday and weekends. Admission, free.

Dallas Zoo
621 E. Clarendon   Dallas 75203
214/946-5154

A large collection of animals, located three miles south of downtown Dallas on I-35 (take the Ewing Avenue exit).

Open from 9 A.M. to 6 P.M. daily. Admission, adults $2, children 6 to 11 $1.25, under 6 free. Parking, $1.

Interior of the Wise County Heritage Museum, Decatur. Photograph by William Howze.

DECATUR
Map 1

Wise County Heritage Museum

1602 S. Trinity   Decatur 76234
817/627-5586   T, B, N, HABS

The administration building of old Decatur Baptist College is the home for the Wise County Heritage Museum, which features exhibitions of Indian artifacts, local history and art, and the old post office wall and windows from Chico.

Open 9 A.M. to 4:30 P.M. Monday through Saturday, 1 to 4:30 P.M. on Sunday. Admission, adults, $.50; children, school groups, and senior citizens, $.25.

DEER PARK
Map 4

Battleship Texas

See Houston, San Jacinto Battleground

Deer Park Independent School District Historical School Museum

204 Ivy   Deer Park 77536
713/479-2831, Ext. 135   H

Housed in the Administration Building Annex, the Deer Park School Museum traces the history of the school district from its beginning in 1931 to the present. Items from each school in the district are on exhibit, and two video tapes interpret the history of the school.

Open on school days from 8 A.M. to 4 P.M. and the first Sunday of each month from 1 to 5 P.M. Admission, free.

San Jacinto Museum of History

See Houston, San Jacinto Battleground

The Deer Park Independent School District Historical School Museum.

Whitehead Memorial Museum

1308 S. Main Street   Del Rio 78840

512/774-3611, Ext. 244   H, B, T, N

The Whitehead Memorial Museum contains several buildings and sites, including a hacienda and chapel; the Perry Store, which was the largest mercantile store between San Antonio and El Paso during the 1870s; the Hal Patton Labor Office, which now contains an exhibit relating to black history and the Seminole scouts of the area; the shepherd's wagon; a twentieth-century log cabin; a replica of Judge Roy Bean's famous saloon; and the graves of Roy Bean and his son, Sam.

Open Tuesday through Saturday from 9 A.M. to 12 P.M., 1 to 4:30 P.M. Closed Sunday and Monday. Admission, adults $1; children $.25.

Eisenhower Birthplace State Park

208 E. Day   Denison 75020

214/465-8908   H, T

The restored home where President Dwight David Eisenhower was born on October 14, 1890, is a modest structure. The Eisenhower family lived in Denison for three years while "Ike's" father worked as an engine wiper for the Missouri, Kansas and Texas Railroad. On display is a quilt made by Eisenhower's mother, as well as other period furnishings.

Open daily from 10 A.M. to noon, 1 to 5 P.M.; June through Labor Day, 8 A.M. to 5 P.M. Closed New Year's Day and Christmas Day. Admission, adults $.50; children $.25.

Grayson County Frontier Village
Loy Park on Loy Lake Road   Denison 75020
214/463-2487   B (in the planning), T

Founded in 1966 as a replica of an 1880s town, the Grayson County Frontier Village now contains seven structures, including the Bullock-Bass House (1850s), the Holder-Cold Springs Log School House (1855), and the Davis-Ansely Cabin (1839), one of the oldest historical buildings in the county. The cabin, which has bullet holes from Indian raids in the outer walls, is the site where the Rev. Sumner Bacon organized the first congregation in Grayson County. Also in the Village is the W. T. Lankford house (1847), which is believed to be the first house in Grayson County built of milled lumber. Other artifacts of pioneer life include horse-drawn farm machinery, a road camp jail wagon, and a courting sleigh. Plans call for the structures to be furnished with antiques representative of the period during which they were used.

Open Sunday from 2 to 5 P.M. and other times by appointment. Admission, free.

Courthouse-on-the-Square Museum
The Square   Denton 76201
817/566-1487   H, B, T, N, HABS

The Courthouse-on-the-Square Museum is located on the second floor of the old Denton County Courthouse, which was completed in 1896. One of the spectacular Texas courthouses, it was designed by Central Texas architect W. C. Dodson and was probably inspired by the French Cathedral in Florence, Italy.

Exhibitions depict life as it was lived by ordinary people about the turn of the century in Denton County. There are special changing exhibits from time to time.

Open Monday through Thursday from 2:00 to 5:00 P.M. Closed Friday through Sunday and on major holidays. Admission, free.

Historical Collection
North Texas State University
Avenue A & Mulberry Street   Denton 76203
817/565-2386   B

Begun in 1925 by Dr. J. L. Kingsbury, the Historical Collection now contains material relating to the life of early regional settlers, firearms, a doll collection, and ethnographic, archaeological, and prehistory materials. There is also a section of material relating to early ranching history. Temporary exhibits interpret university research and educational activities.

The Historical Collection is located in the Historical Building, constructed in 1913 and the oldest structure on the North Texas State University campus.

Open from 1:00 to 5:00 P.M. Monday through Friday and by appointment. Call for information on tours.

Texas Woman's University
Texas' First Ladies Historic Costume Collection
Ground floor, College of Nutrition, Textiles, and Human Development Building Denton 76204
817/382-8821

The collection includes either the actual garments or faithful copies of the gowns worn by the wives of the Governors of Texas and the Presidents of the Republic of Texas, in addition to dresses worn at formal events by the wives of three Presidents of the United States and a wife of a Vice President of the United States. There are dresses or copies of dresses worn by Mrs. Sam Houston, Mrs. Dan Moody, and Mrs. Lyndon B. Johnson, among others.

Open from 8 A.M. to 5 P.M. Monday through Friday. Admission, free.

Texas Woman's University
Texas Woman's University Art Museum
1 Circle Drive Denton 76204
817/382-8923

An ongoing schedule of art exhibitions is presented in the Art Museum of Texas Woman's University throughout the year. The museum is located in the completely renovated East Wing and West Wing Galleries of the Fine Arts Building.

Open from 9 A.M. to 4 P.M. when school is in session. Admission, free.

Texas Woman's University
Texas Woman's University State Historical Collection: History of Texas Women
Old Main Building Denton 76204
817/387-1215 T

The history of Texas Woman's University goes back to the Girls' Industrial Institute and College of Texas, which was created in 1901. The cornerstone for the Old Main Building was laid January 10, 1903, and classes began in September. The school went through several name changes before it became Texas Woman's University in

Courthouse-on-the-Square Museum, Denton. Photograph by Todd Webb. Courtesy Amon Carter Museum, Fort Worth.

Old Main, on the Denton campus of Texas Woman's University, houses exhibits from the State Historical Collection: History of Texas Women.

1957. Exhibits relate to the history of Texas women and include artifacts, photographs, manuscripts, and publications.

Open Tuesday from 9 A.M. to noon, Thursday from 1 to 4 P.M. Closed when school is not in session. Admission, free.

DIMMITT
Map 9

Castro County Historical Museum

404 W. Halsell Street   Dimmitt 79027
806/647-2611

A general museum focusing on the history and pioneer crafts of the area, the Castro County Historical Museum features demonstrations of soap-making, quilting, spinning, and a County Fair each September.

Open Monday through Friday from 1 to 5 P.M., Saturday and Sunday by appointment. Admission, free.

DUBLIN
Map 10

Lyon Museum

113 E. Blackjack   Dublin 76446
817/445-2582   T

Located in a historic building, the Lyon Museum displays artifacts pertaining to local, pioneer history. The structure was built in 1880 and veneered with native stone in 1895.

Open Saturday from 2 to 4 P.M. Admission, free.

Lyon Museum, Dublin.

Moore County Historical Museum
Lew Haile Annex
Dumas Avenue & East 8th   Dumas 79029
806/935-3113   H

The museum features exhibits that relate to life in Moore County, the wildlife as well as the people. There are exhibits on Indians in the Panhandle, barbed wire, early kitchen implements, and a general store, doctor-pharmacist office, and early day schoolroom.

Open during winter Monday through Friday from 1 to 4:30 P.M.; summer, Tuesday through Saturday from 10 A.M. to 5 P.M., Sunday from 2 to 5 P.M.

Fort Duncan Museum
Fort Duncan Park   Eagle Pass 78852
512/773-6057   T, HABS

This restored nineteenth-century fort complex includes the post headquarters, powder magazine, and six other restored buildings. In the headquarters building is the museum, which features archaeological exhibits as well as displays on local and pioneer history. Fort Duncan, established on the Rio Grande near Eagle Pass, was one of the important frontier posts during the mid-nineteenth century.

Open September through May, weekends from 2 to 5 P.M., June through August, daily except Sunday, 10 A.M. to 5 P.M. A $1 donation is requested for admission.

Edgewood Heritage Center
North Main   Edgewood 75117
214/896-4253   T

Sponsored by the Edgewood Historical Society, the Heritage Center contains a dog-trot cabin, a log barn, a turn-of-the-century cottage, a syrup mill, and a bank building. The cabin is furnished with artifacts contemporary with its construction.

Open the first and third Saturdays of the month, and by appointment. A donation is requested for admission.

Hidalgo County Historical Museum
121 E. McIntyre (on Courthouse Square)
Edinburg 78539
512/383-6911   H, B

The Hidalgo County Historical Museum tells the long history and cultural heritage of the Lower Rio Grande Valley region. Exhibits include archaeology, Spanish exploration and settlement, river steamboats, and ranch life. The

Hidalgo County Historical Museum, Edinburg.

turn-of-the-century "Old Town" features exhibits on farming and the Valley boom days of the early 1900s. The museum is partly housed in an old jail; its hanging room and trap door can be inspected by visitors. Exhibits nearby tell of early lawmen and bandit raids. Downstairs, the "Country Store" gift show uses turn-of-the-century store fixtures, including an antique cash register.

Public programs such as lectures, demonstrations, and films are given on most Sunday afternoons in the fall, winter, and spring months. Puppet shows and docented tours for school groups are available.

Open Tuesday through Friday from 9 A.M. to 5 P.M., Sunday from 1 to 5 P.M. Closed Monday and Saturday.

EDNA
Map 4

Texana Museum and Library
403 N. Wells Street (U.S. 111 N)   Edna 77957
512/782-5431   H, T

Founded in 1963, the museum displays material pertaining to the history of Jackson County and the early history of Texas, including an authentic country store. There are special traveling exhibits several times each year.

Open Tuesday through Friday from 1 to 5 P.M., Saturday from 8 A.M. to noon. Admission, free.

Egypt Plantation

Egypt 77436

409/677-3562   T

The brick house that William Jones Elliott Heard, an original member of Stephen F. Austin's colony, built in 1849–1854 is today a museum housing photographs, furniture, manuscripts, and artifacts and other memorabilia of early life in Texas. The plantation got its name when Austin's colonists said that they "went down into Egypt for corn," during the 1827 drought, a reference to the Biblical story of Jacob's and his sons' visits to Egypt. Captain Heard must have recalled his Tennessee youth when he built the house, for it is Georgian in its basic style and used brick made on the site in 1850.

Open weekdays from 8 A.M. to noon and 2 to 4 P.M. by reservation. Tours of groups of twelve or more are available by reservation for $5 per person.

Entrance hall of the Captain W. E. Heard House, Egypt. Photograph by Todd Webb. Courtesy Amon Carter Museum, Fort Worth.

El Campo Museum of Art, History & Natural Science

201 E. Jackson Street   El Campo 77437
409/543-2713   H, B

The collection consists of world record animal trophies in background habitats, including the Africa Room, the Jungle Cats Exhibit, the Mountain Rams Exhibit, and the Alaskan Exhibit. The white rhinoceros is one of the few in a U.S. museum, and there is an example of every kind of ram. A section of the exhibit relates to the history of the El Campo area, and changing exhibitions are also presented from time to time.

Open weekdays from 9 A.M. to 5 P.M.; Saturday and Sunday from 1 to 5 P.M. Admission, free.

Schleicher County Museum

Menard highway and U.S. 277   Eldorado 76936
915/853-2709   H

Housed in an old hardware store building constructed of native rock, the Schleicher County Museum emphasizes the history of the county, which was founded in 1901.

Open Monday through Thursday from 2 to 4:30 P.M. and at other times by appointment.

Bullfight Museum

Del Camino Restaurant
5001 Alameda (U.S. 80E)   El Paso 79905
915/772-2711

Housed in the corridors and dining rooms of the Del Camino Restaurant, the Bullfight Museum contains costumes, artifacts, and memorabilia associated with bullfighting in both Mexico and Spain. The displays include historic prints, newspaper and magazine clippings, and photographs as well as personal memorabilia and clothing of famous toreadors.

Open daily when the restaurant is open. Admission, free.

Chamizal National Memorial Museum

800 S. San Marcial   El Paso 79944
915/541-7780 or 541-7880   H, B, N

The Chamizal National Memorial was established in 1973 to commemorate the peaceful settlement of boundary disputes between the United States and Mexico. The permanent exhibition recounts the history of the boundary survey between the two countries, made during the 1850s. Temporary exhibitions, changed monthly, feature artists of the United States and Mexico and traveling displays developed by the

National Park Service or local staff.

The Memorial is also a theater of performance arts dedicated to the exchange of cultural ideas between Mexico and the U.S. Special events are the Siglo de Oro Drama Festival in March, the Fiesta of the Arts during the summer, and the Border Folk Festival in October. Call for information on performances.

Open daily from 9 A.M. to 5 P.M. and frequently during the evening. Admission to the museum is free. There is a modest charge for some performances.

Church Heritage Center
Trinity United Methodist Church
Corner of Mesa and Yandell   El Paso 79922
915/532-2674   T

The Heritage Center depicts the first 100 years in the life of the Trinity United Methodist Church, the oldest church in El Paso, which was founded in January 1882. Special exhibitions are sometimes arranged.

Tours on request. Call for information.

El Paso Centennial Museum
University of Texas at El Paso
University and Wiggins Avenue   El Paso 79968
915/747-5565   H, B

Founded in 1936 as one of the Texas Centennial Museums, the El Paso Centennial Museum features exhibits pertaining to the human and natural history of El Paso, the American Southwest, and northern Mexico. Noteworthy collections include wooden tools, basketry, and sandals from the cave dwellers of the El Paso area, pottery from Casas Grandes (Mexico), Southwestern Indian baskets, Colonial Spanish ironwork and textiles, the Ben Wittick Collection of nineteenth-century photographs, and the Josephine Clardy-Fox Fine Art Collection. Also in the collection are numerous rocks, minerals, and meteorites, Cretaceous marine fossils, dinosaur bones from the Big Bend, and a large collection of stuffed birds and eggs.

Open Tuesday through Friday 10 A.M. to 4:30 P.M., Sundays 1:30 to 5:30 P.M. Closed Monday and Saturday and on university holidays. Admission, free.

*El Paso Museum of Art
1211 Montana Avenue   El Paso 79902
915/541-4043   H, B

The El Paso Museum of Art is best known for its Kress Collection, made up of fifty-seven

El Paso Centennial Museum, University of Texas at El Paso. Photograph by Russell Banks.

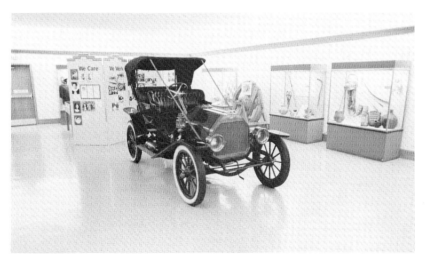

Interior of the El Paso Centennial Museum, on the campus of the University of Texas at El Paso. Photograph by Russell Banks.

paintings and two sculptures by European masters such as Bellini, Botticelli, Crespi, Tiepolo, Ribera, and Van Dyck and created between the years 1200 and 1800. The collection also includes pre-Columbian art of the Americas, post-Columbian decorative arts, and American art, including a fine painting by the American Western artist Frederic Remington, *Sign of Friendship*. The Old Master collection is exhibited in the west wing of the museum; the east wing is reserved for traveling exhibitions and changing exhibits from the museum's permanent collection.

The museum is housed in the 1910 residence of Senator and Mrs. W. W. Turney, who donated the house to the city in 1940. The two wings were added after the gift of the Kress collection in 1959–1960.

Open Wednesday through Saturday from 10 A.M. to 5 P.M., closed Monday and Tuesday. Admission, free.

The El Paso Museum of Art is located in the old Turney House. Photograph by Ron Tyler.

El Paso Museum of History
I-10 East, Avenue of the Americas exit
12901 Gateway West   El Paso 79927
915/858-1928

The El Paso Museum of History features material relating to the history of El Paso, Texas, and the Southwest, including seven life-size dioramas depicting events from El Paso's history: the building of the missions, the coming of the railroad, and General Pershing's expedition into Mexico, among others. Also on display are boot-making tools, weapons, saddles, and quilts and coverlets from the permanent collection. Various other items such as a handgun collection and *charro* equipment are on long-term loan.

Open Tuesday through Saturday 9 A.M. to 5 P.M., Sunday from 1 to 5 P.M. Admission, free.

Fort Bliss
Fort Bliss Replica Museum
U.S. Army Air Defense Center
Fort Bliss 79916
915/568-2804 or 568-4518   T

Founded in 1954, the museum consists of four adobe buildings that contain items relating directly to the history of the U.S. Army, Fort Bliss, and the El Paso area. Exhibitions include military and western-type small arms dating from 1848 to the present, photographs, maps, paintings, and prints, and uniforms and other artifacts relating to the military.

Open daily from 9 A.M. to 4:30 P.M. Closed holidays. Admission, free.

Fort Bliss
Third U.S. Cavalry Regimental Museum
Building 2407
Headquarters
3d Armored Cavalry Regiment
Fort Bliss 79916
915/568-7783 or 568-1922   H (exhibitions only), B

Devoted to the history of the regiment from its founding, the Third U.S. Cavalry Regimental Museum is located in a small, one-story building behind the Regimental Headquarters. On display are uniforms, weapons, equipment, photographs, documents, and trophies, as well as a complete collection of regimental standards that trace the history of the customs and traditions of the Third Armored Cavalry Regiment. Several vehicles and aircraft are on display in a small park behind the museum.

Fort Bliss Replica Museum, Fort Bliss, El Paso. U.S. Army photograph.

Third U.S. Cavalry Regimental Museum, Fort Bliss, El Paso.

Open from 7:30 A.M. to 4:30 P.M. Monday through Friday, noon until 4 P.M. on weekends and holidays. Closed Christmas, New Year's, Easter, and Thanksgiving.

Fort Bliss
*U.S. Army Air Defense Artillery Museum
Building 5000, Pleasanton Road
Fort Bliss 79916
915/568-5412 or 568-6848   H, B

Exhibitions relate to military history, science, and technology of the U.S. Army Air Defense Artillery. The main gallery houses the permanent exhibit of the history of Air Defense Artillery depicted by dioramas, weapons, ammunition, models, and various other artifacts. The School and Training Center Room contains an exhibit of the history of the U.S. Army Air Defense School and the development of training techniques and targets. The outdoors weapons park contains a selection of antiaircraft weapons and equipment from World War II until the present.

A mini theater features a twelve-minute visitor operated audiovisual program that is changed monthly. The programs are generally related to military history, but also feature museum related subjects.

Open daily from 9 A.M. to 4:30 P.M. Closed New Year's Day, Easter, Thanksgiving, and Christmas. Admission, free.

Fort Bliss
U.S. Army Museum of the Noncommissioned Officer
Building 11331   Fort Bliss 79918
915/568-8609   H

This small building houses the Army's Museum of the Noncommissioned Officer, which depicts, through exhibits of uniforms, photographs, and other material, the history of the noncommissioned officer.

Open Monday through Friday from 9 A.M. to 4 P.M., Saturday and Sunday from noon to 4 P.M. Admission, free.

Insights: El Paso Science Center, Inc.
303 N. Oregon   El Paso 79901
915/542-2990   B

Located in the basement of the El Paso Electric Company in the historic Mills Building, Insights is a science museum with emphasis on "hands-on," educational science exhibitions. More than eighty exhibits actively involve the visitor in exploring the principles and wonders of the world of science and technology.

Open 1 to 5 P.M. Tuesday through Friday, 10 A.M. to 5 P.M. Saturday. Admission, free.

Los Portales

San Elizario Plaza   San Elizario 79849
No telephone   T, HABS

    Thought by some to be the first El Paso
County Courthouse and probably constructed
before 1850, this adobe and stucco structure
was donated to San Elizario for use as a school
c. 1885. It was restored in 1967.

    Write for information on open hours and
admission.

Magoffin Home State Historic Site

1120 Magoffin Avenue   El Paso 79901
915/533-5147   H, T, N

    The Magoffin Home contains nineteenth-
century Mexican and American Victorian furniture as well as a small photographic and painting
collection. The house is a rare Texas example of
what became known as the Territorial style. It
was built of sun-dried adobe bricks in 1875 by
Joseph Magoffin, the second son of James Wiley
Magoffin, a Kentuckian of Irish ancestry who
settled on the northern bank of the Rio Grande
in 1849 (opposite the Mexican village of Paso del
Norte, present-day Ciudad Juárez) and established Magoffinsville. Some time before 1887,
the home was covered with a lime plaster scored
to resemble masonry. Magoffin's descendants

Entrance to the Magoffin House, El Paso. Courtesy Texas Parks and Wildlife Department.

have occupied the home continuously since its completion.

Open Wednesday through Sunday from 9 A.M. to 4 P.M., closed Monday and Tuesday. Guided tours are available, with special tours available if a reservation is made in advance. Admission, adults $.50; children 6 to 12 $.25.

Third U.S. Cavalry Regimental Museum
See Fort Bliss

U.S. Army Air Defense Artillery Museum
See Fort Bliss

U.S. Army Museum of the Noncommissioned Officer
See Fort Bliss

Wilderness Park Museum
2000 Transmountain Road   El Paso 79924
915/755-4332   H, B

Established in a seventeen-acre park where the original environment has been preserved, the Wilderness Park Museum tells the story of human adaptation to the desert. Five dioramas show human development, from the time of the mammoth hunters to the cave dwellings of Olla Cave in the Chihuahuan sierra. Permanent exhibitions trace the development of humans in the El Paso area from Folsom Man to today's Apaches. Changing exhibitions, such as Anasazi and pre-Columbian pottery, are also presented.

The nature trail winds through the park for a mile, past a pithouse, a kiva, and a replica of a Pueblo ruin. The visitor can also get a good view of the Franklin Mountains from the trail.

Open Tuesday through Sunday from 9 A.M. to 5 P.M. Admission is free except for special exhibitions, for which a modest charge may be levied.

Ysleta del Sur Pueblo Museum
119 S. Old Pueblo Road   El Paso 79907
915/859-3916   H, B, R

Located in the suburb of Ysleta, fifteen miles east and south of downtown El Paso, the Ysleta del Sur Pueblo Museum is housed in the historic Alderette-Candelaria House, built circa 1840, and tells of the story of the Tigua Indian Tribe of Texas. Nearby is the historic Ysleta Mission, built in 1682, and the modern Tigua Indian Reservation Arts & Crafts Center.

Open daily from 9 A.M. to 5 P.M. during April to October, 8:30 A.M. to 5:30 P.M. during November through March. Admission, free.

EOLA
Map 6

Barrow Foundation Museum

Nineteen miles east of San Angelo on S.H. 765
Eola 76937
915/655-4187

The Barrow Foundation complex is dedicated to the history and culture of West Texas. Two modern facilities contain artifacts, relics, and nostalgia. Special displays emphasize fossils and wildlife, Indian artifacts, farm implements, and period interiors such as the old Eola Post Office and a turn-of-the century operating room. A third building is under construction. The Barrow Ranch, a working ranch specializing in longhorns, may be toured.

Open by reservation only. Admission, free. School tours may be arranged.

FAIRFIELD
Map 3

Freestone County Historical Museum

302 East Main   Fairfield 75840
214/389-3738   B, T

The museum is housed in the old county jail, which was originally constructed of hand-made bricks in 1857 with outer walls 30 inches thick and 18-inch inner walls. The exhibits, which relate to the history of Freestone and surrounding counties, consist of uniforms, documents, and other memorabilia of the seven wars in which men from Freestone County have participated. The Carter Log House (1845) and the Potter-Watson Log Cabin (1852) have been restored and placed on the museum grounds. The old Valverde cannon, captured by Sibley's Texas Brigade at the battle of Valverde, New Mexico, in 1862 is

Interior of the Carter Cabin, Freestone County Museum, Fairfield.

authentically remounted and standing in front of the nearby courthouse.

The museum is open Wednesday and Saturday from 10 A.M. to 4 P.M., Sunday from 1:30 to 4 P.M. Admission, adults $.50; children $.25.

FALFURRIAS
Map 5

Heritage Museum

Falfurrias 78355
512/325-2907

The Heritage Museum features exhibitions relating to the Falfurrias area, including a Texas Ranger room and farm equipment.

Open Tuesday through Friday from 11 A.M. to 5 P.M., Saturday from 1 to 5 P.M. Admission, free.

FANNIN
Map 4

Fannin Battleground State Historic Site

Nine miles east of Goliad on U.S. 59
Fannin 77960
512/645-2020   H (but not the gazebo), T

The Fannin Battlefield is the site of the Battle of Coleto Creek, March 19–20, 1836, where more than 350 Texas troops under the command of Colonel James W. Fannin surrendered to superior Mexican forces under General José Urrea. The Texans were executed on the orders of Mexican President Antonio López de Santa Anna. The Texas Centennial Commission erected the Goliad Memorial Shaft at the burial spot of the victims of what became known as the Goliad Massacre, and a small exhibit in the park gazebo summarizes this event as an element of the Texas war for independence.

Open from 8 A.M. to 5 P.M. daily. Admission, free.

FLOYDADA
Map 9

Floyd County Historical Museum

105 E. Missouri (north of the courthouse)
Floydada 79235
806/983-2415

Located in a downtown commercial building that is now completely turned over to the museum, the Floyd County Historical Museum features exhibitions relating to the history of Floyd County and area. Exhibits include a replica of the Thomas Montgomery Ranchhouse built in 1887, which was headquarters for the T-M Bar Ranch (furnished as it would have been while in use), blacksmith tools, Indian artifacts, early household items and furnishings, and a small art collection.

Open Monday through Friday from 1 to 5 P.M. Admission, free.

Parade in front of the Floyd County Historical Museum, Floydada.

Fort Bliss
See El Paso

FORT DAVIS
Map 8

Fort Davis National Historic Site
S.H. 17   Fort Davis 79734
915/426-3225   B, HABS

Fort Davis, established in 1854 as a link in the frontier defense system on the El Paso–San Antonio Road, was used by the army until 1891. The post, now partially restored, features collections relating to the U.S. Army during the period the fort was in use. Archival collections concentrate on military records of the fort, units stationed there, and historic photographs of officers, enlisted men, and fort structures. On-site living history demonstrations are presented June through August, and a slide program on the history of the fort and an audio program of an 1875 Dress Retreat Parade are available daily.

Open daily from 8 A.M. to 5 P.M.; June through August, 8 A.M. to 6 P.M. Admission, $1 per carload or $.50 per person.

Officers' Row at Fort Davis. Photograph by Todd Webb. Courtesy Amon Carter Museum, Fort Worth.

Interpretive Center
Davis Mountains State Park
Four miles northwest of Fort Davis on S.H.
118   Fort Davis 79734
915/426-3337

Founded in 1967, the Interpretive Center contains information on the Davis Mountains, an extinct volcanic range rising high above the surrounding desert. There is a diorama depicting the regional geology, plants, animals, and local ecology as well as a wildlife viewing window, through which one may watch birds and mammals as they come to the feeding and watering station outside. A four-mile hiking trail connects to Fort Davis National Historic Site. State and National Park personnel present evening programs at the amphitheater during summer months.

Open daily from 10 A.M. to 6 P.M. June through August. Admission, $2 for car park and entrance fee.

McDonald Observatory
18 miles northwest of Fort Davis on S.H. 118
Fort Davis 79734
915/426-3423   B, T

Established in 1932 with a bequest from a Paris, Texas, banker named W. J. McDonald, the University of Texas McDonald Observatory is today one of the world's major centers for astronomical research. The 6,800 feet high Mount Locke in the Davis Mountains was chosen as the site because of its altitude, the distance from artificially-lighted cities, its high ratio of clear nights, and its latitude, which permits observation of the southern skies. Astronomers from around the world use the 82-inch reflector telescope (the second largest in the world when it was dedicated in 1939), the 107-inch reflector telescope (the third largest in the world when it was dedicated in 1969), or one of the other three telescopes now in operation.

The W. L. Moody, Jr., Information Center is located at the foot of the mountain and provides slide shows designed to acquaint the visitor with the history of the Observatory and the work done here. A self-guided tour begins at the visitors' parking area near the large domes. Information is available at the nearby Information Stand. The tour includes a public telescope viewing area, where you can observe the 82-inch dome as well as the surrounding mountains through the public telescopes, and the 107-inch telescope, which is sometimes not available because of maintenance. There is a Visitors' Gallery on the fifth floor of the 2.7-meter telescope building, which provides exhibits as well as viewing of the telescope area.

The Observatory has set aside the last Wednesday evening of each month for public viewing through the 2.7-meter telescope. A total of *only 150* persons can be accommodated. Persons interested in attending may request reservations by writing at least six months in advance to: Visitors' Center, c/o Mary Dutchover, McDonald Observatory, Box 1337, Fort Davis, Texas 79734. Please include a self-addressed, stamped envelope with your request. Specify the desired month and the number in your group.

Open Monday through Saturday from 9 A.M. to 5 P.M., and Sunday from 1 to 5 P.M. September 1 through May 31; Monday through Saturday from 9 A.M. to 7 P.M., and Sunday from 1 to 7 P.M. June 1 through August 31. Closed New Year's Day, Thanksgiving Day, and Christmas Day. Admission, free.

Neill Museum
Seven blocks west of the Courthouse
Fort Davis 79734
915/426-3969   T

The museum is located in the historic Trueheart House (1899) and exhibits period furnishings, an extensive collection of more than 300 dolls, and antique toys made in Texas.

Open June 1 through September 7 and by appointment. Admission, adults $1; children $.50.

Overland Trail Museum

Fort Davis 79734
915/426-3999   H, B

Exhibitions relate to local and pioneer history of the Fort Davis area. The museum is housed in the home of Nick Mersfelder, Fort Davis barber, justice of the peace, and photographer, who was to the Fort Davis area what Judge Roy Bean was to Langtry—the law west of the Pecos. The living room, barbershop, and kitchen are furnished for display, including a number of Mersfelder's photographs.

Open from June through September 15 Wednesday through Sunday from 1 to 5 P.M. and by appointment. Admission, free, but donations are accepted.

Fort Hood
See Killeen

FORT MCKAVETT
(Map 6)

Fort McKavett State Historic Site

23 miles west of Menard on U.S. 190 and F.R. 864   Fort McKavett 78641
915/396-2358   H, T, N, HABS

Established in 1852 for frontier protection, Fort McKavett was abandoned shortly before the Civil War but was reoccupied in 1868. It was a base of military operations against Indian tribes in western Texas until it was finally closed in 1883. The site consists of the majority of the fort grounds. With fourteen restored buildings and many stabilized structures, McKavett is the best representation of a nineteenth-century fort site within the state park system. An interpretive exhibit in one wing of the post hospital building presents the history of the site. Guided group tours are available with advance notice.

Open daily from 8 A.M. to 5 P.M. Admission, free.

Fort Sam Houston
See San Antonio

FORT STOCKTON
Map 7

Annie Riggs Memorial Museum

301 S. Main Street   Fort Stockton 79735
915/366-7106 or 336-2167   T

Built of adobe bricks and wood, the Annie Riggs Memorial Museum opened near the courthouse square in 1899 as the Riggs Hotel. Today

Overland Trail Museum, Fort Davis.

Annie Riggs Hotel, Fort Stockton. Photograph by Todd Webb. Courtesy Amon Carter Museum, Fort Worth.

it houses exhibits related to the history of West Texas. Displays feature pioneer clothing, arrowheads and Indian artifacts, a cowboy room, a geology room, the history of Fort Stockton, religious artifacts from the first church (1875), and a library.

Open Monday through Saturday from 10 A.M. to noon, 1 to 5 P.M., Sunday from 1:30 to 5 P.M. There are special summer hours. Admission, adults $.50; children under 12 $.25; children under 6 free.

Amon Carter Square
*Amon Carter Museum of Western Art
3501 Camp Bowie Boulevard
Fort Worth 76107
817/738-1933   H, B

Opened in 1961 to house the collection assembled by Fort Worth newspaperman Amon G. Carter, the Carter Museum has developed into one of the finest museums of American art in the country. In addition to Carter's collection of paintings and sculpture by Frederic Remington and Charles M. Russell, the two best known Western artists of the late nineteenth and early twentieth century, the museum presents a variety of exhibitions related to nineteenth- and twentieth-century American art. To Carter's original collection have been added paintings by American artists such as Martin Johnson Heade, William Michael Harnett, William T. Ranney, Jasper F. Cropsey, and William Merritt Chase, as well as famous Western American painters such as Thomas Moran, Albert Bierstadt, John Mix Stanley, Charles Deas, and Seth Eastman. The collection also includes an impressive group of twentieth-century paintings and sculpture, including works by Elie Nadelman, Marsden Hartley, Arthur Dove, John Marin, Stuart Davis, Charles Sheeler, and Georgia O'Keeffe.

The museum has a significant photographic and print collection including original photographs by nineteenth-century masters William Henry Jackson, Edweard Muybridge, Carleton Watkins, and Paul Strand and Ansel Adams of the twentieth century, as well as Santa Fe photographer Laura Gilpin's photographic estate, including negatives, prints, books, and papers. The print collection includes work by John James

Amon Carter Museum, Fort Worth.

Frederic Remington, A Dash for the Timber, *1889. Oil on canvas, 48¼ × 84⅛ in. Courtesy Amon Carter Museum, Fort Worth.*

Fitz Hugh Lane, Boston Harbor, *1856, from the collection of the Amon Carter Museum, Fort Worth.*

Audubon, Currier & Ives, and a large collection of historic bird's-eye views of cities, as well as the Tamarind Workshop collection of contemporary prints.

Recent temporary exhibitions have included "Charles Willson Peale and His World" and retrospectives of the work of *trompe l'oeil* painter John Frederick Peto and photographer Carleton E. Watkins.

The research library is open by appointment to scholars and researchers, and exhibitions from the library collection are frequently featured in the library foyer. Traveling exhibitions relating to nineteenth- and twentieth-century American art are presented in the galleries, and a regular schedule of films, lectures, and other public programs are presented in the theater.

The museum building, designed by New York architect Philip Johnson, is constructed of honey-colored Texas shellstone. A sculptural grouping by the English artist Henry Moore is the focal point of the plaza, which also features native Texas shrubs and trees.

The Amon Carter Museum is one of four museums located in Amon Carter Square, along with Casa Manana Theater and the Will Rogers Memorial Coliseum, where the annual Southwestern Exposition and Fat Stock Show and Rodeo is held each January and February. It is easy to park on Lancaster Street, between the Amon Carter and the Fort Worth Art Museum, and walk to all the attractions in the area, which also include the Fort Worth Museum of Science and History and the Kimbell Art Museum. Tours may be arranged for any of the three art museums by calling 817/738-6811.

Open Tuesday through Saturday from 10 A.M. to 5 P.M., Sunday from 1 to 5:30 P.M. Admission, free.

Amon Carter Square
*Fort Worth Art Museum
1309 Montgomery   Fort Worth 76107
817/738-9215   H, B

Twentieth-century art and performing arts are the focus of the Fort Worth Art Museum, which traces its beginnings to 1892, when a committee of interested persons decided to establish a library and art gallery in Fort Worth. With a gift from Andrew Carnegie, the dream came true, and a library, with space for an art gallery, was constructed in 1901. *Approaching Storm* by George Inness was the museum's first acquisition in 1904. In 1925, the Friends of Art assisted in purchasing one of Thomas Eakins's most famous paintings, *The Swimming Hole.*

The Fort Worth Art Museum obtained its own quarters in 1954 when it moved into a Herbert Bayer structure and grew to include works by artists such as George Grosz, Paul Klee, Max Weber, and Ben Shahn. Recent acquisitions have continued to emphasize the modern masters

Andy Warhol, **Twenty-five Colored Marilyns,** *1962. Acrylic on canvas, 89 × 69 in. Photograph by David Wharton. Courtesy Fort Worth Art Museum.*

Thomas Eakins, **The Swimming Hole,** *1883. Oil on canvas, 27 × 36 in. Photograph by David Wharton. Courtesy Fort Worth Art Museum.*

with acquisitions of work by Lyonel Feininger, Hans Hofmann, and Pablo Picasso, as well as work by Red Grooms, Frank Stella, and Robert Rauschenberg.

Following renovation and an addition, designed by O'Neill Ford & Associates, the museum expanded its program to include the performing arts and now presents a year-round schedule of lectures, symposia, films, modern dance, and experimental music. Tours may be arranged by calling 817/738-6811.

Open Tuesday through Saturday from 10 A.M. to 5 P.M., Sunday from 1 to 5 P.M. From September through May the museum is also open Tuesday until 9 P.M. Admission, free.

The Fort Worth Museum of Science and History.

Amon Carter Square
*Fort Worth Museum of Science and History
1501 Montgomery   Fort Worth 76107
817/732-1631   H, B, R

Established as the Children's Museum in 1941, the Fort Worth Museum of Science and History has grown from two rooms in the De Zavala Elementary School to the largest museum of its kind in the Southwest. Its 120,000 square-foot facility contains seven exhibit galleries, the Noble Planetarium, and a new Omni Theater.

The museum's collection of more than 100,000 specimens and artifacts ranges from fossils to computers. Two Jurassic dinosaur skeletons over 150 million years old highlight exhibits that trace the geological history of the earth. In other galleries, cultures the world over are traced through 6,000 years of recorded history, from pre-Columbian pottery to an astronaut's space suit. The history of Texas and early Fort Worth is told in an exhibition that features six pioneer period rooms. The gallery of Medicine and Man traces the development of medicine from prehistoric surgery to the present. Participatory exhibits include Human Physiology, which uses models, color, light, and sound to explain how the body functions. Antique Calculators and Computer Technology are explained in another gallery, where visitors are encouraged to learn Spanish, play games, and talk to computers. Smaller exhibits on dolls, laser technology, and the history of the museum are highlighted along the museum's hallways.

In the Noble Planetarium a light and sound show called Laser Magic is offered to the public. The new Omni Theater, a 30,000 square-foot facility opened in 1983, features an 80 foot tilted dome and seats 360 persons. The Omnimax film projector creates 180-degree images that visually surround the audience. Programmed controls and multiple image projectors make the Omni Theater one of the most advanced educational facilities in the Southwest.

Exhibit galleries are open Monday through Saturday from 9 A.M. to 5 P.M., Sunday from 2 to 5 P.M. Admission, free. Planetarium shows, Laser Magic, and Omnimax films are also presented in the evening. Call for times and admission fees.

Amon Carter Square
*Kimbell Art Museum
1101 Will Rogers Road West   Fort Worth 76107
817/332-8451   H, B, R

Opened in 1972 in a building designed by Louis I. Kahn, the Kimbell Art Museum has recently been called the finest small museum in the country. Fort Worth industrialist Kay Kimbell's personal collection consisted of important eighteenth- and nineteenth-century works, primarily by British artists. Major works by British and European masters of all ages have been added to the collection since the museum opened: the *Barnabas Altarpiece*, the earliest known English painting, probably done between 1250 and 1260; Duccio di Buoninsegna's *The Raising of Lazarus*; Georges de La Tour's *Cheat with the Ace of Clubs*; Diego Velázquez's *Portrait of Don Pedro de Barerana*; Rembrandt Van Rijn's *Portrait of a Young Jew*; and nineteenth-

Gallery of the Kimbell Art Museum, Fort Worth, showing the stairway to the lower, operational level of the museum, with the bookstore on the left.

Georges de la Tour, The Cheat with the Ace of Clubs, *no date. Oil on canvas, $38\frac{1}{2} \times 61\frac{1}{2}$ in. Courtesy Kimbell Art Museum, Fort Worth.*

Diego Velázquez, Don Pedro de Barberana, *c. 1631–1633. Oil on canvas, 78 × 43⅞ in. Courtesy Kimbell Art Museum, Fort Worth.*

and twentieth-century works by Paul Cézanne, *Peasant in a Blue Smock;* Pablo Picasso, *Nude Combing Her Hair;* Edouard Manet, *Portrait of Georges Clemenceau;* and Odilon Redon, *The Birth of Venus,* for example. In addition, the museum has added pre-Columbian, African, and Oriental works as well as a number of significant prints to the collection. The Kimbell has recently organized a stunning series of temporary exhibitions, including exhibitions on the work of Jusepe de Ribera and Jean-Baptiste Oudry, so call ahead to see what special exhibitions might be on view. Tours may be arranged by calling 817/738-6811.

Kahn's building is equal to the collection. Formed by a series of parallel cycloid vaults, the museum allows for interludes of garden space. In one such space is Maillol's *L'Air*; in another, Antoine Bourdelle's *Penelope*; in another, a seating area where patrons can eat lunch outside. One of the most pleasing aspects of the building is the innovative lighting system that Kahn designed in an attempt to take advantage of natural light supplemented by artificial light, but the most lasting feeling is the intimacy of galleries that permit up close inspection of the individual works while not cramping the viewer in a small space.

The museum offers an active program of lectures, films, music, theater productions, and seminars, and a research library is open by appointment.

Open Tuesday through Saturday from 10 A.M. to 5 P.M., Sunday from 1 to 5 P.M. Admission, free.

Amon Carter Square
Special Collections, Health Sciences Library
Seventh Floor, Medical Education Building I
Texas College of Osteopathic Medicine
Camp Bowie at Montgomery
Fort Worth 76107
817/735-2593
Exhibitions in the Special Collections area of the Health Sciences Library tell the history of osteopathic medicine in Texas since 1900 and the history of the Texas College of Osteopathic Medicine since its opening in 1970. Exhibits include medical memorabilia such as early instruments and medications and rare medical books.

Open Monday through Friday from 8 A.M. to 5 P.M. Admission, free.

Brown-Lupton Gallery
See Texas Christian University

Cattleman's Museum
Texas and Southwestern Cattle Raisers Foundation
1301 W. Seventh   Fort Worth 76102
817/332-7064   H
Housed in the new headquarters building of the Texas and Southwestern Cattle Raisers Foundation, the Cattleman's Museum admirably supplements Fort Worth's long-lived "Cowtown" image. The exhibitions focus on the men and women who built the cattle industry from the early 1880s to the present, and on the brand inspectors who, as a result of the cattlemen's asso-

ciation, helped curb the theft of cattle. The museum exhibits historic photographs as well as tools of the cowboy's trade, from a pair of Colt revolvers and a set of spurs donated by Watt R. Matthews, noted Albany rancher, to the silver-mounted saddle, chaps, and vest worn in countless rodeo parades by the late William R. Watt, who was the head of the Fort Worth Southwestern Exposition and Fat Stock Show and Rodeo.

In addition, the museum presents short video programs on the history of the older Texas ranches, including the Burnett Estates, the Waggoner Ranch, and the King Ranch. Adjoining the museum is the Cattle Raisers Memorial Hall, which honors individual cattlemen whose contributions enriched the history of the industry. Samuel Burk Burnett, Cornelia Adair, Charles Goodnight, and Captain Richard King are among the ranchers in the Memorial Hall. Sculptor Jim Reno has cast a 12-foot-high bronze, entitled *The Brand Inspector*, to highlight the landscape facade of the building.

Open Monday through Friday from 8 A.M. to 5 P.M. except public holidays. Admission, free.

Charles D. Tandy Archaeology Museum
Southwestern Baptist Theological Seminary
2001 Broadus   Fort Worth 76122
817/923-1921

This museum, named for Charles D. Tandy, founder and chairman of the board of the Tandy Corporation of Fort Worth, brings to life the study of early biblical periods. Included in the exhibition are artifacts from the seminary's continuing archaeological expeditions at Tel Batash-Timnah, Israel. The displays include many items shared with the Hebrew University of Jerusalem.

Also located in the museum is a heritage room, which recreates early history of the seminary, including the desk and library of early presidents as well as other historical material. Some of the library's rare books are featured in changing displays.

Open Monday through Friday from 8 A.M. to 5 P.M. Admission, free.

Eddleman-McFarland House
1110 Penn Street   Fort Worth 76102
817/332-5875   T, N

Built in 1898 by Sarah Ball, the widow of the wealthy Galveston banker George Ball, this picturesque late Victorian home sits on a bluff over-looking the Trinity River. Frank Hays McFarland purchased the house for his family in 1907, and it was continuously occupied by the family until 1978. The upstairs serves as office space for the current owner, the Junior League of Fort Worth, while the first floor, which retains the original woodwork, flooring, and fixtures, is open to the public.

Guided tours are available on Tuesday and Thursday from 10 A.M. to 2 P.M., Sunday from 2 to 5 P.M., or by appointment. Admission, $2. Group rates are available.

Forest Park
Fort Worth Zoological Park
2727 Zoological Park Drive
Fort Worth 76110
817/870-7050   H, B

The Fort Worth Zoo offers, in addition to traditional outdoor animal viewing, a primate building, an African diorama, a tropical aviary, and a herpetarium with an aquarium with 2,000 fresh and salt water creatures. Founded in 1909, the zoo provides weekday guided tours and films at the education center and summer classes in zoology and zoo art.

Open from 9 A.M. to 5 P.M. daily. Admission, adults $1.50; children under 12 free. Group rates are available. Call 817/870-7055 for reservations and information.

Rhinocerous in the Fort Worth Zoo.

Forest Park
Log Cabin Village
University Drive at Log Cabin Village Lane
Fort Worth 76109
817/926-5881 B, T

Log Cabin Village consists of seven log houses, all more than 100 years old, that have been restored and furnished in keeping with their nineteenth-century heritage. One of the houses serves as headquarters for the Village, while another has been turned into a working grist mill. One of the highlights of the Village is the Isaac Parker house, a good example of a dog-trot house, which was the home of Isaac Parker, for whom nearby Parker County (county seat Weatherford) was named.

Open Monday through Friday from 8 A.M. to 4:30 P.M., Saturday from noon to 4:30 P.M., and Sunday from 1 to 4:30 P.M. Admission, adults $.60; children under 12 $.35.

Fort Worth Art Museum
See Amon Carter Square

Fort Worth Botanic Garden
3220 Botanic Garden Drive (north of I-30)
Fort Worth 76107
817/870-7686 H, B

The Fort Worth Botanic Garden, with its thousands of feet of rock walkways, terraces, and shelterhouse, was built by relief laborers be-

The Harry A. Foster House in Fort Worth's Log Cabin Village. Photograph by Elna Wilkinson.

tween 1933 and 1935. The 114.62-acre garden has approximately 3,500 bushes, 2,000 different plants, and more than 150 varieties of trees adapted to the Fort Worth area. Seasonal color can be enjoyed throughout the year when daffodils, daylilies, annual flower beds, chrysanthemums, and flowering trees are in bloom. Special areas include the rose gardens, the Fragrance Garden for the Blind, the Test Garden, the Japanese Garden, the Perennial Garden, and the azalea plantings. Changing exhibitions display artistic representations of plant material and explanations of plants' uses and techniques.

The Garden is open daily from 8 A.M. to sundown, the Garden Center and exhibition greenhouse from 8 A.M. to 5 P.M. The 7.5-acre Japanese Garden is open Tuesday through Saturday from 10 A.M. to 5 P.M. and Sunday from 1 to 5 P.M. Closed on Monday. Summer hours for the Japanese Garden are Tuesday through Saturday from 9 A.M. to 7 P.M., Sunday from 1 to 7 P.M. Admittance up to thirty minutes prior to closing time. Admission for the Japanese Garden only: $1 for 12 years old and up. Children under 12 with parent or sponsor, no charge. Unsponsored children under 12 not admitted. One adult may sponsor five children.

Fort Worth Interpretative Center
See Sundance Square

Fort Worth Museum of Science and History
See Amon Carter Square

Fort Worth Zoological Park
See Forest Park

Heritage Room
Tarrant County Junior College
Northeast Campus
828 Harwood   Hurst 76053
817/281-7860   H

Although primarily a research center for the study of local history, the Heritage Room has gathered some furniture, objects, and artifacts in addition to the photographs and manuscripts relating to the history of Tarrant County, primarily the northeast quadrant.

Open Monday through Thursday from 8 A.M. to 10 P.M., Friday from 8 A.M. to 5 P.M., and Sunday from 2 to 6 P.M. Admission, free.

J. M. Moudy Exhibition Space
See Texas Christian University

Kimbell Art Museum
See Amon Carter Square

Log Cabin Village
See Forest Park

Museum of Aviation Group
300 North Spur 341 (just south of the main gate
of General Dynamics)   Fort Worth 76108
No telephone

Aircraft on display in this park area are a B-36,
B-58, KC-97, F-105, F-89, and F-84.

Open Wednesday through Saturday from 10
A.M. to 3 P.M., closed Sunday through Tuesday.
Admission, free.

Pate Museum of Transportation
U.S. 377 between Fort Worth and Cresson
Fort Worth 76101
817/396-4305   B, T

All modes of transportation are included in
the Pate Museum of Transportation, including
automobiles, airplanes, trains, boats, and artifacts and library pertaining to the evolution and
development of transportation. The museum is
located on the Texas Refinery Corporation
ranch, west of Fort Worth and just off U.S. 377.

Open daily except Monday from 9 A.M. to
5 P.M. Admission, free.

Sid Richardson Collection of Western Art
See Sundance Square

1929 Packard in the Pate Museum of Transportation, near Fort Worth.

**Special Collections, Texas College of
Osteopathic Medicine**
See Amon Carter Square

Sundance Square
Fort Worth Interpretative Center
Fire Station No. 1
2nd and Commerce Streets   Fort Worth 76102
817/732-1631   H

The Fort Worth Interpretative Center, housed
on the first floor of an historic fire house located
one block from Sundance Square in downtown
Fort Worth, is designed as the gateway to the
newly-restored downtown area. In 2,200 square
feet of exhibit space, the Center portrays the
city's colorful history, from a frontier military
post, through Cowtown and the arrival of the
railroad, to a modern oil and aerospace center in
the twentieth century. Designed and administered by the Fort Worth Museum of Science
and History, the Center was funded by the City
of Fort Worth and the Bass Brothers Enterprises.

Open daily from 10 A.M. to 5 P.M. Admission,
free.

Sundance Square
Sid Richardson Collection of Western Art
309 Main Street   Fort Worth 76102
817/332-6554   H, B

The Sid Richardson Collection of Western Art
consists of a magnificent group of paintings by
Frederic Remington and Charles M. Russell that
were acquired by the Fort Worth oilman Sid W.
Richardson from 1942 until shortly before his
death in 1959. Richardson's interest in Western
American painting grew, like his friend Amon
G. Carter's, from his personal experience and
impressions of the old West.

The collection, which continues to grow, is
housed in a reconstructed turn-of-the-century
building in Sundance Square, just two blocks
south of the handsome, newly-restored Tarrant
County Courthouse (1894). The nearby shops
and offices along Main Street have been restored
to the grace and elegance of their original
facades.

Open Tuesday through Friday from 10 A.M. to
5 P.M., Saturday from 11 A.M. to 6 P.M., and Sunday from 1 to 5 P.M. Admission, free.

The Sid Richardson Collection of Western Art, in the Sundance Square area of Fort Worth.

*Frederic Remington, **Self Portrait on a Horse**, c. 1890. Oil on canvas, 29³⁄₁₆ × 19⅛ in. Courtesy Sid Richardson Collection of Western Art, Fort Worth.*

*Charles M. Russell, **When Blackfeet and Sioux Meet**, 1908. Oil on canvas, 20½ × 29⅞ in. Courtesy Sid Richardson Collection of Western Art, Fort Worth.*

Texas Christian University
Brown-Lupton Gallery
Student Center   Fort Worth 76129
817/921-7926   H

Changing exhibitions, mostly regional, professional artists, group exhibits, student works, and traveling shows are presented in the Brown-Lupton Gallery. There is a regular schedule of films and lectures, mostly on Monday at noon. Call for information and current exhibits.

Open weekdays from 11 A.M. to 4 P.M., weekends from 1 to 4 P.M. Admission, free.

Texas Christian University
J. M. Moudy Exhibition Space
J. M. Moudy Building for Visual Arts and Communication
Fort Worth 76129
817/921-7643

The J. M. Moudy Building for Visual Arts and Communication, housed in a strikingly modern structure designed by Kevin Roche and opened in 1982, contains one exhibition space, which presents monthly exhibitions of living artists' works, supported by lectures and educational programs.

Open weekdays from 11 A.M. to 4 P.M., weekends from 1 to 4 P.M. Admission, free.

The J. M. Moudy Building for Visual Arts and Communication, Texas Christian University, Fort Worth.

Texas Railroad Museum
Quartermaster Depot
Fort Worth Federal Center
5051 James Street   Fort Worth 76100
817/261-2480   H, B

Locomotive No. 610, built in 1927 and the only engine of its kind left in Texas, sits on exhibit in the Texas Railroad Museum in the Fort Worth Federal Center. A gift to Amon Carter, Sr., in 1951, the engine was restored and pulled the American Freedom Train through Texas during the nation's Bicentennial. The engine previously was on display, first, at Will Rogers Coliseum, then near the stockyards on the north side of the city. It is now on display on the weekends in a shelter that is designed to keep it operative for exhibitions and special trips.

Also on exhibit are porters' hats, conductors' punches, dining car menus and china, old-fashioned lanterns, signs and pictures, baggage wagons, waiting-room double benches, coal-fired caboose and depot stoves, and an intricate, hand-built model train set from the C. B. Baird estate.

Open Saturday and Sunday from 1 to 5 P.M.

The restored Thistle Hill recalls Fort Worth's cattle baron days. Photograph by Ron Tyler.

Thistle Hill
1509 Pennsylvania   Fort Worth 76104
817/336-1212   T, B, N, HABS

Called a "historic cattle baron's mansion," Thistle Hill was constructed in 1903 for the young, soon-to-be wed Electra Waggoner (of the well-known W. T. Waggoner ranching family). Situated on the peak of what was then known as "Quality Hill," the house was purchased in 1910 by Winfield Scott, also a cattleman and promi-

111

nent citizen. Today the house is being restored and furnished to recall the cattle baron days of Fort Worth.

Guided tours available Monday through Friday from 10 A.M. to 3:15 P.M., Sunday from 1 to 4:30 P.M. Admission, adults $1.50; children age 6 to 14 $.50. Group rates are available, and the house may be rented for various functions.

The Western Company Museum
6100 Western Place   Fort Worth 76107
817/731-5261 or 731-5217   H

Located in the international headquarters of the Western Company of North America, The Western Company Museum tells the story of petroleum as one of our energy sources. The geology of hydrocarbons, chemistry, physics, and astronomy are utilized in the presentation. Multimedia techniques, including rig sounds, motion, light, cinema projection, voice, photomural backgrounds, and "talking faces" assist in bringing the petroleum industry, and the Western Company's role in it, to life.

Open Monday through Friday from 8:30 A.M. to 4:30 P.M. Closed holidays. Admission, free.

FREDERICKSBURG
Map 6

Admiral Nimitz State Historical Park
340 East Main Street   Fredericksburg 78624
512/997-4379   H, B, N (historic district)

Located in the birthplace of Fleet Admiral Chester Nimitz, Commander-in-Chief in the Pacific during World War II. This State Historical Park pays tribute to him and to those who served with him during World War II. The Pacific War History Walk exhibits rare planes, guns, and tanks. The Japanese Garden of Peace is a gift from the people of Japan, and the Museum of the Pacific War, in the restored Steamboat Hotel (constructed in 1852), includes exhibits and audio-visual programs as well as a research library and bookstore.

Open daily from 8 A.M. to 5 P.M. Closed Thanksgiving and Christmas days. Admission, adults over age 18, $1.

Pioneer Memorial Museum
309 West Main Street   Fredericksburg 78624
512/997-2835   H, B, T, N

The Pioneer Memorial Museum is a complex of several buildings dating from the mid-1800s and including an authentic Sunday House (a unique Fredericksburg institution where members of the rural/ranching family stayed when they came to town on the weekend), the Fassel

The unique Nimitz Steamboat Hotel on Main Street, Fredericksburg, is being carefully restored to house the Museum of the Pacific War. Courtesy The Admiral Nimitz State Historical Park.

Gallery of The Western Company Museum, Fort Worth.

House, and the Kammlah House, which contains the museum. Constructed of stone, the Kammlah House served as a home and store through the 1920s. It has nine rooms, a wine cellar, and a picturesque Hof (yard). The John O. Meusebach Room (honoring the founder of Fredericksburg) contains a number of historical objects of interest.

Open Monday through Saturday from 10 A.M. to 5 P.M. and Sunday from 1 to 5 P.M. from May 1 through Labor Day; weekends only during the remainder of the year. There is a small admission charge.

Schandua House
111 East Austin Street   Fredericksburg 78624
512/997-2835   H, T

This miniature house without electricity, gas, or running water has been authentically restored to give a picture of life in the 1890s. The front room served as living and sleeping quarters, the back room was for cooking and eating. It is furnished with a mix of German primitive and mid-Victorian furniture.

Open by appointment and frequently for the Christmas and Easter tours of homes.

FRITCH
Map 9

Alibates Flint Quarries and Texas Panhandle Pueblo Culture National Monument
Alibates Road southwest of Fritch off U.S. 136
Fritch 79036
806/857-3151

For thousands of years the bluffs and ridges of the Canadian River breaks were quarried for Alibates flint to make stone tools and weapons. Although flint normally has one characteristic shade, Alibates flint, which comes from a relatively small section on the Canadian River, has a multitude of bright colors in endless variations and patterns. Using nothing more elaborate than a fine antler tip, a skilled flint chipper can chip and flake an astonishing variety of everyday tools of survival. Archeologists have found knives, hammers, chisels, drills, axes, awls, fishhooks, buttons, hoes, scrapers, and gravers as well as arrowheads made of Alibates flint in many different places in the Great Plains and the Southwest, indicating prehistoric trade patterns and popularity of the multicolored flint.

The quarries can be seen only on a guided tour limited to twenty persons. The tours are free and are conducted daily at 10 A.M. and 2 P.M. from

Memorial Day through Labor Day. Departure is from the Bates Canyon information station. Off-season tours are provided on request. Write to the Superintendent, Lake Meredith National Recreational Area, P.O. Box 1438, Fritch, Texas 79036, at least five days in advance.

Lake Meredith Aquatic & Wildlife Museum
104 N. Robey (under the water tower)
Fritch 79036
806/857-2458   B

Located near Lake Meredith and the Alibates Flint Quarries National Monument, the Lake Meredith Aquatic & Wildlife Museum contains several large, realistic dioramas depicting animals in their natural habitat as well as five giant aquariums filled with native fish, such as catfish, walleye, perch, carp, small- and large-mouth bass, sand bass, and blue gill.

Open Monday through Saturday from 10 A.M. to 5 P.M., Sunday from 2 to 5 P.M. A donation is requested for admission.

FULTON
Map 4

Fulton Mansion State Historic Structure
Henderson Street and Fulton Beach Road
Fulton 78358
512/729-0386   H, T, N, HABS

Completed in 1876, this house was the home of George W. Fulton, cousin of Robert Fulton and prominent cattle raiser and businessman of the Texas Coastal Bend. The house was built in the French Second Empire style and contains such innovations as central heating, gas lighting, and indoor plumbing, which were rare for Texas in the late nineteenth century. Several rooms have been restored and furnished in the mid-1880s style and are included on a guided tour.

Open Wednesday through Sunday from 10 A.M. to noon, 1 to 4 P.M. Closed Christmas. Advance reservations requested for groups of ten or more. Admission, adults $.50, children age 6 to 12, $.25.

GAIL
Map 9

Borden County Historical Museum
Gail 79738
915/856-4602

Founded in 1967, the Borden County Historical Museum is devoted to local history. On exhibit is a medicine case from the old drugstore (1891), a bar, stoves, costumes, saddles, and old photographs.

Open by appointment. Admission, free.

The George W. Fulton House, Fulton Beach. Photograph by Todd Webb. Courtesy Amon Carter Museum, Fort Worth.

The Morton Museum of Cooke County, Gainesville.

Morton Museum of Cooke County

210 S. Dixon Street at Pecan Street
Gainesville 76240
817/668-8900   B, T

Housed in the city's 1884 fire station/city hall, the museum exhibits memorabilia pertaining to Cooke County pioneers and history. A brochure is available at the museum for a tour of historic homes and churches in Gainesville.

The museum is open Tuesday through Saturday from 12 to 5 P.M., Sunday from 2 to 5 P.M. Admission, free.

American National Insurance Tower

19th and Market Street   Galveston 77553
409/763-4661, Ext. 216

On the twentieth floor of the American National Insurance Tower is an archives exhibit as well as a pictorial history of Galveston. Part of the company's well-known art collection is also included in the tour. The fine view from the top of the tower is also a good way to orient yourself for seeing the rest of the city.

Open Monday through Friday. Call for information about free, guided tours.

Antique Dollhouse Museum

1721 Broadway   Galveston 77550
409/762-7289   B

The Antique Dollhouse Museum is located in the historic John Z. H. Scott house and contains a large collection of dolls, from pre–Civil War to the present. Included are American folk dolls, French and German, Chinese, and Hawaiian dolls, both in settings and in custom-made cases.

The Antique Dollhouse is located in an historic classical revival raised cottage that was first owned by Walter Gresham (in the 1850s) and originally located on the site of the Bishop's Palace. J. Z. H. Scott, a prominent attorney, purchased the house in 1887 and employed Nicholas Clayton, a well-known Galveston architect, to make additions. The house was purchased from Scott's heirs in 1981 and restored.

Open Tuesday through Saturday from 10 A.M. to 6 P.M., Sunday from 1 to 6 P.M. (October–March). Admission, adults $3; children $2.

Ashton Villa

2328 Broadway   Galveston 77553
409/762-3933   H (film and first floor only), B, T, N, HABS

Designed and constructed in 1859 by James M. Brown, social and civic leader of Galveston, nineteenth century "Queen City of the Gulf," Ashton Villa is built in the Italianate style marked by low roofs, deep-bracketed eaves, and tall, narrow windows and doors. This antebellum house was one of the first in Texas to presage the new style and probably created quite a stir in Galveston, which was much more congenial to Greek Revival. It survived the Civil War, the 1900 hurricane, and threatened demolition to become a symbol of historic preservation in Galveston. It is authentically furnished.

Open daily from 10 A.M. to 4 P.M., weekends, noon to 5 P.M. Closed Tuesdays September through May and on Thanksgiving and Christmas. Admission, adults $3, students and senior citizens $2.50, children 6 to 12 years of age $1.50, children under 6 free.

Bishop's Palace

1402 Broadway   Galveston 77550
409/762-2475   B, T, N, HABS

Designed by the noted Galveston architect Nicholas J. Clayton, the Bishop's Palace was constructed in 1886 for Walter Gresham, a wealthy Galveston attorney, and his wife. The four story Victorian structure, built of granite, limestone, and red sandstone and considered the finest turreted Victorian mansion in the state, took seven years to complete and involved materials from around the world. Features include imported fireplaces, ornate stained-glass windows, and a beautiful, handcarved main staircase, among other works of craftsmanship. The American Institute of Architects named the house one of the 100 outstanding buildings in the United States in 1956. It is listed by the Library of Congress as one of the fourteen structures representing early American architecture. The house got its popular name—the Bishop's Palace—when it was sold to the Catholic Diocese of Galveston three years after Mr. Gresham's death in 1920 and was used by Bishop Christopher E. Byrne as the official Episcopal residence and Diocesan office. It continued in that function until Bishop Byrne's death in 1950.

Open Monday through Saturday from 10 A.M. to 5 P.M., Sunday from noon to 5 P.M. during the summer; Wednesday through Saturday and Monday from 1 to 5 P.M., Sunday from noon to 5 P.M. during the winter. Closed on Tuesday. Admission, adults $2.50, teenagers $1.50; children, $.50. Subject to change.

Ashton Villa, Galveston.

Staircase in the Bishop's Palace, Galveston. Photograph by Todd Webb. Courtesy Amon Carter Museum, Fort Worth.

Center for Transportation & Commerce
See The Strand
Elissa
See The Strand
Galveston Arts Center Gallery
See The Strand

Galveston County Historical Museum
2219 Market Street   Galveston 77553
409/766-2340   T

Housed in the 1919 City National Bank, built by W. L. Moody, Jr., the Museum is devoted to the history of Galveston. Exhibits from the permanent collection as well as temporary and traveling exhibitions pertain to the history of both the city and the county. The building retains many of its original features, including a magnificent painted plaster barrel-vault ceiling. The museum sponsors the annual re-enactment of the Civil War Battle of Galveston.

Open Wednesday through Saturday from 10 A.M. to 5 P.M., Sunday from 12 to 5 P.M. Admission, free.

Galveston Garden Center
Sydnor Powhatan House
3427 Avenue O   Galveston 77550
409/763-9374   B, R, T, N, HABS

John Seabrook Sydnor, a pioneer business and civic leader in Galveston, built his authentic Greek Revival hotel in 1847. Located on 21st Street between avenues M and N, the Powhatan Hotel was home to Sydnor and his family for nearly three decades. Sydnor had the pre-cut timbers brought in from Maine by sailing ships. The hotel became unprofitable because it was located too far from the city center and was closed to become a school, a military academy, and then an orphanage. It was later moved to its present location and the Galveston Garden Club acquired it in 1965. It has now been restored to some of its former elegance and is open for tours.

Open Tuesday through Saturday from 1 to 5 P.M. A donation is requested for admission.

Rosenberg Library
2310 Sealy Avenue   Galveston 77550
409/763-8854   H, T

The Rosenberg Library is Texas' oldest free public library in continuous operation. In addition to galleries for changing exhibitions, the library contains the James M. Lykes Maritime Gallery, the Harris Gallery, which features special exhibitions, and the Hutchings Gallery, which shows historic exhibitions. The library contains more than 200,000 books, 1,233,900 manuscripts, 219,000 documents, and extensive collections of paintings, drawings, and graphics of the nineteenth and twentieth centuries.

Open Monday through Thursday from 9 A.M. to 9 P.M., Friday and Saturday from 9 A.M. to 6 P.M. The Archives division is open Tuesday through Saturday from 10 A.M. to 5 P.M., and the Rare Books division is open Tuesday through Friday from 1 to 5 P.M. and 9 A.M. to 5 P.M. on Saturday. Admission, free.

Samuel May Williams Interpretive Center

3601 Avenue P   Galveston 77553
409/765-7834

Samuel May Williams was Stephen F. Austin's secretary, Texas's first banker, and a founder of Galveston. His home, which was prefabricated in Maine and shipped to Galveston, was erected in 1839–40. It is a raised cottage surrounded by broad galleries and topped with a stunning cupola and widow's walk. It has recently been restored and filled with authentic furnishings. Audiovisual programs tell the story of Williams and early Texas.

Call for open hours and information.

The Rosenberg Library, Galveston.

The Strand
2000–2500 Strand Street   Galveston 77553
409/765-7834   N

This ten-block area of The Strand, the "Wall Street of the Southwest," has been declared a National Historic Landmark because of its architecturally significant nineteenth-century commercial structures. Many of the buildings have been restored and are active with shops, restaurants, galleries, apartments, and offices, as well as the Center for Transportation and Commerce (railroad museum). Nearby are the restored 1877 square-rigged sailing ship *Elissa* at Pier 22 and Pier 19, with shrimp boats and wharf access.

The Galveston Historical Foundation provides an audio-tour of The Strand, beginning from The Strand Visitors Center, 2016 Strand. Pictorial signs mark significant landmarks. "Dickens's Evening on The Strand" is presented the first weekend in December. Write or call for information.

The Strand
Center for Transportation & Commerce
123 Rosenberg   Galveston 77550
409/765-5700   H, B, R

The Center for Transportation & Commerce, located at the foot of The Strand on Rosenberg Street, recalls Galveston's earlier days as a transportation center and crossroads of the world when square-rigged sailing ships docked in its deep-water port and locomotives moved quickly in and out of the Santa Fe Railroad's Union Station. Thirty-five restored railroad cars are on display on four of the station's five tracks.

Perhaps the most unusual display—and the focal point of the museum—is a group of thirty-nine historically accurate, life-size sculptures in The People's Gallery entitled *A Moment Frozen in Time*. The group includes conductors impatiently watching the time, businessmen waiting for the next train, a beauty queen posing for a reporter, and sailors, children, and many other figures. The sculpture group is accompanied by conversations, which can be heard through "hearphones" located throughout the gallery, which help evoke the atmosphere of a 1932 train station.

Other attractions include a working HO-gauge model railroad traveling around a model of the Port of Galveston, four audiovisual presentations on the history of Galveston, and an interpretive display on railroad history.

The Strand, Galveston.

A Moment Frozen in Time *at the Center for Transportation and Commerce, Galveston.*

Open daily from 10 A.M. to 6 P.M. Admission, adults $4.00; senior citizens $3; children 12 and under, $2.00. Group rates available with advance reservation.

The Elissa at Pier 22, adjacent to The Strand in Galveston.

The Strand
Elissa
Pier 22 (adjacent to The Strand)
Galveston 77553
409/763-0027   B, N

This "Tall Ship for Texas" is a masterfully-restored, three-masted, square-rigged sailing ship built in 1877 by Alexander Hall & Son in Aberdeen, Scotland. It is typical of the cargo ships calling on the Port of Galveston in the late nineteenth century. *Elissa* herself sailed to Galveston in 1883 and 1886. Interpretive displays offer visitors a self-guided tour. A color film on *Elissa's* restoration is on view in the Strand Visitor's Center, 2016 Strand. There is also a Children's Activity Area which includes a shoreside mock sailing ship. *Elissa*, a restoration project of the Galveston Historical Foundation, is the only square-rigger between Baltimore and San Diego.

Open Wednesday through Monday from 10 A.M. to 6 P.M. Admission, adults $3; children $2.50; senior citizens and military $2; children under 3, free.

The Strand
Galveston Arts Center Gallery
2127 Strand   Galveston 77550
409/763-2403   H, B, T, HABS

Located at the corner of 22nd (Kempner) and the historic Strand, the Galveston Arts Center Gallery occupies a rare Victorian building with a premium gallery exhibition area fourteen feet high with long, uninterrupted walls. The gallery features local, regional, and nationally-known artists. The Galveston County Cultural Arts Council, which sponsors the Gallery, also has restored the Grand Opera House to its 1894 splendor and sponsors various performing arts there. Call for information on exhibitions and programs.

The Gallery is open Wednesday through Saturday and Monday from 10 A.M. to 5 P.M. and Sunday from 1 to 5 P.M. Closed Tuesday, New Year's Day, Thanksgiving, and Christmas. Admission, free.

Trube House
1627 Sealy Avenue   Galveston 77550
409/763-5205

The Trube House is a thirty-nine room Danish-castle inspired home designed in 1890 by Alfred Muller. It is a replica of a castle in Keil, Denmark, now Germany.

Open by appointment. Admission, $2.50 for tours. Group rates are available.

The Trube House, Galveston. Photograph by Todd Webb. Courtesy Amon Carter Museum, Fort Worth.

GARLAND
Map 1

Landmark Museum

920 W. Avenue D   Garland 75040
No telephone

The history of Garland, as it evolved from a farming outpost to an industrialized suburb, is told in the Landmark Museum. Housed in a restored 1900 vintage Santa Fe depot, the museum displays include farming and agricultural items, clothing, personal housewares, photographs, and newspapers and documents. A 1910 Pullman car in the process of restoration is located next door, as is the Lyle House, a representative late nineteenth-century frame house.

Open from 3 to 5:30 P.M. Sunday and by appointment. Admission, free.

GEORGETOWN
Map 3

Mood Heritage Museum

Southwestern University   Georgetown 78626
512/863-1997   H, B

The Mood Heritage Museum features an exhibit of early Indian material as well as material on the University itself. Southwestern University is one of the older colleges in the state, being a merger of Rutersville College, Wesleyan College, McKenzie College, and Soule University in 1873. It was called Texas University until it was incorporated as Southwestern University in 1875. The museum is located in Mood Hall (1908), one of the more historic buildings on the campus. There is also space devoted to changing exhibitions, such as the current exhibit on the early history of Georgetown.

Open Tuesday, Thursday afternoon, and Friday morning. Admission, free.

The Mood Heritage Museum is located on the first floor of Mood-Bridwell Hall at Southwestern University, Georgetown.

Cactus Park and Museum

U.S. 281 (1 mile south of George West)
George West 78022
512/449-1448

Historic collections relating to the people of Live Oak County are housed in a ten-room white stucco house that was donated to the city for the purpose of establishing a museum. The park provides facilities for camping.

Open from 9 A.M. to 12 P.M. Monday and Tuesday, other times by appointment. Admission adults, $1.50, eighteen years old and under $.25. An adult must accompany small children.

GLEN ROSE
Map 1

Dinosaur Valley State Park

Off F.R. 205   Glen Rose 76043
817/897-4588

Dinosaur tracks found in the Paluxy River near Glen Rose have proven to be of great interest. The prints were long known, but were finally recognized in the 1930s to be sauropod, ornithopod, and therapod tracks, the print of a flatfooted reptile that walked on its heels, by Roland T. Bird of the American Museum of Natural History in New York City. There is no museum in the park, but visitors can view the tracks.

Open year round. Admission, $2 per vehicle.

Somervell County Museum

Vernon and Elm Streets   Glen Rose 76043
817/897-2739 or 897-4529   B

The Somervell County Museum features fossils discovered in Texas, many in Somervell County, including teeth and bones from mammoths and the mastodon bone from the Giant Ground Sloth. Also on display are fiberglass dinosaur tracks and a cast of a tyrannosaur's jaw bone.

Also on display is historic material relating to the history of Somervell County, including a large collection of barbed wire.

Open June to Labor Day Monday through Saturday from 10 A.M. to 5 P.M., Sunday from 1 to 5 P.M.; Labor Day to June Saturday from 10 A.M. to 5 P.M. and Sunday from 1 to 5 P.M. Open at other times, and for school groups, by appointment. Admission, free.

GOLDTHWAITE
Map 10

Mills County Historical Museum

Third and Fisher Streets   Goldthwaite 76844
No telephone   H

Displays include material relating to the history of Mills County, including schools,

Mission Espíritu Santo, Goliad.

churches, businesses, farm equipment, and a typical kitchen, bedroom, and parlor of an earlier period. There are small changing exhibitions of material relating to local history.

Open Monday, Wednesday, Friday, and Saturday from 1 to 5 P.M. There is no charge for admission, but donations are accepted.

GOLIAD
Map 4

Mission Espíritu Santo

U.S. 183/77A, 1/2 mile south of Goliad
Goliad 77963
512/645-3405   H, T

Located in an area rich in Texas history, Mission Espíritu Santo has been restored to much of its former beauty. The Mission church, granary, and workshop have been reconstructed on the ruins of the original, which was established in 1749 and was active until 1830. Exhibitions include artifacts, memorabilia, and dioramas of the Spanish mission period in Texas.

The ruins of Mission Rosario, which was founded in 1754 and finally secularized in 1831, are located about four miles west of Goliad off U.S. 59. The birthplace of Ignacio Zaragoza, the Mexican general whose victory over the French in 1862 is celebrated each Cinco de Mayo (May 5), is located south of the park near the restored Presidio La Bahía and Colonel James Fannin's grave marker.

Open daily from 8 A.M. to 12 noon, 1 to 5 P.M. Admission to the park is $2 per vehicle. Senior citizens, free. "Parklands passport" available. Group tour reservations required.

Old Market House Museum
Corner of Franklin and Market streets
Goliad 77963
512/645-3563   T, HABS

The Old Market House was constructed as a farmer's market in the early 1870s and originally contained stalls which were rented to farmers and stockmen for the sale of their produce and meat. In 1886 a council room and hook and ladder room for the horse drawn fire engines were added.

The Market House has now been designated a Texas Archaeological Landmark and contains a museum that houses documents, pictures, household items, and farm appliances from the nineteenth and early twentieth centuries.

Open Monday through Friday from 10 A.M. to noon and 1 to 4 P.M. Admission, free.

Presidio La Bahía Museum
Two miles south of Goliad on U.S. 183/77A
Goliad 77963
512/645-3752   B, T, N, HABS

Established in 1749 to protect the missions around La Bahía (as Goliad was then known), the Presidio La Bahía has been restored and is still an active church. The museum contains artifacts from nine different civilizations, beginning with the Indians who camped on the site before the Spaniards arrived. The name of the settlement was changed from La Bahía to Goliad in 1829, and the village was the third largest Mexican settlement in Texas. Colonel James Fannin's men were imprisoned in the chapel of the presidio prior to their execution on Palm Sunday, 1836 (see entry under Fannin, Texas).

Open daily from 9 A.M. to 5 P.M. Closed Good Friday and Christmas. Admission, adults $1, children $.25.

Zaragoza Birthplace
Goliad State Historical Park   Goliad 77963
512/645-3405   H, T

This reconstructed, three-room building commemorates the Goliad birthplace of Ignacio Zaragoza, who later became a military hero in Mexico. On May 5, 1862, at the age of 33, Zaragoza led his poorly equipped army to victory over the elite French forces of Napoleon III at Puebla. An exhibit in two rooms of the birthplace structure details the life of Zaragoza and the significant events leading to the famous battle that is now celebrated as Cinco de Mayo.

Open by appointment. Admission, free.

Eggleston House

St. Louis Street   Gonzales 78629
No telephone   T

A "dog-run" style log house, the Eggleston House was built in 1840 near the banks of the Guadalupe River by Jesse K. Davis, a member of Stephen F. Austin's colony, for Horace Eggleston. Called by Drury Blakeley Alexander "undoubtedly the finest remaining log house in Texas," the Eggleston House has been painstakingly restored and is in excellent condition.

Open Thursday through Saturday from noon to 4 P.M. Admission, free.

Gonzales Memorial Museum

St. Louis and St. Lawrence streets
Gonzales 78629
512/672-6350   B

Founded in 1936, the museum was constructed to honor the men from Gonzales who died at the Alamo. It traces Southwestern and Civil War history through its exhibitions and collections, which include pioneer artifacts and clothing as well as the "Come and Take It" cannon that was fired at Gonzales on October 2, 1835, setting off the Texas Revolution.

The site where the "come and take it" cannon was fired is located south of the city near Independence Park. The Gonzales Municipal Building has a WPA mosaic commemorating the event.

Open Monday through Saturday from 10 to noon and from 1 to 5 P.M. and Sunday from 1 to 5 P.M. Closed Christmas. Admission, free, but donations are accepted.

Old Jail Museum

414 St. Lawrence Street   Gonzales 78629
512/672-6532   T, N, HABS

Architect Eugene T. Heiner designed the Gonzales County Jail according to a cruciform plan to hold 150 to 200 prisoners in case of a riot. It was constructed in 1885–1887 and was in use until 1975. Six hangings occurred in the jail, but the present gallows is a reproduction, the last authentic one having been torn down in 1954. Items relating to the history of Gonzales County are also on display.

Open Monday through Friday from 9 A.M. to 5 P.M., Saturday from 9 A.M. to 4 P.M., and Sunday from noon to 4 P.M. Guides available Monday through Thursday from 9 A.M. to 3:30 P.M. and on Saturday and Sunday. Admission, free.

The Eggleston House, Gonzales. Photograph by Todd Webb. Courtesy Amon Carter Museum, Fort Worth.

The Old Jail Museum is located in the Gonzales County Jail, Gonzales. Photograph by Phil Martin.

GRANBURY
Map 1

Hood County Museum

115 North Houston   Granbury 76048
817/443-3781 or 573-9921   B

Opened in 1976, the Hood County Museum is located on the second floor of Ratliff Gallery and includes both history and art in the permanent collection. Work on display is primarily by contemporary Western American artists such as Melvin Warren, James Boren, and John Free, among others.

Open Tuesday through Saturday from 11 A.M. to 5 P.M. Admission, free.

Museum of Time
211 West Pearl (one block west of the square)
Granbury 76048
817/573-1556

The Museum of Time contains more than 300 clocks from Germany, England, France, Holland, Switzerland, and the United States. There are more than 150 watches on display.

Open Monday through Saturday from 10 A.M. to 5 P.M. Closed on Sunday. Admission, adults $1.50; children under 12 $.50. All children must be accompanied by an adult.

Texas American Indian Museum
213 North Crockett   Granbury 76048
817/573-8341

The Texas American Indian Museum features more than 5,000 artifacts about the Indian, from arrowheads, war bonnets, costumes, and beadwork to maps and paintings.

Open Monday through Saturday from 9 A.M. to 5 P.M. Closed on Sunday. Admission, free, but donations are accepted.

GRAND PRAIRIE
Map 1

Dr. H. V. Copeland Historic Home
125 S.W. Dallas   Grand Prairie 75051
214/264-1571   T

This historic house contains the memorabilia of the doctor who served the city for more than fifty years, as well as medical paraphernalia, books, and furniture of Dr. Copeland and other important individuals.

Open by appointment and on special occasions. Admission, free.

Fire Museum of Texas
702 Safari Parkway (just off I-30)
Grand Prairie 75050
214/263-1042   H

With exhibits of fire fighting vehicles, equipment, and memorabilia, the Fire Museum of Texas attempts to preserve the history and heritage of the Fire Service in Texas and the United States.

Open daily from 9 A.M. to 5 P.M. June through Labor Day, same hours Wednesday through Sunday May and September. Admission, adults $2.50; children 4 to 12, $1.50; firemen, active military, and senior citizens, $2. Group rates are available for twelve or more persons. Call for information.

Texas Sports Hall of Fame

401 E. Safari Parkway (just off I-30)
Grand Prairie 75050
214/263-4255   H, B, R

Sports memorabilia and biographies of the
more than 100 sports heroes of Texas who have
thus far been inducted into the Hall of Fame are
the subject of this new museum. Beginning with
Tris Speaker, the Boston Red Sox and Cleveland
Indians outfielder of the 1910s and 1920s, the
museum has exhibits relating to baseball slug-
gers Ernie Banks and Rogers Hornsby, Mildred
"Babe" Didrekson Zaharias, Sammy Baugh,
Doak Walker, Davey O'Brien, Bob Lilly, and
many others. On the second floor, four theaters
show custom-produced films on Texas high
school, college, and professional football (nar-
rated by Don Meredith), Texas sports from World
War I to the moon landing, Texas Bowls (the
Cotton, Sun, and Bluebonnet), and baseball.
Highlights in the exhibits are Davey O'Brien's
1938 Heisman Trophy, the shot with which
Randy Matson broke the world's shot put record,
and Bobby Morrow's gold medal from the 1956
Olympics. Also on the second floor are computer games, hand-to-eye coordination tests, and
a "Dial-a-Moment" radio room where you can

*Interior of the restored 1913 streetcar in the historical area of the Texas Sports Hall of Fame,
Grand Prairie.*

recall the climax of the 1969 "shootout" between Texas and Arkansas.

The state sports hall of fame concept was originated in 1949 by a Beaumont sports writer, Thad Johnson. In 1951 Texas sports writers began electing no more than six amateur or professional athletes to the hall of fame. Currently there are 134 inductees.

Open 10 A.M. to 7 P.M. from Memorial Day through Labor Day; the rest of the year, Tuesday through Friday 10 A.M. to 5 P.M., Saturday and Sunday 10 A.M. to 6 P.M., and closed Monday. Admission, adults $3; children between 4 and 12 years of age $1.50. Prices subject to change.

Wax Museum
601 E. Safari Parkway (just off I-30)
Grand Prairie 75050
214/263-2391   H, B, R

The Wax Museum of the Southwest, located in a modern structure on I-30 between Dallas and Fort Worth, contains 182 life-like figures of famous as well as infamous personalities. It is the largest and oldest wax museum in the Southwest and one of the largest in the country. There are also collections of antique guns, antiques, and Indian artifacts on display.

Open Memorial Day through Labor Day from 9 A.M. to 9 P.M.; the remainder of the year, Monday through Friday 10 A.M. to 5 P.M., Saturday and Sunday 10 A.M. to 6 P.M. The box office closes one hour before closing time. Admission, $3.95, children 3 and under, free when accompanied by an adult.

Wax Museum, located on I-30 in Grand Prairie.

GRAND SALINE
Map 1

Grand Saline Public Library and Museum

201 E. Pacific   Grand Saline 75140
214/962-5516

The museum consists of some antique furniture and a porcelain doll collection made by a local resident.

Open Tuesday through Friday from 9 A.M. to 5 P.M., Saturday from 9 A.M. to 12 P.M. Admission, free.

GRAPEVINE
Map 1

Grapevine Historical Museum

231 S. Ball Street   Grapevine 76051
817/488-8521

The museum is located in the old depot for the Cottonbelt Railroad, itself a historic structure. With exhibits that relate to local history, the museum has also acquired the old Grapevine jail and the Torian Log Cabin, which is located on Main Street.

Open Saturday and Sunday from 1 to 5 P.M.

Grapevine Historical Museum, located in Heritage Park.

GREENVILLE
Map 1

Audie Murphy Room

W. Walworth Harrison Public Library
3716 Lee Street   Greenville 75401
214/455-2205   H, T

The Audie Murphy Room honors America's most decorated soldier, who was a native of Hunt County. Audie Murphy's letters and historical mementos, including family photographs, Murphy's uniform and foot locker, and replicas of his decorations are on display.

Open Monday from 10 A.M. to 8 P.M. and Tuesday through Thursday from 9 A.M. to 8 P.M., Friday from 9 A.M. to 5 P.M., and Saturday from 9 A.M. to 4 P.M. Admission, free.

Limestone County Historical Museum

210 W. Navasota   Groesbeck 76642
817/729-5064   B

Groesbeck was founded in 1870 by the Houston and Texas Central Railroad and named for Abram Groesbeeck, a director of the company. The spelling of the name was changed during President Theodore Roosevelt's push to simplify spelling. Exhibitions are related to the history of Limestone County.

Open Monday 8 A.M. to 5 P.M., Wednesday and Thursday 8 A.M. to noon, Friday 1 to 5 P.M. Closed Tuesday, Saturday, and Sunday. Admission, adults $.50; children $.25.

Old Fort Parker State Historic Site

Five miles north of Groesbeck on S.H. 14
Groesbeck 76642
817/729-5253

Old Fort Parker is a replica of the fort where Cynthia Ann Parker, a nine-year old white girl, was captured by Comanches. The fort had been constructed by James and Silas Parker in 1834. In the spring of 1836, while most of the men were away tending the fields, Comanches raided the fort, killing five and capturing five, three of them children. Cynthia Ann and her brother, John, quickly adapted to the Indian life, she as the wife of Quanah, who later became a famous chief, and he as a skilled and effective warrior.

Cynthia Ann's story is told at the fort in a self-guided tour. She was recaptured by Texas Ranger Captain Lawrence Sullivan Ross in 1860. She could not readjust to white society and, following several unsuccessful attempts to escape to the Indians, died in 1865.

Open daily from 8 A.M. to 5 P.M. Open until 8 P.M. on weekends between Memorial Day and Labor Day. Admission, adults $.50; children 6–12 $.25; children under 6 free. Guided tours are available by reservation.

Guadalupe Mountains National Park

110 miles east of El Paso on U.S. 62/180
Pine Springs 88220
915/828-3385   B

Guadalupe Mountains National Park is one of the more remote parks in Texas, located 110 miles east of El Paso and 55 miles south of Carlsbad, New Mexico, on U.S. 62/180. Geology and natural history exhibits are currently housed in a trailer at the Frijole Visitor Center. Planning on a new building is underway but not yet com-

pleted. There is a ten-minute slide show to describe the Permian Reef, which explains the
many interesting natural features of the region,
including Carlsbad Caverns. With Guadalupe
Peak, El Capitan, McKittrick Canyon, and numerous other spectacular natural sites, Guadalupe Mountains National Park is recommended
for hikers and campers. You should write ahead
for information. The mailing address is Star
Route 1, Box 480, Carlsbad, New Mexico 88220.

Open daily from 8 A.M. to 4:30 P.M., and 8
A.M. to 6 P.M. from Memorial Day to Labor Day.
Admission, free.

HAMILTON

Map 10

Hamilton County Museum

Hamilton County Courthouse
On the square   Hamilton 76531
No telephone

A general museum devoted to the history of
Hamilton County, which was organized in 1858
with Hamilton as the county seat.

Open weekdays from 8 A.M. to 5 P.M.

HARLINGEN

Map 5

Confederate Air Force Flying Museum

Rebel Field
Valley International Airport   Harlingen 78550
512/425-1057   H, B

Famed for the Ghost Squadron that flies
vintage World War II airplanes (1939–1945), the
Confederate Air Force Flying Museum is a
sprawling exhibition of World War II history and
artifacts as well as more than 100 historic aircraft, with a few replicas of enemy planes added
to make the mock air battles look more realistic. The collection, all airworthy and owned in-
dividually by the members of the CAF, includes
the Royal Air Force Spitfire, the U.S. Army Air
Force P-51 Mustang, the B-17 Flying Fortress,
the A-26 Invader, and a B-29 Superfortress,
among others.

Open Monday through Saturday from 9 A.M.
to 5 P.M., Sunday and holidays from 1 to 6 P.M.
Call or write for information on forthcoming air
shows. The annual, four-day homecoming air
show is held each October. Admission, adults
$3; students age 6–18, $1.50.

Industrial Air Park

Harlingen Hospital Museum

Industrial Air Park
Boxwood Street   Harlingen 78550
512/423-3979   T

The Harlingen Hospital Museum is the city's
first hospital, built on the corner of F Street and

Tyler in 1923 and used until 1927, when a larger hospital was constructed. Moved to Industrial Air Park, near the Rio Grande Valley Museum, the hospital was restored and furnished as a historic medical museum, with an early twentieth-century operating room, dental office, medical library, patient room, and examining room.

Open Tuesday through Friday from 9 A.M. to noon and 2 to 5 P.M., and Sunday from 2 to 5 P.M. Admission, free, but a donation may be made.

Industrial Air Park
Rio Grande Valley Museum
Industrial Air Park
Boxwood Street   Harlingen 78550
512/423-3979

The Rio Grande Valley Museum contains exhibits emphasizing the Lower Valley's bicultural heritage. Exhibits pertain to early life in Texas, from the Karankawa and Coahuiltecan Indians through the Spanish period, the Mexican Republic, and the Texas Republic. The museum also includes natural history exhibits, and early farm equipment and furnishings.

A recent addition features textiles and clothing, including quilts, lace, doilies, wedding clothes, and children's clothes from the nineteenth and early twentieth centuries. The museum is located in the old jail of the former Army Air Force base.

A part of the same complex is the Paso Real Stagecoach Inn, built in the late nineteenth century on the shores of nearby Arroyo Colorado as a stage stop. Abandoned in 1904 when the railroads came to the Valley, it was salvaged, moved to the park, and restored in 1973. It contains an exhibition of nineteenth-century furniture.

There is also a garden for the blind which contains plants, shrubs, and trees that may be touched.

Open Tuesday through Friday from 9 A.M. to noon and 2 to 5 P.M., Sunday from 2 to 5 P.M. Admission, free, but a donation may be given.

Lon C. Hill Home
Lon C. Hill Park   Harlingen 78550
512/423-3979

Located across the street from the city auditorium, the Lon C. Hill Home is the first home built in Harlingen by the city's founder in 1904. It was the headquarters of the Hill plantation. Restored in 1971 and donated to the city in

1974, the two-story frame structure contains turn-of-the-century furnishings.

Open Wednesday from 10 A.M. to noon and 2 to 5 P.M., Thursday from 2 to 5 P.M. December through March open Sunday from 2:30 to 5 P.M. Admission, free.

HASKELL
Map 10

J. U. and Florence B. Fields Museum of Fine Living

401 N. Avenue E (U.S. 277) Haskell 79521
817/864-3898 T

The Fields Museum of Fine Living contains the collection assembled over a number of years by members of the Fields family. It includes various pre–Civil War artifacts as well as pressed glass and Victorian furniture that belonged to Mrs. Fields.

Open Tuesday and Saturday from 2 to 5 P.M. Admission, free.

HELENA
Map 4

Karnes County Museum

Courthouse Square Helena 78118
512/780-2868 B

Local memorabilia, old photographs, antique clothing, and many other historical artifacts are displayed in the Karnes County Museum, which is located in the building which served as the Karnes County Courthouse from 1873 to 1894. Upstairs room settings depict the home life of the early settlers.

Open Tuesday through Saturday from 8 A.M. to 5 P.M., Sunday from 1 to 5 P.M. Admission, free.

HENDERSON
Map 2

The Howard-Dickinson House

501 South Main Street Henderson 75652
214/657-6925 T

The first brick house in Rusk County, the two-story Howard-Dickinson House has been completely restored and contains authentic period furniture. It was constructed by the Howards in 1855; the frame wing was added in 1905 by the Dickinsons.

Open Sunday from 1 to 5 P.M. and by appointment. Admission, adults $1; students $.50.

HEREFORD
Map 9

Deaf Smith County Historical Museum

400 Sampson Street Hereford 79045
806/364-4338

Emphasizing the pioneer history of Deaf Smith County, the museum includes exhibitions of Indian artifacts, household equipment, farming and ranching implements, a general store, and a chapel. A Santa Fe caboose is on exhibi-

The Howard-Dickinson House, Henderson.

tion in the yard, as well as a genuine wooden windmill and a reconstructed dugout, typical of the type of housing in which many High Plains pioneers lived. The museum also owns a good collection of historic fashions.

Open Tuesday through Saturday from 10 A.M. to 5 P.M., Sunday from 2 to 5 P.M. Closed Mondays, Thanksgiving, Christmas, and New Year's Day. Admission, free.

E. B. Black Historical House

508 W. Third Street   Hereford 79045
806/364-4338   T, N, HABS

An excellent example of West Texas residential architecture, the Black House marks the advent of classic revival in the Texas Panhandle. Constructed in 1909 by E. B. Black, who operated a family furniture store in the city, the one-and-one-half-story house remained in the family until it was donated to the Deaf Smith County Historical Society in 1977.

Open by appointment for tours, club meetings, and special occasions. Admission, free.

National Cowgirl Hall of Fame and Heritage Center

Pittman House   Hereford 79045
806/364-5252

The National Cowgirl Hall of Fame includes memorabilia of prize-winning cowgirls, from early greats such as Jackie Worthington, Lucille Mulhall, Tad Lucas, and Fern Sawyer to such recent champions as Sue Pirtle. Saddles, boots, chaps, spurs, and photo albums constitute a large part of the collection.

There are currently fifty-three elected members of the Hall of Fame. Rodeo championships are important; but so, too, are pioneer accomplishments; hence the famous Justin Boot Company owner Enid Justin is also a Hall of Fame honoree.

The Center also has a Western art collection and features different Western artists each month.

Open Monday through Friday from 9 A.M. to 5:30 P.M. Admission, $2. Call for information.

HILLSBORO
Map 1

Confederate Research Center and Audie L. Murphy Gun Museum

Hill Junior College   Hillsboro 76645
817/582-2555   H, B

The Confederate Research Center features an extensive collection of books, magazines, artifacts and records, including photographs, maps, correspondence, and data on microfilm. This material relates generally to Texas in the Confederacy and specifically to Hood's Texas Brigade, which was organized in Richmond, Virginia, in the summer of 1861 and served with Robert E. Lee's Army of Virginia and James Longstreet's Second Corps throughout the Civil War. Under the leadership of General John B. Hood, the brigade fought in at least twenty-four battles of the war.

The Audie L. Murphy Gun Museum displays rare Confederate and Texas firearms and edged weapons. It also features memorabilia pertaining to Audie L. Murphy, the most decorated combat soldier in World War II. The Gun Museum contains an extensive special library on weaponry.

Open weekdays from 8 A.M. to 5 P.M. when college is in session. Admission, free.

HONDO
Map 6

Medina County Museum

2202 18th Street   Hondo 78861
512/426-2271

Located in the old Southern Pacific Depot, the Medina County Museum contains memorabilia from the pioneers of Medina County. There is a carriage, a one-room school house, and several other historical exhibitions.

Open weekdays from 10 A.M. to 5 P.M. and Sunday from 2 to 6 P.M. from Memorial Day to Labor Day. Admission, adults, $1; children under 6, free.

R. F. Voyer Regional Museum

Downtown square, U.S. 82
Honey Grove 75446
214/378-7171 H

Named for R. F. Voyer, former administrator of the David Graham Hall Foundation, one of the sponsors of the museum with Paris Junior College, the museum is dedicated to interpreting the history of the four county region—Fannin, Lamar, Delta, and Red River—along the Red River Valley of northeast Texas. "When Cotton was King in the Red River Valley," theme of the basic permanent exhibit, is subject to various interpretations of the role cotton played in the life of the people of Northeast Texas during the first quarter of the twentieth century. Other exhibits relate to the life of Dr. David Graham Hall, doctor, philanthropist, and founder of the David Graham Hall Trust and Foundation.

Open Tuesday through Saturday from 1:30 to 4 P.M., Wednesday from 10 A.M. to noon and 1 to 3:30 P.M., Saturday from 1:30 to 4 P.M. Closed on Monday and holidays. Admission, free.

The Art League of Houston Gallery

1953 Montrose Blvd.   Houston 77006
713/523-9530 H

The Art League of Houston Gallery exhibits paintings, sculpture, ceramics, drawings, and wall hangings by local artists. Exhibitions change frequently. The League also sponsors an annual juried competition, "Dimensions Houston."

Open Tuesday through Friday 10 A.M. to 4 P.M., Saturday noon to 4 P.M. Admission, free.

Battleship Texas

See San Jacinto Battleground

*Bayou Bend

1 Westcott Street   Houston 77019
713/529-8773 H, T

Designed by Houston architect John F. Staub and built in 1927, this 24-room mansion is filled with the greatest collection of decorative arts and paintings in the state. Spanning 200 years of American history, from the mid-seventeenth century to the mid-nineteenth century, the collection, along with the mansion, was donated to the Museum of Fine Arts by Miss Ima Hogg, only daughter of James Stephen Hogg, Texas Governor from 1891 to 1895. The Bayou Bend collection, begun by Miss Hogg in 1920 with the intention of giving it to a Texas museum, con-

Bayou Bend, a part of the Museum of Fine Arts, Houston.

The Drawing Room, Bayou Bend, Houston. Photograph by Allen Mewbourn. Courtesy The Museum of Fine Arts, Houston, Gift of Miss Ima Hogg.

tains American furniture dating back to the seventeenth century along with eighteenth- and nineteenth-century paintings, decorative arts, porcelains, metalware, books, and glass. "I cannot remember when I was not interested in old things with a history," Miss Hogg wrote, and she continued to collect for the mansion until her death in 1975. Included are paintings by the American masters Gilbert Stuart, Charles Willson Peale, John Singleton Copley, Robert Feke, and Edward Hicks, among others. Various rooms in the mansion recall fashionable American styles, from the early eighteenth-century wood paneling of New England to the Georgian style drawing room and the early Victorian Belter Parlor of the mid-nineteenth century.

The mansion is located on fourteen acres of small gardens and natural woodlands overlooking the bend in Buffalo Bayou. The Hogg family assisted in developing some 1,500 acres along the bayou that are now known as River Oaks, an exclusive residential section.

Open by advance reservation only. Tuesday through Friday 10 to 11:45 A.M., 12:45 to 2:30 P.M. Saturday 10 A.M. to 12:45 P.M. Two-hour guided tours begin every 15 minutes, both morning and afternoon. Second Sunday of each month, except March and August, open from 1 to 5 P.M. with no reservations required. Admission, free, but a refundable $1 deposit per person is required to hold reservation. Closed during August, New Year's Day, Independence Day, Thanksgiving, and Christmas.

Contemporary Arts Museum
See Montrose Area

Edith L. Moore Nature Sanctuary
440 Wilchester   Houston 77079
713/932-1392   B

Sponsored by the Houston Audubon Society, the Moore Nature Sanctuary consists of almost eighteen acres with nature trails, native flora and fauna, and a 1932 log cabin with exhibits of birds nests and stuffed birds.

The nature trails are open from dawn to dusk; the cabin is open from 9 A.M. to noon weekdays. Admission, free.

*Harris County Heritage Society
Sam Houston Park
1100 Bagby   Houston 77002
713/223-8367   H, B, R, T (Kellum-Noble House), N (Kellum-Noble House), HABS (Kellum-Noble

House, Shelter House, and Nichols-Rice-Cherry House)

Within view of the downtown skyscrapers, the Harris County Heritage Society has restored some of the earliest and finest buildings in Houston's history. The Long Row recalls that Houston's first business building was a long row of small stores and shops originally constructed in 1837. The row was destroyed by fire in 1860; this reconstruction was completed in 1967. A number of houses have been restored and moved to Sam Houston Park, including the Kellum-Noble House, the Nichols-Rice-Cherry House, the Pillot House, the San Felipe Cottage, and The Old Place, a cabin moved from the west bank of Clear Creek and thought to be the oldest structure in Harris County (1824). Also included in the park are the St. John Church, constructed in the northwest part of Harris County by German farmers in 1891, and the Bandstand, a copy of the original turn-of-the-century Houston City Park bandstand.

Open Tuesday through Friday from 10 A.M. to 4 P.M., Saturday from 11 A.M. to 3 P.M., and Sunday from 2 P.M. to 5 P.M. An admission is charged, with special rates for students and children.

Hermann Park
Houston Museum of Natural Science
1 Hermann Circle Drive
Houston 77030
713/526-4273   H, B

Founded in 1909, the Houston Museum of Natural Science has grown to one of the largest natural science museums in the Southwest, containing some 120,000 square feet of exhibits, shows, study rooms, auditorium, and 232-seat Burke Baker Planetarium. One of the most striking exhibits is the 70-foot-long skeleton of a *Diplodocus*, a herbivorous dinosaur, that presides over the Alfred C. Glassell, Jr. Hall. Nearby are exhibits of Indian materials from the Western Hemisphere, the porcelain Boehm Birds, the Harry C. Wiess Hall of Petroleum Science and Technology, and an area for temporary exhibitions.

On the second floor are a series of exhibits on the coastal habitats of Texas as well as the G. W. Strake Hall of Texas History, which brings to life events from Texas's past from 1543 to 1907. The Frensley African Hall, which contains examples of African birds, plants, animals, and artifacts is also on the second floor, as is the Farish Hall of Texas Wildlife, featuring habitat groups from the Big Bend to the Big Thicket.

The ground floor contains the Arnold Hall of Space Science, which includes artifacts from the Mercury, Gemini, and Apollo space missions. Here also is the Moody Foundation Hall of Chemistry, which features exhibits by the Robert A. Welch Foundation chronicling the history of chemistry. The Eby Hall of Gems and Minerals, the Cullen Hall of Communications, and the Fondren Hall of Energy are also on the ground floor.

The Burke Baker Planetarium programs feature a seasonal variety of educational and entertaining events, and the Frensley Hall of Astronomy provides information and additional programs on astronomy and space science.

Open Tuesday through Saturday from 9 A.M. to 5 P.M., Sunday and Monday from noon to 5 P.M., and Friday evenings from 7:30 to 9. Closed on New Year's Day, Thanksgiving, and Christmas. Admission, free.

Hermann Park
Houston Zoological Gardens
1 Zoo Circle Drive   Houston 77030
713/523-3211

The Houston Zoo is large, consisting of 520 species of reptiles, 261 species of birds, and 128 species of mammals. Lectures, guided tours, and educational programs for children make the zoo more accessible for the public.

Open daily from May through October from 9:30 A.M. to 8 P.M.; November through April 9:30 A.M. to 6 P.M. Admission, free.

Hermann Park
Museum of Medical Science
Second Floor of the Museum of Natural Science
5800 Caroline   Houston 77030
713/529-3766   H

Exhibits explain, in both English and Spanish and with graphic models, various phases of life functions and birth. Special exhibits permit the visitor to view the beat of his or her own heart, check lung capacity and eyesight, touch and examine a human skeleton, and measure height and weight. Especially interesting is the life-size, transparent model of a woman, accompanied by a ten-minute program that explains the various parts of the body. An educational computer game is available for public participation.

New wing of the Houston Museum of Natural Science.

Entrance to the Museum of Medical Science, Houston.

Open Tuesday through Saturday from 9 A.M. to 4:45 P.M., Sunday and Monday from noon to 4:45 P.M. Admission, free. There is no charge for school group tours, but they must be booked two weeks in advance.

Hermann Park
Pioneer Memorial Log House Museum
1510 Outer Belt Drive
Houston 77025
713/528-9344 or 665-4473   B

Built in 1936 by the Daughters of the Republic of Texas, San Jacinto Chapter, in conjunction with the Texas Centennial, the Memorial Log House Museum contains furniture, artifacts, letters, paintings, and other items that relate to pioneer Texas.

Open the first Thursday of each month from 1 to 4 P.M. Admission, free.

Houston Center for Photography

1440 Harold   Houston 77006
713/663-6373

Founded in 1981, the Center presents a variety of photographic exhibitions and is in the process of building a permanent collection ranging from documentary to fine art photographs, classical images to the avant-garde. Various educational programs accompany the exhibitions. The Center now has approximately 800 square feet of exhibit space, but has plans for larger quarters in the near future.

Open Saturday and Sunday from 12 to 5 P.M. Admission, free.

Houston Museum of Natural Science

See Hermann Park

Houston Police Department Museum

17000 Aldine-Westfield Road   Houston 77073
713/230-2300, Ext. 361

The Houston Police Department Museum is the focal point of the Department's community service, training, recruiting, and outreach program. There are a number of exhibits related to the function and life of a police officer. The history of the Houston police force is traced from 1837 to the present using old artifacts and equipment, including a three-wheel motorcycle, a police car, and a 300C Hughes helicopter. The various divisions of the department are illustrated, such as the Homicide Detectives, the Bomb Squad, and the Accident Division, and there is an Evidence Maze, which demonstrates the process of collecting and processing evidence.

An Archival Research Center is being established, and community service officers are available upon advance request for civic groups, neighborhood groups, etc. Please call the museum for more information. Admission, free.

Houston Public Library

500 McKinney   Houston 77002
713/224-544   H

The Houston Public Library downtown is composed of two buildings connected by an outside plaza and an underground tunnel. The old library (the Julia Ideson Building) houses the Special Collections, the Texas and Local History Department, and the Houston Metropolitan Resource Center. The new library is the widely used area with regular library departments.

The Houston Public Library.

Exhibitions are changed each month in both buildings. These exhibits are usually drawn from artists and collections in Houston, and traveling exhibits. Programs relating to the exhibitions are presented at noon on Wednesday.

The Julia Ideson Building is open Monday through Saturday from 9 A.M. to 6 P.M.; the central building Monday through Saturday from 9 A.M. to 9 P.M., Sunday from 2 to 6 P.M. Admission, free.

Houston Zoological Gardens
See Hermann Park

Lyndon B. Johnson Space Center
Three miles east of I-45 on NASA Road 1
Houston 77058
713/483-4321 or 483-4241   H

The Johnson Space Center is in charge of our manned space flights from launch through landing. It is also in charge of selecting and training the astronauts as well as developing technology for manned space flight, managing the industrial efforts in design and fabrication of spacecraft, and managing the experiments during the space flights. Much of the story of space flight can be seen in the exhibits here.

Lunar module and lunar rover on view in the Olin E. Teague Visitor Center of the Johnson Space Center, Houston. NASA photograph.

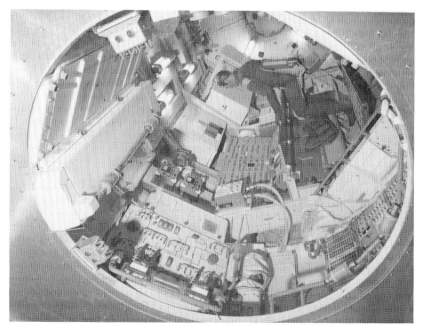

An interior view of the Skylab Multiple Docking Adapter trainer, Johnson Space Center. NASA photograph.

A self-guided tour with no reservations required begins in the Olin E. Teague Visitor Center, where moon rocks, spacecraft, and other exhibits are on display. Astronaut Gordon Cooper's Mercury capsule and the Apollo 17 spacecraft are only two of the many historical artifacts exhibited. NASA films are shown regularly. The Visitor Center closes at 4:45 P.M.

Follow the green signs to the following buildings: in the Mission Simulation and Training Center (Building 5), the Skylab trainers used by the astronauts to practice for the Shuttle missions are on display. In Building 9A, just a short drive away, Space Shuttle Orbiter Training is in progress, and most of the more than 800 pounds of lunar material brought back by the astronauts is being tested and examined in the Lunar Sample Building (31A) nearby. Actual space vehicles can be viewed in Rocket Park.

Briefings through the Mission Control Center are available on a first-come first-served basis everyday of the year except Christmas. Check in at the Visitor Center Information Desk for the next available briefing. Tours requiring special arrangements may be made by calling 713/483-4241.

The Johnson Space Center is located southeast of downtown Houston, almost on Galveston Bay, and is open daily, except Christmas, from 9 A.M. to 4 P.M. Admission, free. Allow 2 1/2 to 3 hours for your tour. Begin at the Visitor Center in Building 2, where you can get information and brochure for the self-guided tour.

These spacesuits are a part of the historical exhibit in the Teague Visitor Center, Johnson Space Center, Houston. NASA photograph.

Montrose Area

Contemporary Arts Museum

5216 Montrose Blvd.   Houston 77006
713/526-3129   H, B

Since its founding in 1948, the Contemporary Arts Museum has devoted itself to the presentation of the best in contemporary arts, both from this area and other parts of the country. The museum presents from twelve to fourteen changing exhibitions each year, accompanied by scholarly publications and educational activities which include lectures by exhibiting artists, films, tours, and classes for both children and adults.

The museum was designed by Gunnar Birkets and Associates and is built of stainless steel in the form of a parallelogram. A long ramp leads the visitor into what appears to be a minimal metal block sculpture, but inside the vast spaces accommodate huge sculptures or small print exhibitions equally well.

Open Tuesday through Saturday from 10 A.M. to 5 P.M., Sunday noon to 6 P.M. Closed Mondays, New Year's Day, Independence Day, Columbus Day, Thanksgiving, and Christmas. Admission, free.

Contemporary Arts Museum, Houston. Photograph by Rick Gardner.

Montrose Area

*The Museum of Fine Arts, Houston

1001 Bissonnet at Main   Houston 77265
713/526-1361   H, B

One of the finest art museums in the state, the Museum of Fine Arts grew out of the Houston Public School Art League, founded in 1900. The museum opened in 1924 in a building designed by William Ward Watkin. Wings were added in 1926 and 1953. The internationally famous architect Ludwig Mies van der Rohe com-

152

Fra Angelico, Predella: "Scene from the Life of St. Anthony," *c. 1437. Tempera on wood, 7⅜ × 11⅛ in. Photograph by Allen Mewbourn. Courtesy The Museum of Fine Arts, Houston, The Edith A. and Percy S. Straus Collection.*

Pablo Picasso, Standing Woman, *1961. Painted iron, 70¼ × 67¼ in. Photograph by Allen Mewbourn. Courtesy The Museum of Fine Arts, Houston, Gift from the Esther Florence Whinery Goodrich Foundation.*

pleted the master plan of the museum in 1954, with the additions being completed in 1958 and 1974, more than doubling the museum's gallery space.

The collections have kept pace with the expanding building. Beginning with a relatively modest bequest from the Houston Art League, the collection soon grew to include art from ancient Egypt, Greece, and Rome, Oriental works, Early Christian and Medieval objects, and pre-Columbian and Tribal arts. Today the museum is strong in Renaissance works, Impressionist and post-Impressionist paintings, sculpture, and American decorative arts, Frederic Remington paintings, and American and European photographs in the post-1945 period. Especially popular are works by Fra Angelico, Cézanne, Renoir, and Picasso.

A growing interest in photographs and prints has permitted the museum to accumulate important collections in these areas, especially the Target collection of twentieth-century photographs, and frequent exhibitions from this increasingly popular part of the collection are shown in the print gallery.

In addition to continuing exhibitions from the permanent collection, the museum presents approximately 25 special exhibitions each year as well as an active series of films, lectures, and special events. Bayou Bend (see separate entry) is also a part of the museum.

Open Tuesday through Saturday from 10 A.M. to 5 P.M., Sunday from 1 to 6 P.M. Admission, free.

Museum of American Architecture and Decorative Arts
Houston Baptist University
7502 Fondren Road   Houston 77074
713/774-7661   H

The Museum of American Architecture and Decorative Arts features displays of early Texas furniture and decorative arts, early American textiles and furniture, and groups of antique dolls, probably the most fascinating of which depicts the coronation of Napoleon.

Open Tuesday through Thursday from 10 A.M. to 4 P.M. Closed Easter; first three weeks of August; Christmas vacation. Admission, free. Special tours may be arranged by appointment.

The Museum of Fine Arts, Houston
See Montrose Area

Museum of Medical Science
See Hermann Park

Museum of Printing History
1324 West Clay   Houston 77019
713/522-4652   B

Located in the east wing of the Graphic Arts Conference Center, the Museum of Printing History is a showcase for the history of printing as well as for the tools of the trade. On display are many rare examples of printing, including the oldest printed piece in the world, the Hyaku-manto Dharani Scroll, which was printed in Nara, Japan, in 764 A.D. Examples such as one of the earliest pieces printed in the Western Hemisphere, as well as documents from both Texas and U.S. history, and a number of antique printing presses are also included in the exhibit. The museum, which is sponsored by Houston-area graphic arts companies and printers, features a series of printing demonstrations with each new exhibit.

Open Monday through Friday (except holidays) from 10 A.M. to 4 P.M. Admission, free.

O'Kane Gallery
University of Houston Downtown Campus
1 Main Street   Houston 77002
713/749-1950   H

Established in 1970, the O'Kane Gallery has proved to be a showplace for young and little-known artists. Gallery exhibits present a rich and varied fair of mixed media works by Houston area artists as well as Texas artists. Changing exhibitions of art, photography, and craft.

Open Monday through Friday from 10 A.M. to 5 P.M. Admission, free.

Pioneer Memorial Log House Museum
See Hermann Park

Rice University
Rice Museum
University Boulevard & Stockton Street
Houston 77005
713/522-0886   H, B

Tucked into entrance 7 on the Rice University campus is the Rice Museum, which features a program of temporary art exhibitions drawn from the Menil Foundation Collection (cycladic to modern), as well as traveling exhibitions. Recent exhibitions have included the work of contemporary French painters as well as that of master printmakers from the sixteenth through the nineteenth centuries.

Open Tuesday through Saturday from 10 A.M. to 5 P.M., Sunday noon to 6 P.M. Closed Monday. Admission, free.

Rice University
Sewall Art Gallery
Sewall Hall, entrance 2
6100 S. Main   Houston 77251
713/527-8101, Ext. 3502   H

Sewall Art Gallery, located on the main floor of Sewall Hall, functions principally as an extension of the teaching activities in the Department of Art and Art History of Rice University. The Gallery actively collects art works which are used for research, loan, and exhibitions. Four to six exhibitions are mounted during the academic year, which correlate with the Art Department's course offerings, focusing on historical and contemporary presentations of painting, sculpture, graphic, video, and performance arts.

Open Monday through Saturday from noon to 5 P.M. Admission, free.

Robert A. Vines Environmental Science Center
Spring Branch Independent School District
8856 Westview Drive   Houston 77055
713/465-9628   H, B

The Environmental Science Center contains exhibits on native wildlife, geology, oceanography, and exotic wildlife as well as an arboretum that includes approximately 200 species of trees, shrubs, and vines native to southeast Texas.

Open weekdays from 8:30 A.M. to 5 P.M. Closed two weeks at Christmas, Memorial Day, July 4, Labor Day, and Thanksgiving.

Rothko Chapel
1401 Sul Ross at Yupon
St. Thomas University   Houston 77006
713/524-9839   H

This small, nondenominational chapel designed by Philip Johnson contains fourteen dark and abstract paintings done by Mark Rothko shortly before his death. Visitors are welcome to view the paintings and meditate. At the end of a small reflecting pool is Barnett Newman's sculpture *Broken Obelisk*.

Open daily from 10 A.M. to 6 P.M. Admission, free.

San Jacinto Battleground
Battleship Texas
3527 Battleground Road   Houston 77571
713/479-2411   H (limited), B, N

Proud veteran of two world wars, the U.S.S. *Texas*, a dreadnought class battleship, was decommissioned from service and presented to the State of Texas in 1948. Today the battleship *Texas* rests peacefully near Houston on the Ship Channel in the San Jacinto Battleground Park and is a museum as well as a memorial to those who served in our nation's military.

The *Texas*, which was launched in 1914 at a cost of $5,830,000, is 573 feet long, and had a speed of 21 knots. Expenses for bringing the ship to Texas, towing, docking, etc., were borne by public contribution. The Admiral Nimitz Room, the Cruiser Houston Room, the Trophy Room, the Engine Room, and the Texas Navy Museum are dedicated to informing visitors about past glories and sacrifices. An audio system has been installed to give detailed highlights of the ship's equipment and performance. The ship has been designated a Mechanical Engineering Landmark by the American Society of Mechanical Engineers.

Open daily from 10 A.M. to 5 P.M. There is an admission charge.

San Jacinto Battleground
San Jacinto Museum of History
San Jacinto Battleground State Historical Park (off S.H. 225)   Houston 77571
713/479-2421   H, B, N

Housed in the San Jacinto Monument, which was constructed in 1938–39 on the site of the 1836 Battle of San Jacinto in which Texas won its independence from Mexico, the San Jacinto Museum of History contains 15,000 square feet of exhibition space and interprets Texas history from the early Indian civilizations to Texas's growth through the end of the nineteenth century. The museum is strong in material relating to the Republic of Texas (1836–1845) and the contributions to the development of the state by Spanish, Mexican, and French colonists.

A prime attraction is the observation floor on the top of the 570 feet high Monument, which provides a striking view of the battlefield, the Houston Ship Channel, and the battleship U.S.S. *Texas*.

The Anglo-American room of the San Jacinto Museum of History in Houston. Four centuries of Texas history are documented in the two large exhibit galleries, research library, and archives.

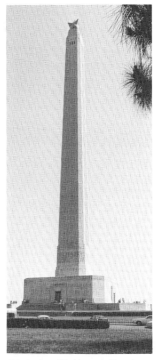

San Jacinto Monument, Houston.

The Monument itself was built as the tallest masonry structure in the world and commemorates the heroes of the Battle of San Jacinto. It is made of Texas Cordova cream limestone reinforced by a concrete innerlining. The building is 125 feet square, with the shaft tapering from 47 feet square to 30 feet square at the observation tower. The 35-foot high star weighs approximately 220 tons.

There is a self-guided tour of the battleground.

The museum is open Tuesday through Sunday from 9:30 A.M. to 5:30 P.M. and the Monument's entrance foyer and observation floor are operated seven days a week. Closed Christmas Eve and Christmas Day. Admission to the Monument and museum is free, but there is a charge of $1.50 for adults and $.50 for children under 12 to use the elevator to go to the observation floor.

Sarah Campbell Blaffer Gallery

114 Fine Arts Building
University of Houston
4800 Calhoun   Houston 77004
713/749-1329   H, B

Exhibitions at the Blaffer Gallery are planned for a diverse audience and include historic as well as contemporary works. Items in the Blaffer Foundation include major paintings from the fifteenth century to the present as well as contemporary prints, and pre-Columbian sculpture and Mexican graphics.

Open Tuesday through Saturday from 10 A.M. to 6 P.M., Sunday from 1 to 6 P.M. Admission, free.

Sewall Art Gallery

See Rice University

University of Houston Gallery
Lawndale Annex
5600 Hillman   Houston 77023
713/749-4953   H

The University of Houston Gallery, located in the Lawndale Annex, exhibits changing exhibitions of contemporary art and architecture. The Gallery serves as an alternative space for new and upcoming artists whose works cannot be easily adapted to normal gallery spaces. Although national artists are represented in the exhibitions, one of the goals of the Gallery is to promote regional art. Performance art is presented in an auditorium adjacent to the Gallery.

Open Tuesday through Saturday from 10 A.M. to 3 P.M. and by appointment. Admission, free.

HUMBLE
Map 4

Humble Historical Museum
Next to the library, between Main Street and Higgins Street   Humble 77338
713/446-9881

Located in a building constructed during the Bicentennial year, the Humble Historical Museum exhibits general items and artifacts relating to area farming, ranching, and the early oil industry. The exhibits are a "hands-on" group of everyday objects reminiscent of the turn-of-the-century.

Open Tuesday, Thursday, Friday, and Sunday from 2 to 5 P.M., Saturday from 10 A.M. to 4 P.M. Closed on federal and state holidays. Admission, free.

HUNTSVILLE
Map 3

Sam Houston Memorial Museum
1804 Sam Houston Avenue   Huntsville 77340
409/295-7824   T, B

The Sam Houston Memorial Museum houses the world's largest collection of memorabilia relating to the first president of the Republic of Texas. Through the exhibits, Sam Houston's career unfolds: hero of the Battle of San Jacinto, first president of the Republic, first U.S. Senator from Texas, governor of Texas.

In addition to the main museum, Woodland Home, the house where Margaret Lea and Sam Houston lived, plus Houston's log law office and frontier kitchen, occupy the fifteen acres of historic park grounds. The Steamboat House, built by Dr. Rufus Bailey in 1858 and donated to the state, has been moved to the site. Here the hero of San Jacinto died.

Woodland Home, or the Wigwam, as Houston called it, is a good example of a Texas house that started as a one-room log house and gradually developed into a six-room house of typical Texas dog-trot style.

Open daily from 9 A.M. to 5 P.M., except Thanksgiving and Christmas. A donation is requested for admission.

Hurst

See Fort Worth, Heritage Room

INDEPENDENCE
Map 3

Texas Baptist Historical Center Museum

Corner F.R. 50 and F.R. 390
Independence 77833
409/836-5117   H, B, T, HABS

Three years after Texas obtained its independence from Mexico in 1836, a Baptist church was founded in Independence, one of the first such churches in the new republic. The present structure replaced the original adobe building that burned in 1872. Independence was known as "the Athens of Early Texas," because Baylor University for men and Baylor College for women were founded there in 1845. After his baptism in 1854, Sam Houston was counted among the members of the Independence church. In 1886 Baylor University moved to Waco and Baylor College to Belton. The only remnants of the schools are the columns of the Administration Building of the Female Department that stand on the hill west of the church. The museum of the Texas Baptist Historical Center, located by the church, contains a collection of historical records and books, family in-

The Sam Houston Memorial Museum, adjacent to the campus of Sam Houston State University, Huntsville.

formation, and history of the town's educational heritage.

Open Wednesday through Saturday from 10 A.M. to 4 P.M. and 1 to 5 P.M. on Sunday. Donations are requested for admission.

IRAAN
Map 7

Iraan Museum
Alley Oop Park in west city limits, off S.H. 29
Iraan 79744
915/639-2832   H

The exhibitions relate to the history of the city of Iraan, which received its name when the names of the owners of a prized lot, Ira and Ann Yates, were combined. Exhibits include artifacts relating to Indians in the area as well as fossils and historical objects, such as old photographs and memorabilia.

Open Saturday from 10 A.M. to noon, 1 to 6 P.M., and Sunday from 2 to 6 P.M. during April, May, September, October, and November; open Wednesday through Sunday from 1 to 6 P.M. June through August. Closed Monday and Tuesday and January through March. A donation is requested for admission.

ITASCA
Map 1

Itasca Historical Museum and Recreation Center
300 Hooks Street   Itasca 76055
817/687-2685   B

The old Missouri, Kansas, and Topeka Railway Station, formerly located in downtown Itasca, was purchased and moved to this location to house the museum. It contains a collection of artifacts and historical material relating to the families of the area. On display are clothing, books, and an old dental office.

Open on July 4, during Homecoming in October, and by reservation. Admission, free.

JACKSBORO
Map 10

Fort Richardson State Park
Jacksboro 76056
817/567-3506   H, T, N

Fort Richardson was northernmost in the chain of federal posts established to defend the frontier of Texas. The Sixth Cavalry first set up quarters near Jacksboro in 1866, but unhealthy conditions at Buffalo Springs forced them to move some twenty miles north to the site of Fort Richardson the following year. The fort was abandoned in 1878. Exhibits in the interpretive center detail the history of the post, including the so-called Salt Creek Massacre, when a group of Kiowas led by Chiefs Satanta, Satank, and Big Tree killed a wagon master and six teamsters.

Open daily from 10 A.M. to 5 P.M. during the summer; tentatively from Friday through Monday during the fall and spring; and tentatively Saturday and Sunday during the winter. Call for information.

Vanishing Texana Museum

310 S. Bolton   Jacksonville 75766
214/586-4152

Located in the Jacksonville Public Library, the Vanishing Texana Museum consists of several display cases of memorabilia relating to Texas history. Items on exhibit range from Indian pottery to pioneer tools and turn-of-the-century machines.

Open Monday from noon to 8 P.M., Tuesday through Thursday from 9:30 A.M. to 5:30 P.M., Friday from 9 A.M. to 5 P.M., and Saturday from 9 A.M. to 2 P.M. Closed Sunday. Admission, free.

Epperson House

Delta and Alley Streets   Jefferson 75657
No telephone   T, HABS

Now called the House of the Seasons because of the different colored glass—red, green, yellow, and blue—on different sides of the cupola, the Epperson House is an elegant example of the transition between Greek Revival and Victorian architecture in Texas. Period furnishing and paintings make the large house an interesting visit, as do the open hall well, which rises from the ground floor to the cupola giving the appearance of a dome, and the cupola itself. Looking through the various colored glasses colors the landscape to resemble scenes from the four seasons.

Write for information about open hours and admission.

Freeman Plantation

Jefferson 75657
214/665-2606 or 665-2320   T, N, HABS

Built in 1850 by Williamson M. Freeman, cotton planter and manufacturer, this antebellum Greek Revival style home shows a trace of Louisiana influence in the architecture. Constructed of pine, cypress, and hand-made clay bricks, the house, located about a mile out of Jefferson on Highway 49 West, is furnished with antebellum antiques.

Open for tours daily except Wednesday from 1:30 to 5 P.M. Group tours can be arranged at other times by appointment. Admission, adults $3; children under 12 $1.

Jay Gould Private Railroad Car & Excelsior House

Austin Street   Jefferson 75657
214/665-2513   H (but a 6-inch step at the door), B, T, R (in the hotel for hotel guests; minimum group required; call for information and reservations), HABS (Hotel)

The Excelsior House, probably built by William Perry c. 1858–1859, has been a continuously operating hotel since its opening. Restored in 1961 to its former elegance, the hotel is reminiscent of the days when Jefferson was a river port and steamboats plied the Big Cypress River between Jefferson and the Red River in Louisiana.

Jefferson was at one time the largest inland shipping point in Texas, with 226 steamboats landing at its port in 1872. When the Corps of Engineers broke up the Red River raft (a major log jam) in 1874, there was no longer enough water in the Big Cypress to float a steamboat, and Jefferson became an isolated village in the middle of Marion County. The decline was almost as rapid as the ascent. With the arrival of the Texas & Pacific Railroad in nearby Marshall, the economic doom of the city was complete.

The Excelsior guest register, along with other mementos of Jefferson's glory days, is on dis-

Jay Gould Railroad Car, Jefferson. Courtesy Jessie Allen Wise Garden Club, Jefferson. Photograph by Ken Everett.

play in the lobby of the hotel. The 88-foot, four-stateroom railroad car on display across the street was the car in which Jay Gould and his family crisscrossed the country. A "palace on wheels," with a lounge, dining room, kitchen, butler's pantry, and bath, it is a physical reminder of the Jefferson that could have been.

The railroad car is open daily from 9 A.M. to 4 P.M. Admission, $.50, paid at the desk of the hotel. The hotel facilities must be booked far in advance because of demand.

Jefferson Historical Museum
223 W. Austin Street   Jefferson 75657
214/665-2775   B, HABS

Located in the old federal courthouse and post office, a handsome red brick building constructed in 1888 in the Romanesque Revival style, the Jefferson Historical Museum contains historical memorabilia, objects, and documents relating to the history of Jefferson and the state.

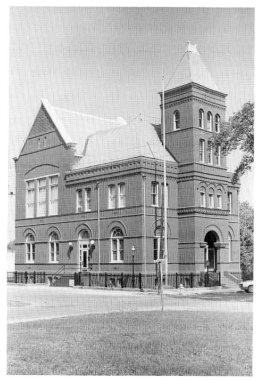

Jefferson Historical Museum. Photograph by Todd Webb. Courtesy Amon Carter Museum, Fort Worth.

Maps, manuscripts, clothing, and furniture assist in telling the story of the settlement of this part of Texas. One of the more unusual items is a bird's-eye view of Jefferson during its heyday. There is also a collection of Caddo Indian artifacts, paintings, and guns and weapons.

Open daily from 9:30 A.M. to 5 P.M. Admission, adults $1, students $.50, children under 6 free.

The Magnolias
209 E. Broadway   Jefferson 75657
214/665-2754   T, N, HABS

This Greek Revival house was built in 1867 by Dan N. Alley, Sr., a co-founder of Jefferson, as a dowry for his daughter, Victoria. It was sold in 1876 to W. B. Ward, a leading businessman. The "1881 Club," the oldest chartered club in Texas, was founded here in October 1881. The house is distinctive for its hexastyle Doric portico shelters and elaborately carved entrance with sidelights and fan-shaped pilaster opposite each end column. It is authentically furnished.

Open for tours daily from 9:30 to 11 A.M. and 1:30 to 4 P.M. and at 2:30 P.M. on Sunday. Call for information and admission.

JOHNSON CITY
Map 6

Lyndon B. Johnson National Historical Park
Lyndon B. Johnson Boyhood Home
1 block south, U.S. 290 West
Johnson City 78636
512/868-7128   H, B, T

Lyndon B. Johnson lived in this one-story white framehouse from about 1914 to 1934. It was the scene of his first political rally in 1937. The house has been restored and furnished with Johnson family furniture and memorabilia. The Johnson City Unit also includes the Johnson Settlement, which has a restored dog-trot cabin used by President Johnson's grandparents during the cattle drive era. The Johnson Settlement is accessible by horse-drawn wagon or walking trail. The LBJ Ranch Unit, including the Birthplace and Texas White House, is located in Stonewall.

Open daily from 9 A.M. to 5 P.M. Admission, free.

Lyndon B. Johnson National Historical Park
Lyndon B. Johnson Ranch
U.S. 290   Stonewall 78671
512/868-7128   H, T, HABS

Visitors tour President Lyndon B. Johnson's LBJ Ranch via National Park Service tour bus.

President Johnson grew up in this white frame house in Johnson City. It is now a part of the Lyndon B. Johnson National Historical Park. National Park Service photograph.

The birthplace of President Lyndon B. Johnson, Stonewall. National Park Service photograph.

Points of interest include the President's Texas White House, ranchlands, the President's birthplace, and the gravesite in the Johnson Family Cemetery. The Park's Johnson City Unit includes the Boyhood Home.

Open daily from 10 A.M. to 4 P.M. Admission, free.

Lyndon B. Johnson State Historical Park
U.S. 290   Stonewall 78671
512/644-2252   H, B, R

Located directly across the Pedernales River from President Johnson's ranch house, the LBJ State Historical Park was established in 1970. The focal point of the park is the Visitor Center, which contains memorabilia from President Johnson's boyhood and a wide variety of items representative of Hill Country ethnic groups. One exhibit presents photographs of famous visitors to the LBJ Ranch.

Attached to the Visitor Center is the Behrens Cabin, a two-room dog-trot cabin built by German immigrant Johannes Behrens during the 1840s. The furnishings are typical of the mid-nineteenth century.

An auditorium in the Visitor Center will accommodate 234 persons for state performances or films; an outdoor amphitheater is used for a variety of programs.

Free bus tours, conducted by the National Park Service, begin at the State Park Visitor Center. Included in the tour is the one-room Junction School first attended by the four-year-old Lyndon B. Johnson in 1912, his reconstructed birthplace, and the nearby Johnson family cemetery, where the former President is buried. A brochure at the Visitor Center contains information on other tours.

Open daily from 9 A.M. to 6 P.M. May through Labor day, 8 A.M. to 5 P.M. the remainder of the year. Admission, free.

JUNCTION
Map 6

Kimble Historical Museum
4th and College Street   Junction 76849
915/446-3067 or 446-2129   H

The museum houses exhibits relating to Kimble County. On display are farm and ranch articles used in the early days, such as tools, cattle brands, a spinning wheel, and a loom. Also on exhibit are documents, photographs, household items, and World War I relics.

Open Sunday from 2 to 5 P.M. in the summer months and by appointment. Admission, free, but a donation is appreciated.

KARNACK
Map 2

Caddo Lake State Park
14 miles northeast of Marshall on S.H. 43
Karnack 75661
214/679-3351   T

Situated on Cypress Bayou, a tributary of the Red River, Caddo Lake was used for navigation from Shreveport to the commercial port of Jefferson in the mid-nineteenth century. A Caddo Indian legend attributes the formation of the lake to an earthquake. A small exhibit in the park headquarters building highlights the historical and biological setting of the park.

Open daily from 8 A.M. to 5 P.M. Admission, $2 for car park and entrance fee.

KENEDY
Map 4

Kenedy Museum
Kenedy 78119
512/583-3761

The museum, with exhibitions that relate to the history of Karnes County, is housed in a 1940 vintage caboose that was used by the Southern Pacific Railroad.

Open by appointment. Admission, free.

KERMIT
Map 7

Kermit's Medallion Home
North side of Winkler County Park
Kermit 79745   T
915/586-2365

The Baird-Mosley Home, also called the Medallion Home, is the oldest existing structure in Kermit. Built in 1910 by W. H. Seastrunk, the house was moved to its present location in Pioneer Park in 1969. It has been furnished with period pieces belonging to families in the area. Also in the park are a homesteader's one-room

Rolls-Royce PIII Sedanca de Ville at the Classic Showcase in Kerrville. Photograph by Warren E. Warner.

shack, which was originally located twelve miles northwest of town, and a standard cable tool derrick with walking beam, the last active equipment of its type in Texas.

Open Sunday from 3 to 5 P.M. and weekdays by appointment. The park is open daily from 9 A.M. to 4 P.M. Admission, free.

KERRVILLE
Map 6

Classic Showcase

I-10 at Harper Road, exit 505   Kerrville 78028
512/895-5655   H, B

The Classic Showcase is an excellent collection of classic automobiles, including a 1932 Model J. Duesenberg Straight-8, a Rolls-Royce PIII Sedanca de Ville, and an Italian 8A Isotta Fraschini Coupe Roadster, among others.

Open Monday and Wednesday through Saturday from 10 A.M. to 5 P.M., Sunday from noon to 5 P.M. Closed on Tuesday. Admission, adults $1.75; children $1.00; children under six, free.

Cowboy Artists of America Museum

Bandera Highway (S.H. 173)   Kerrville 78028
512/896-2553

The Cowboy Artists of America established the Cowboy Artists of America Museum to serve as their headquarters as well as their showcase. Each member has three or four paintings and/or sculptures on exhibit in the large, main gallery, while smaller galleries have been set aside to exhibit the work of regional Western artists, students, and one-man shows. CAA memorabilia is also on exhibit. For membership in the CAA, an artist must make a significant contribution toward what is believed to be high quality in Western American art, which, to the CAA, focuses around the subject of life on the American frontier, past and present.

Open Tuesday through Saturday from 9 A.M. to 5 P.M., Sunday from 1 to 5 P.M. Admission, adults $2, children $.50.

KILGORE
Map 2

Kilgore College
East Texas Oil Museum

U.S. 259 at Ross Street   Kilgore 75662
214/984-1445   H, B

The East Texas Oil Museum, on the campus of Kilgore College, is a tribute to the pioneers of the oil industry. The museum houses exhibits, audiovisual presentations, photographs, and oil field tools that recreate the discovery and production of oil in the East Texas fields in the early 1930s. Columbus Marion "Dad" Joiner, a seventy-year-old wildcatter, had already drilled two dry holes when he brought in the Daisy Bradford #3 in Rusk County in May, 1929. A drill stem test the following year resulted in a gusher, and oil fever mounted as leasehounds, oil speculators, drillers, roughnecks, and camp followers descended on East Texas. Kilgore's population went from a few hundred to over 10,000 in just twenty-four hours.

The museum includes handpainted murals of early oil production and portraits of famous men. Exhibits include East Texas Boom Towns, Civic, School, Church, Home Life, and Transportation. A Memorial Room (where the career of H. L. Hunt, one of the most famous of the East Texas oilmen, is recounted), and Boomtown USA, a full-scale town including stores, people, animals, and machinery depicting the lively activity of an oil boom town. Boomtown's museum includes a geology exhibit as well as a simulated ride to the center of the earth—3,800 feet below the surface, where the oil deposits lie.

Open Tuesday through Saturday from 9 A.M. to 4 P.M. (5 P.M. from June 1 through August 31), Sunday from 2 to 5 P.M. Closed Monday, Easter, and Thanksgiving. Special holiday schedule from December 20 to January 1. Guided tours are available by reservation, and a nominal admission fee is charged.

Kilgore College
Rangerette Showcase-Museum
Physical Education Complex
1100 Broadway at Ross   Kilgore 75662
214/984-8531, Ext. 301   H, B

Organized in 1940 by Gussie Nell Davis, who originated the precision dance-drill, the Kilgore College Rangerettes, along with their performing colleagues the Ranger Band, have appeared across the nation as well as on three international tours. The Rangerette Showcase-Museum tells their story, from the first group in 1940 to the present. Included in the exhibit are a mechanized display of Rangerette props, a display of costumes from the spring stage show, thousands of photographs and clippings, and short films and slide shows of the Rangerettes in performance.

Open Tuesday through Friday from 10 A.M. to noon and 1 to 4:30 P.M., Saturday and Sunday from 2 to 5 P.M. Closed Monday, Thanksgiving and following day, and Christmas–New Year's week.

East Texas Oil Museum, Kilgore.

Display in the Rangerette Showcase-Museum, Kilgore College, Kilgore.

KILLEEN
Map 3

Fort Hood
1st Cavalry Museum
2218 Headquarters Avenue   Fort Hood 76545
817/685-7415

Exhibitions relate to the history of the 1st Cavalry Division and its regiments from 1855 to the present.

Open Monday through Friday from 9 A.M. to 4:30 P.M., Saturday and Sunday from 12 to 4 P.M. Admission, free.

Fort Hood
2nd Armored Division Museum
Battalion Avenue at 27th Street
Fort Hood 76546
817/685-5632 or 685-3570   H, B, T

The history of the 2nd Armored Division
("Hell on Wheels"), which was organized on July
15, 1940, at Fort Benning, Georgia, under the
command of General George S. Patton, Jr., and
served with distinction in Africa, Italy, and western Europe, is told in the exhibitions. Also included are captured enemy equipment from
World War II, Korea, and Vietnam and displays
on the history of the 6th Cavalry Brigade.

Open Monday, Tuesday, Thursday, and Friday
from 9 A.M. to 5 P.M., Wednesday from noon to 5
P.M., and Saturday and Sunday from noon to 4
P.M. Closed Christmas and New Year's Day. Admission, free.

KINGSVILLE
Map 5

John E. Conner Museum
820 W. Santa Gertrudis
Texas A & I University   Kingsville 78363
512/595-2819   H, B

The museum includes exhibitions of natural
history, local and pioneer history, ranching, ethnic culture, and archaeology. There is a collection of 900 branding irons, the King Ranch Natural History Collection, and archival material,
including photographs, on South Texas and regional county records. There is also a changing
exhibits gallery. The museum is adding new exhibition space as its collections and interpretative programs continue to grow.

The museum sponsors a "Bring Your Brown
Bag" lecture series each Monday November
through April.

Open weekdays from 10 A.M. to 5 P.M., Sunday from 2:30 to 5 P.M. Admission, free.

LA GRANGE
Map 3

Fayette Heritage Museum and Archives
855 S. Jefferson Street   La Grange 78945
409/968-6418   H (first floor only), B

The Fayette Heritage Museum exhibitions relate mostly to the history of Fayette County and
change seasonally. There is an invitational art
show in the spring. Archival holdings consist of
genealogical documents, records of local organizations, and back issues of the *La Grange
Journal.*

Open Tuesday through Friday from 10 A.M. to
5 P.M., Saturday from 10 A.M. to 1 P.M., Sunday
from 1 to 5 P.M.

N. W. Faison Home and Museum

822 S. Jefferson Street, seven blocks south of the U.S. 77 intersection   La Grange 78945
732/968-3898   T

Constructed in 1845 and owned by members of the N. W. Faison family since 1866, this house contains period furnishings, pioneer memorabilia, and oil paintings. It is a good example of a simple Texas house that has been decorated almost to excess, particularly at the top and bottom of the columns.

Open Saturday and Sunday from 1 to 5 P.M. Admission, adults $1, children under 12 $.10.

LAJITAS
Map 8

Lajitas Museum and Desert Garden

P.O. Box 40   Terlingua 79852
915/371-2267   H, B, R

Located just outside Lajitas on F.M. 170 en route to Terlingua, the Lajitas Museum and Desert Garden is devoted to the history of the Chihuahuan Desert region, with exhibits on archaeology, botany, and geology as well as history.

Call for open hours and admission.

LAMESA
Map 9

Lamesa–Dawson County Museum

South 2nd Street and Avenue M   Lamesa 79331
No telephone

The Lamesa–Dawson County Museum is housed in the first three-story house built in the city by Ulyss Dalmont in 1917. Furnishings and items relate to Dawson County history, going back to the city's founding as Chicago on the

N. W. Faison House, La Grange. Photograph by Todd Webb. Courtesy Amon Carter Museum, Fort Worth.

Pecos and Northern Texas Railroad in 1905.
When the post office was granted, the name was
changed to Lamesa, the Spanish term for the flat
tableland on which the community is located.

Open Sunday from 1 to 5 P.M. Tours by appointment. Admission, free.

LAMPASAS
Map 3

Cauthen House

3rd and Walnut   Lampasas 76550
No telephone

A historic house museum.

Open each Sunday from 2 to 4 P.M. May
through August.

LANGTRY
Map 7

Judge Roy Bean Visitor Center

Loop 25   Langtry 78871
512/291-3340   H (visitor center and gardens
only), T, HABS

When Roy Bean arrived west of the Pecos at
Langtry, he threw up a tent saloon along the
tracks of the Southern Pacific Railroad. A Texas
Ranger captain requested that the commission-
ers court of Pecos County appoint him justice of
the peace in 1882, and Bean's famous Jersey Lily
Saloon became the symbol of the "Law West of
the Pecos." Bean's brand of justice attracted national fame in 1896 when he staged the Fitzsim-
mons-Maher heavyweight championship fight,
which no one else would sponsor, on a sand bar
in the bed of the Rio Grande just below Langtry.
(Fitzsimmons was the easy winner.) The saloon
really was named after the well-known British
singer, Lily Langtry, whom Judge Roy idolized
but never met, but the town, which was established when the railroad came through in 1882,
was named for one of the Southern Pacific's civil
engineers. The visitor center exhibits Roy Bean's
law book, notary seal, and personal belongings
as well as dioramas with sound and a cactus
garden.

Open daily from 8 A.M. to 5 P.M., except December 24–26. Admission, free.

LAREDO
Map 5

Nuevo Santander Museum

West End Washington Street
Laredo State College   Laredo 78040
512/722-8351   H, B, N

The Nuevo Santander Museum, a unit of
Laredo State College, is devoted to the history
of the Rio Grande Valley area.

Open Monday through Friday from 8 A.M. to 5
P.M., Sunday from 1 to 5 P.M. Admission, free.

LEVELLAND
Map 9

South Plains Museum

608 Avenue H (west of the Courthouse)
Levelland 79336
806/894-7547

Exhibits deal with the history of Hockley County, the South Plains, and the cattle and farming industry, including a display of horse-drawn agricultural items. Also on display is a collection of mounted North American Big Game animals.

Open Tuesday through Saturday from 2 to 5 P.M. Admission, free.

LEXINGTON
Map 3

Pioneer Village Museum

On the Square   Lexington 78947
409/773-2305   B

Several 1850s era log cabins have been restored and contain period furnishings that recall the early days of Lexington, the oldest settlement in Lee County.

Open Monday through Saturday from 9 to 11 A.M. and 2 to 4 P.M. Admission, free.

LIBERTY
Map 4

Geraldine Humphreys Cultural Center

1710 Sam Houston Avenue   Liberty 77575
409/336-8901

Two nineteenth-century period rooms have been recreated on the second floor of the Cultural Center to depict two different periods of early Texas. The bell in the tower at the rear

Judge Roy Bean's Jersey Lily Saloon, Langtry.

of the museum was the first one cast from the 1752 mold of the Liberty Bell. There are occasional changing exhibitions in the Center, which is named for Geraldine Humphreys, a descendant of early Liberty County settlers.

Open Monday through Friday from 10 A.M. to 6 P.M. and Saturday from 10 A.M. to noon and 1 to 4 P.M. Closed Sunday. Admission, free.

Sam Houston Regional Library
F.R. 1011 (about 3/4 of a mile off S.H. 146)
Liberty 77575
409/336-7097

The library and research center collects material relating to all ten counties of the Atascosito District. On display are a large number of pictures of Sam Houston, the desk that he used at the Battle of San Jacinto, and other unique items, such as Jean Laffite's journal, a letter from Andrew Jackson introducing Houston to Thomas Jefferson, and correspondence of Houston and David G. Burnett, the first president of the Republic of Texas.

Open Monday through Saturday from 8 A.M. to 5 P.M. Closed Sunday and all state holidays. Admission, free.

LIVINGSTON
Map 2

Alabama-Coushatta Indian Reservation
17 miles east of Livingston on U.S. 190
Livingston 77351
409/563-4391   B, R

Located on the Alabama-Coushatta Indian Reservation, the museum shows the history of the Alabama and Coushatta tribes, who migrated to East Texas from the Southeastern U.S. in 1807, and other Texas Indians. The reservation dates from 1854, when the state of Texas set aside land for the two tribes at the behest of Sam Houston, a great friend of Texas Indians. Natural history dioramas of Tupelo Gum Swamp and the Big Thicket are on permanent display. An active schedule of special events, including a summer outdoor drama and an Annual Pow Wow in June, offers educational and recreational opportunities. Lakeside camping is also available on the Reservation. Write the Visitor and Information Center, Indian Reservation, Route 3, Box 640, Livingston, Texas 77351 for information, or call 409/563-4391 or 563-4777 for reservations for "Beyond the Sundown," an outdoor historical drama of the Alabama-Coushatta Tribes of Texas that is presented during the summer months.

Open Monday through Saturday from 10 A.M. to 5 P.M., Sunday from 12:30 to 5 P.M. Admission to the museum is free, but there is a charge for tours and all other activities: adults, $7; children, $5; under three years of age, free. Theater tickets must be purchased separately.

Polk County Memorial Museum
601 W. Church Street (U.S. 190 W)
Livingston 77351
409/327-8192   H, T, HABS

The museum features local history, including historical objects and artifacts, rocks, and minerals. There is a replica of a country store, a period room, early tools, an early logging engine, and an exhibit relating to the Alabama-Coushatta Indians, whose reservation is nearby.

Open weekdays from 12:30 to 5 P.M. A donation is accepted for admission.

Two white-tailed deer with horns locked in combat. Experts say they could never have separated themselves. Photograph by Kathy Brott-Franks. Courtesy Llano County Historical Museum, Llano.

LLANO
Map 6

Llano County Historical Museum
310 Bessamer Avenue   Llano 78643
915/247-4598 or 247-4051

Located in the old drug store that was constructed in 1922 and formerly belonging to the Bruhl family, the Llano County Historical Museum, founded in 1968, features exhibitions of memorabilia relating to local and pioneer history, mineralogy, and natural history. The gift shop features items made from llanite, an intrusive, igneous rock made up of crystals and grains of quartz and feldspar found only in Llano County.

Open in the summer Tuesday through Saturday from 10 A.M. to noon and 1:30 to 5:30 P.M. and Sunday from 1:30 to 5:30 P.M.; in the winter Friday through Sunday from 1:15 to 5:15 P.M. Admission, free.

Lockhart Log Cabin Museum
Lockhart 78644
512/398-3461

The historic log cabin is presently being furnished with contemporary items to recall the early days of Lockhart, which was established as the county seat of Caldwell County in 1848.

Open hours have not yet been set. Call for information. Admission, free.

Mark Withers Trail Driver Museum
Three miles west of Lockhart on Borchert Loop off S.H. 142   Lockhart 78644
512/398-3375

The history of the trail drives is told in the exhibits housed in the former home of Mark Withers, himself a trail driver. Included are pic-

Historic photograph of the Everett Building, which houses the Gregg County Historical Museum, Longview.

tures of early Texas cattlemen and cattle brands.

Call for information on open hours and admission.

LONGVIEW
Map 2

Caddo Indian Museum
Between U.S. 80 and Harrison Road
Longview 75604
214/759-5739   H, T, N

Exhibits include pre-historic and historic Caddo Indian artifacts in addition to eighteenth- and nineteenth-century Spanish trade goods and early Anglo-American documents.

Open daily from 9 A.M. to 6 P.M. A donation is requested for admission.

Gregg County Historical Museum
Fredonia and Bank Streets   Longview 75601
No telephone   B, N

Housed in the newly restored Everett Building (1909), the Gregg County Historical Museum contains historical artifacts relating to the history of the county as well as a gallery for the display of early area art. Settled after the arrival of the railroad in the 1880s, Longview received its name when surveyors for the Texas and Pacific Railroad commented on the great distance that they could see. The Amelia Sparkman Belding Texas Heritage Resource Center is also housed in the museum.

Write for information on hours and admission.

Longview Museum and Art Center
102 West College   Longview 75606
214/753-8103   H

The Longview Museum permanent collection contains paintings, sculpture, drawings, and graphics by contemporary American artists, including many Texas and Southwestern artists. Exhibits, other than the permanent collection, change bi-monthly, and the museum holds an annual invitational competition.

Open Monday through Friday, 9 A.M. to 5 P.M., Sunday from 1 to 3 P.M. Docent tours are available. Admission, free.

LUBBOCK
Map 9

Municipal Garden and Arts Center
4215 University Avenue   Lubbock 79418
806/762-6411, Ext. 363   H, B

The Arts Center features continually changing art exhibitions as well as an occasional history exhibit.

Open Monday through Friday from 9 A.M. to 5 P.M., Saturday from 8 A.M. to 5 P.M., and Sunday from 1 to 5 P.M. Admission, free.

Longview Museum & Arts Center.

The Museum, Texas Tech University, Lubbock. Photograph by Richard Tyler.

Historical and Creative Arts Center, Lufkin.

Texas Tech University
The Museum
4th Street & Indiana Avenue   Lubbock 79409
806/742-2442   806/742-2498 (Ranching
Heritage Center)
H, B, HABS (Ranching Heritage Center)
The museum is a large, interpretive complex
that includes the main building, which houses
exhibitions and collections of scientific, historic,
and artistic merit; the Lubbock Planetarium; the
Natural Sciences Research Lab; and the Ranching Heritage Center, which consists of more
than 20 authentically restored and furnished
buildings selected to represent the West Texas
ranching industry from the early Spanish period
to the "elegant ranch house" of the early 1900s.

The main building is open Monday, Tuesday,
Wednesday, Friday, and Saturday from 9 A.M. to
4:30 P.M.; Thursday from 9 A.M. to 8:30 P.M.;
and Sunday from 1 to 4:30 P.M. The Moody
Planetarium is open Monday, Tuesday, Wednesday, and Friday at 2:30 P.M.; Thursday at 2:30
and 7:30 P.M.; and Saturday and Sunday at 2 and
3:30 P.M. The Ranching Heritage Center is open
Monday through Saturday from 9 A.M. to 4:30
P.M.; Sunday from 1 to 4:30 P.M. Admission, free
to the museum; for the planetarium, adults $1;
children $.50.

LUFKIN
Map 2

Historical and Creative Arts Center
Corner of 2nd and Paul Streets   Lufkin 75901
409/639-4434 or 639-4435   H, B
Located in the old St. Cyprian's Episcopal
Church (c. 1906), the Historical and Creative
Arts Center offers temporary and permanent exhibitions relating to art, history, and science. It
also houses the Angelina Room of local history,
a turn-of-the-century general store, a multimedia presentation entitled "Lufkin: A Centennial Journey," the Rotary Gallery of Art, and the
memorial courtyard in which one of sculptor
Malcolm Alexander's commemorative monu-
ments for the Alaskan pipeline is displayed.

Open Tuesday through Friday from 10 A.M. to
4 P.M., Sunday from 1 to 5 P.M. Admission, free.

Texas Forestry Museum
1905 Atkinson Drive (S.H. 103 E)
Lufkin 75901
409/634-5523   H (through a back entrance),
B, T
The Texas Forestry Museum describes the history of the East Texas forest industry. Key ex-

181

hibits include a logging locomotive, a high wheeled logging cart, a Martin log wagon, a blacksmith shop, and a fire lookout tower. Some exhibits are housed in the historic Camden Railroad Depot.

Open daily from 1 to 4:30 P.M. Admission, free.

MCALLEN
Map 5

McAllen Hudson Museum

3321 Expressway 83 (between McAllen and Mission) McAllen 78501
512/686-0311 B

Opened in 1981, the Hudson Museum features twenty antique cars, which are Hudsons or related Nash and American Motors cars. Hudson began production in 1909 and continued until the mid-1950s, when it merged with Nash to form American Motors. Among the most unusual exhibits are a 1924 "Super Six" Hudson sedan, a 1931 Essex sport coupe, two 1937 Terraplane pickups, and a matching pair of "his" and "her" 1955 Hudson Hornet sedans. The Essex sport coupe has less than 2,000 actual miles on it and is in virtually mint condition. Included in the exhibit are a Hudson Service Department, complete with parts and service manuals, and an exhibit of glass that was in use while Hudson was making automobiles.

Also on exhibit are a country store, a small gun collection, a coin collection (featuring Mexican coins), some Indian relics, and a player piano.

Open Tuesday through Saturday from 10 A.M. to 6 P.M. and Sunday from 1:30 to 6 P.M. Closed Monday.

*McAllen International Museum

1900 Nolana McAllen 78501
512/682-1564 H, B

Founded in 1967, the McAllen International Museum features exhibitions of art, history, and science. The Hall of Exhibits shows scientific, anthropological, and historical subjects, while art exhibitions are presented in the Art Gallery, a space that also serves as a special programs area. Art, sculpture, and photographic exhibits are presented in the museum's North Gallery, where a lighted map of the Rio Grande Valley that shows places of historical interest is displayed.

Open Tuesday through Saturday from 9 A.M. to 5 P.M., Sunday from 1 to 5 P.M. Closed Monday and major holidays. Admission, free.

Patio of the McAllen International Museum.

McDade Museum

Main Street (off U.S. 290)   McDade 78650
No telephone   T

Housed in a restored 1870s vintage saloon built of native stone, the McDade Museum houses early community artifacts, pioneer farm tools, pottery, a safe, and old wood cookstove, a school desk, and typical household items from the mid-nineteenth century. The saloon was the scene of the famous shoot-out on Christmas morning, 1883, between cattle rustlers and townspeople. Vigilantes lynched eleven outlaws that day.

Open by appointment. Admission, free.

*Heard Natural Science Museum and Wildlife Sanctuary

F.R. 1378, one mile east of S.H. 5
McKinney 75069
214/542-5566   H (but only to the upper floor of the museum), B

The museum features exhibitions on natural history of the North Central Texas area. There are collections of seashells and specimens of marine life and habitat groups illustrating typical upland prairie, bottomland woods, and aquatic habitat. There is also a Rock and Mineral Hall, an Oriental Art Hall, the Heard Family Heritage Room, and a live animal exhibit. Nature exhibits change approximately six times a year.

The Wildlife Sanctuary includes 266 acres with more than 230 species of birds, mammals, reptiles, and amphibians. There are three nature trail loops totalling two and one-half miles. The trails may be visited in guided tours only, for which reservations are necessary. There is an 800-foot paved trail for wheelchair persons.

Open Tuesday through Saturday from 9 A.M. to 5 P.M. and Sunday from 1 to 5 P.M. On Sunday afternoon guides are available for the nature trail tours without reservations. Closed New Year's Day, Easter, Independence Day, Thanksgiving, and December 24 and 25. Admission, free.

Old Post Office Museum

Chestnut at Virginia   McKinney 75069
214/542-0163   H, B

Housed in the old Post Office building, the museum contains exhibitions that relate to early settlers in Collin County, which was settled in 1845, as well as general history of the area, including documents, pictures, photographs, and artifacts.

Open Tuesday from 2 to 5 P.M. and by appointment. Admission, free.

MCLEAN
Map 9

Alanreed-McLean Area Museum
Main Street   McLean 79057
806/779-2731   H

The Alanreed-McLean Area Museum, housed in a building reminiscent of the history of the Panhandle, is composed of period rooms, including a turn-of-the-century family room, an early Gray County bedroom with an 1846 hand-woven bedspread, a pioneer doctor's office, and a farm and ranch room. Also on display are a number of Indian artifacts and antiques from various pioneer families.

Open Monday through Saturday from 11 A.M. to 4 P.M. Admission, free.

MARFA
Map 8

Marfa–Presidio County Museum
221 N. Mesa   Marfa 79843
915/729-4942   H

Contained in a home formerly occupied by R. E. L. Tyler, the Marfa–Presidio County Museum includes exhibits that depict the history and development of Presidio County, from prehistoric through Indian occupation and Indian wars, the coming of the railroad, silver mining, ranching, and the Border Patrol, Army, Air Force, soaring, and other activities of the twentieth century. There is also an area for temporary exhibitions.

Call for information on open hours. Admission, free.

MARLIN
Map 3

Falls County Historical Museum
141 Railroad Street   Marlin 76661
817/883-6707   H, B

On display are a number of items relating to the history of Falls County, including the Bishop F. P. Goddard Indian artifact collection (gathered over a 50-year period in Falls County), the gallows from the county jail, and materials relating to pioneer history. There is also a collection of paintings.

Write for public hours. Admission, free.

Highlands Mansion
One block east of the junction of S.H. 6 and F.R. 147   Marlin 76661
817/936-5234   T

Highlands Mansion was the premier home in Central Texas when Basil C. Clark, a Civil War veteran and Marlin businessman, presented it to his wife in 1900. It has now been restored to

Highlands Mansion, near Marlin.

much of its original elegance. The twin parlors feature high, coved ceilings, richly ornamented, 23-karat gold-leafed emblems and borders with garlands of roses and ribbons, and some of the original gold-leafed French furniture. The silver-plated chandelier is the central feature of the dining room, along with a built-in china cabinet with beautiful beveled and cut-glass doors and silver-plated hardware. The great hall features a 2 1/2-story dome of leaded stained glass.

Open weekdays from 10 A.M. to 4 P.M., Sundays from 1 to 4 P.M. Admission, adults $3, chilren 6–12 $2. Children under 12 must be accompanied by an adult.

MARSHALL
Map 2

Franks Antique Shop and Doll Museum

211 W. Grand Avenue   Marshall 75670
214/935-3065 or 935-3070   T, H

The doll museum and related toys and furniture are displayed in a 1912 double brick garage that has been added to the Hochwald House (1894–1895).

Open by appointment to groups of ten or more. Closed Sunday. Admission, adults $2; children $1. Group rates are available.

The Harrison County Historical Museum is located in the County Courthouse, Marshall. Photograph by Todd Webb. Courtesy Amon Carter Museum, Fort Worth.

Harrison County Historical Museum
Courthouse
Peter Whetstone Square   Marshall 75670
214/938-2680   T, H (elevator), B

The Harrison County Historical Museum is housed in the old courthouse, which was constructed in 1900 of granite, stone, and marble. It has served as the museum since 1965, devoted to telling the history of Marshall (founded in 1839) and surrounding counties. Subjects covered include the Caddo Indians, early pioneers, the Old South, and transportation and communications. Articles on display show the development of the Harrison County area from the Texas War for Independence to the present. Special exhibits relate to Governor Edward Clark, Lady Bird Johnson, and Y. A. Tittle, a professional football player.

Open Sunday through Friday from 1:30 to 5 P.M. Admission, adults $.50; students $.25; sponsored youth groups $.10 each.

MASON
Map 6

Fort Mason Officers Quarters
Spruce Street   Mason 76856
915/347-5725   T

The restored officers quarters of old Fort Mason contains exhibits that tell the story of the fort, which was founded by U.S. Dragoons in 1851 as a part of the frontier defense against marauding Comanche, Apache, and Kiowa Indians. It was finally abandoned in 1869. Included are photographs and memorabilia as well as a miniature of the fort.

Open every day. Admission, free.

Mason County Museum
300 Moody Street   Mason 76856
No telephone   H, T

Located in an 1887 school house that was constructed from the stones removed from the site of Fort Mason, the Mason County Museum features exhibits that relate to early pioneers of the area. Mason grew out of a small settlement near the fort and was named county seat in 1861.

Open daily and by appointment on Saturday and Sunday. Admission, free.

MEMPHIS
Map 9

Hall County Heritage Hall
101 South 6th Street (corner of square)
Memphis 79245
806/259-3345

Local history and natural sciences make up the displays of the Hall County Heritage Hall, which is located in the old First National Bank building that was remodeled to accommodate the historical objects. There is a school room

Hall County Heritage Hall, Memphis. Photograph by Richard Tyler.

area with many pictures on exhibit, some of which recall the founding of the town on the Fort Worth and Denver Railroad in 1890.

Open Monday, Wednesday, and Friday from 1 to 4 P.M. Admission, free.

MENARD
Map 6

Menardville Museum

U.S. 83, north of the San Saba River
Menard 76859
915/396-4318   T, B

Located in the old Frisco Depot, the Menardville Museum houses displays relating to the history of Menard County, which was created from Bexar County in 1858. Antique furniture, including the original safe from the Luckenbach Hardware Store, thought to be the first safe in the county, and the back bar and whiskey cabinet from the Legal Tender Saloon, is on display.

Open Monday through Saturday from 9 A.M. to 5 P.M. Please call for information and admission charges.

MERCEDES
Map 5

Red Horse Museum

Expressway 83 and Virginia Avenue (Vermont Avenue exit from McAllen, F.R. 491 exit from Harlingen)   Mercedes 78570
512/565-6560   B

Exhibits consist of a saloon, a pioneer home, a barn, a livery stable, a barber shop, a collection of musical instruments, and a panorama of South Texas wildlife mounted in their natural surroundings. The Hall of Horns features dozens of freak and trophy specimens, while the siamese calves, born some forty years ago in Dilley, Texas, are on exhibit in the barn.

Open Tuesday through Sunday from 10 A.M. to 6 P.M. Admission, adults $1.50, children $.75.

MERTZON
Map 7

Irion County Museum

Mertzon 76941
No telephone

The exhibits in the Irion County Museum recall the days when the Kansas City, Mexico, and Orient Railroad built through Irion County, with Mertzon as its first stop. Mertzon became a post office and the county seat in 1910.

Open Monday through Friday from 12:30 to 4:30 P.M. Admission, free.

MIAMI
Map 9

Roberts County Museum

U.S. 60   Miami 79059
806/868-3291   H, B, T

The old Santa Fe depot, which was constructed in 1888 and now houses the Roberts

County Museum, was originally located between Main and Birge streets, where the railroad
workers set up a temporary campsite while
building the tracks. The Roberts County Museum acquired the depot and moved it to its
present site in 1979. There have been several
additions since then. On display are the J. A.
Mead Indian and fossil exhibit, a native animal
wild life exhibit, a wedding dress collection, antique dishes, the first tin shop in the area, area
brands, a collection of saddles, a chuck wagon,
buggies, and an old shoe shop with some tools
that are more than 150 years old.

Open weekdays from 1 to 5 P.M., weekends
from 2 to 5 P.M., June through August, 10 A.M.
to noon, 1 to 5 P.M. Closed Wednesday. Admission, free.

MIDLAND
Map 7

Midland County Historical Museum
Midland County Library basement
301 W. Missouri   Midland 79701
915/683-2708

Founded in 1932, the museum exhibits prehistory and history of the region along with memorabilia of the early pioneers. There are more than
3,000 items on exhibit, including old newspapers that depict every phase of the area's
growth, pioneer photographs, a pioneer kitchen,
a replica of Midland Man, the oldest skeletal remains found thus far on the North American
continent, and the gleanings from a chicken's
gizzard. An archives and genealogical section is
available for research.

Open Monday through Thursday from 11 A.M.
to 5 P.M., Saturday from 9 A.M. to noon, 1 to 4
P.M. Admission, free.

Museum of the Southwest
1705 West Missouri   Midland 79701
915/683-2882   B

Dedicated to the collection, preservation, and
interpretation of Southwestern art and culture,
the Museum of the Southwest provides exhibitions from the permanent collection of Taos artists as well as paintings, sculpture, graphics, and
ethnographic materials that reflect the creative
work of Southwestern artists. The Marian
Blakemore Planetarium presents shows and bi-
weekly public programs complemented by astronomy classes.

Open Monday through Saturday from 10 A.M.
to 5 P.M., Sunday from 2 to 5 P.M. Admission,
free. Public programs are presented in the plane-

tarium on Tuesday at 7:30 and 9 P.M. and Sunday at 2 and 3:30 P.M.

Nita Stewart Haley Memorial Library
1805 West Indiana Avenue   Midland 79701
915/682-5785   B

Called a "sanctuary for range history and tradition," the Haley Library contains books, photographs, manuscripts, maps, works of art, and artifacts that relate to the history of Texas and the Southwest, particularly the cattle industry, of which J. Evetts Haley, whose library and archives are housed here, is the preeminent historian. Of special interest are the photographs by Erwin E. Smith of Bonham, one of the best of the early cowboy photographers, and the collection of Argentinian *gaucho* artifacts as well as paintings and bronzes by Western artists.

Open Monday through Friday from 9 A.M. to 5 P.M. Admission, free.

The Alamo Bell, one of the four bells to hang in the Alamo in San Antonio, now in the collection of the Nita Stewart Haley Memorial Library, Midland.

Permian Basin Petroleum Museum, Library, and Hall of Fame
I-20 at S.H. 349 Exit   Midland 79701
915/683-4403   H, B

Devoted to interpreting the history and technology of the oil industry, the Permian Basin Petroleum Museum contains antique drilling equipment, paintings on various historical subjects, modern exploration and producing equipment, and other exhibits. The Library contains approximately 60,000 archival items, including 6,000 old oilfield and boomtown photographs and 300 voice tapes.

Open Monday through Saturday from 9 A.M. to 5 P.M., Sunday from 2 to 5 P.M. Closed

Pipeline patrol plane in the Permian Basin Petroleum Museum, Midland.

Thanksgiving, Christmas Eve and Day. Admission, adults $1.50; children 11 and under $.75; pre-school free.

Z. Taylor Brown–Sarah Dorsey Medallion Home

213 N. Weatherford   Midland 79701
915/682-2931   T, N

Believed to be the oldest house in Midland, which was founded in the 1880s, the Brown-Dorsey Medallion Home has been restored to its turn-of-the-century splendor and furnished with period furnishings. The house was finished in 1900 and served as the family residence until 1968. One of the most unusual features of the house is the wine cellar. Mr. Brown grew his own grapes and made his own wine.

Open by appointment. Admission, free.

MISSION
Map 5

La Lomita Farms Regional Museum

Five miles south of Mission on F.R. 1016
Mission 78572
512/581-2725   T, N

An art museum housed in St. Peter's Novitiate, which still belongs to the Oblate Fathers.

Open daily from 8 A.M. to 5 P.M. Closed on national and state holidays. Admission, free.

MONAHANS
Map 7

Interpretive Center

Monahans Sandhills State Park
I-20/U.S. 80, six miles northeast of Monahans
Monahans 79756
915/943-2092   H, T

The park includes 4,000 acres of sand dunes up to fifty feet high, some shifting, some stabilized. The interpretive center in the park's headquarters has exhibits depicting the plants, animals, archeology, history, and geology of the sandhills area. Visitors may view live birds and animals as they come to the feeding and watering station outside the center.

The park is open from 7 A.M. to 10 P.M. daily. The Interpretive Center is open from 8 A.M. to 5 P.M. Admission to the park is $2 per vehicle, $.50 walk-in or bicycle.

MORAN
Map 10

Moran Historical Museum

Ground Street   Moran 76464
915/945-2942

Located in the old Rockwell Brothers Lumber Company building, which was constructed in 1892, the Moran Historical Museum has hundreds of items on display, including old tools and household items, clothing, antique bottles, Indian artifacts, old photographs, and antique toys. Open by appointment. Admission, free.

NACOGDOCHES
Map 2

Hoya Memorial Library and Museum

211 S. Lanana Street   Nacogdoches 75961
409/564-4693, Ext. 122   T, HABS

Located in the home of Adolphus Sterne, a German immigrant who served in the Texas Revolution, held various local offices, and was a member of both the House and the Senate after Texas became a state, the Hoya Library and Museum displays memorabilia of early Texas, including some furnishings and other belongings of Sam Houston, first president of the republic. Programs of historical Nacogdoches are presented as well. The wooden frame house was built in 1830.

Open Monday through Saturday from 9 A.M. to noon, 2 to 5 P.M. Admission, free.

Millard's Crossing Antiques and Historic Village

6020 North Street
U.S. 59 North   Nacogdoches 75961
409/564-6969

The Millard-Lee House, c. 1837, restored and moved to this site in 1971, contains various antiques, documents, and other Texas memorabilia. A brochure is available, which will direct you on a tour of historic houses, which includes the Millard-Lee House as well as a Victorian home, the Burrows-Millard House (c. 1840), a corn crib, the First Methodist parsonage, a log house, and a chapel (c. 1843).

Tours at 9:30 A.M. and 2 P.M. daily. Sunday at 2 P.M. Admission, $2.50.

Old Nacogdoches University Building

Mound and Hughes Streets
Nacogdoches 75961
409/564-0084   B, T, N

Nacogdoches University was founded in 1845, the first nonsectarian college in Texas. This Greek Revival brick building with a two-story portico and cupola was added in 1858 and served the university as a classroom and administration building until it closed in 1895, with the exception of the Civil War when Confederate soldiers used it as a headquarters and hospital and Reconstruction when it was occupied by Federal soldiers. After years of disrepair, the building was restored in 1960 and made into a museum, which today contains early Texas furniture, vintage clothing, manuscripts, deeds, church furni-

The Hoya Memorial Library and Museum is housed in the Adolphus Sterne home, Nacogdoches. Photograph by Todd Webb. Courtesy Amon Carter Museum, Fort Worth.

ture, farm tools, a schoolroom and desks, and various other artifacts of days gone by.

Open Saturday and Sunday from 10 A.M. to noon and 2 to 5 P.M., daily June through August, same hours. There is no admission fee, but a donation is requested.

Stone Fort Museum
Stephen F. Austin State University
Clark Drive and Griffith Boulevard
Nacogdoches 75962
409/569-2408   H (first floor only), B, T

Originally constructed in 1799 on the town square as a trading post, the Stone Fort was moved during the Texas Centennial of 1936 to the Stephen F. Austin State University campus and reconstructed as a museum. It now contains collections and displays relating to the history and technology of East Texas, from prehistory to 1900.

Open Tuesday through Saturday from 9 A.M. to 5 P.M., Sunday from 1 to 5 P.M. Admission, free, but donations are accepted.

NEDERLAND
Map 4

Dutch Windmill Museum
Tex Ritter Park
1528 Boston Avenue   Nederland 77627
409/722-0279   B, T

The Dutch Windmill Museum was built in 1969 as a tribute to Dutch settlers who came to Nederland in 1898. The forty-foot-tall structure is an exact replica of a Dutch windmill. The museum houses mementos from Holland, artifacts of the region, and items owned by the late Woodward Maurice ("Tex") Ritter, the well-known Country and Western singer, who was from Nederland.

Open Tuesday through Sunday from 1 to 5 P.M. March 1 to Labor Day; Thursday through Sunday from 1 to 5 P.M., Labor Day through March 1. Admission, free.

La Maison des Acadiens

Tex Ritter Park
1520 Boston Avenue   Nederland 77627
409/722-0947   B

La Maison des Acadiens, a replica of an early Acadian home in south Louisiana, was built in 1976 as a reminder of the large number of Acadians who came from Louisiana to make their home in the Nederland area. La Maison has a living room, bedroom, and kitchen in addition to the upstairs room, all furnished with historic, turn-of-the-century objects.

Open Tuesday through Sunday from 1 to 5 P.M. March through August; Thursday through Sunday September through February. Admission, free.

NEW BRAUNFELS
Map 6

Lindheimer Museum

Comal Street   New Braunfels 78130
512/625-7046

Ferdinand Jacob Lindheimer was an internationally known botanist who, like many of his countrymen, fled from an oppressive government in Germany. Lindheimer arrived in Texas in time to help in the fight for independence in 1836 and was one of the advisors who suggested to Prince Carl of Solms-Braunfels that he locate his colony in the Texas hill country. Lindheimer studied Texas flora, and more than thirty varieties carry his name in their botanical titles, but he is best remembered as editor of the *Neu-Braunfelser Zeitung*, the German-language newspaper, which he published in this house.

The house is a good example of the ancient *Fachwerk* (half-timber) style that the German settlers adapted to Texas cedar and limestone. It includes a parlor, a bedroom, a wine cellar and kitchen, and Lindheimer's office and print shop. Some of his botanical specimens and the family Bible are on display, as well as his desk, pewter bowl, and china coffee pot and several pieces of furniture that were made in New Braunfels.

The Dutch Windmill Museum, Nederland.

La Maison des Acadiens, Tex Ritter Park, Nederland.

Open daily from 2 to 5 P.M. except Monday during June through August, Saturday and Sunday from 2 to 5 P.M. during September through May. Admission, $.50. Call for special tours.

Sophienburg Memorial Museum and Archives

401 West Coll Street   New Braunfels 78130
512/629-1572   H, B

The Sophienburg Memorial Museum is built on the site where Prince Carl of Solms-Braunfels, who led a group of German immigrants to their new home in Texas, planned to build a replica of his family castle in Germany. He did construct the administration building for the town, which was settled in 1845, and the pictures, objects, and artifacts on display in the museum recall the history of these intrepid Germans who left their homeland to settle in the new Republic of Texas.

The museum was originally established in the basement of the city hall in 1932, but was moved to the present limestone building in 1933. It got its name from the hill overlooking the new village, which Prince Carl called "Sophienburg" (which translates as "Sophia's Castle"), named for Prince Carl's fiancee, Lady Sophia. Because she would not come to Texas, he returned to Germany to marry her. Included in the exhibitions are German books and manuscripts, a copy of the Solms-Braunfels archives, and a collection of handmade furniture, tools, and crafts, as well as a replica of the Prince's castle in Braunfels, Germany.

Open Monday through Saturday from 10 A.M. to 5 P.M., Sunday from 1 to 5 P.M. Admission, adults $1; children $.25.

NEWCASTLE
Map 10

Fort Belknap Museum

3 miles south of Newcastle   Newcastle 76372
817/846-3222   H, T, HABS

Founded in 1851, Fort Belknap was one of a chain of forts from the Red River to the Rio Grande. All the original buildings were constructed of logs. When the post was relocated in 1856 because of a lack of water, the new buildings were constructed of native sandstone. Fort Belknap was the hub of a series of roads stretching from Fort Worth to El Paso, Fort Phantom Hill (near present-day Abilene) to San Antonio. It was abandoned in 1867 and reconstructed as a part of the Texas centennial in 1936.

The museum in the commissary's store contains frontier weapons, furnishings, and tools that might have been used by the officers stationed at Fort Belknap, whose photographs are also on display. The museum in the "corn house" includes gowns worn by Mrs. Dwight D. Eisenhower, Mrs. Douglas MacArthur, and Mrs. Lyndon B. Johnson. The site contains several other restored buildings and a genealogical library and archives.

Open Thursday through Tuesday, 9 A.M. to 5 P.M. Closed Wednesday. Admission, free.

NOCONA
Map 1

Joe Benton Museum

Just off U.S. 82 (entrance to ranch directly across from boot factory) Nocona 76225
817/825-6557

Benton was a rancher who, early in the twentieth century, began collecting aboriginal and European artifacts that turned up near the site of Spanish Fort, located north of Nocona in a bend of the Red River. Spanish Fort was an important intertribal trading site and, as such, attracted both Spanish and French merchants and military. In the nineteenth century a fork of the Chisholm Trail crossed the Red River nearby. Benton let it be known that he wanted the artifacts that others discovered, so he accumulated quite a collection over the years, much of which is now on display in the museum named for him and tended by his daughter and son-in-law.

Open by appointment only. Call or write Clarice Benton Whiteside for an appointment. Admission, free.

NORDHEIM
Map 4

Nordheim Historical Museum

One block off Main Street behind the Post Office Nordheim 78141
512/938-5886

Located in the old fire station, the Nordheim Historical Museum includes displays that depict the history of the German settlement of Nordheim. Founded in 1895 on the Texas and New Orleans Railroad as Weldon Switch, the city changed its name in 1897 to commemorate the city of the same name in Hanover, Germany. In addition to the historical displays, there is a brass band exhibit.

Call for information on open hours and admission.

ODESSA
Map 7

The Presidential Museum

622 N. Lee Street Odessa 79761
915–332-7123 H, B

Devoted to the office of the presidency and the men who have held it, the Presidential Museum contains exhibitions of portraits, documents, signatures, campaign memorabilia, commemorative items, and original political cartoons that relate to the Presidents, Vice-Presidents, First Ladies, losing candidates, and Presidents of the Republic of Texas. There is also a changing exhibitions program that includes a broader range of subjects.

Open Monday through Friday from 10 A.M. to noon, 1 to 5 P.M. Admission, free.

The Presidential Museum, Odessa. Photograph by Alton's Studio of Photography.

White-Pool Historic House

112 E. Murphy Street   Odessa 79761
915/362-6050   H, B
Constructed in 1887, the White-Pool House was the first substantial structure in Odessa, which was founded on the Texas and Pacific Railroad in 1886. The exhibition portrays the various periods of Odessa's development, including ranching (the White family) and oil (the Pool family).

Call for information on open hours and admission.

O'DONNELL
Map 9

O'Donnell Museum

8th and Doak streets   O'Donnell 79351
806/428-3719   T
The O'Donnell Museum features displays of historical material from the south High Plains, recalling the turn-of-the-century when the city was founded. Downstairs is the old telephone system, showing how calls used to be made. Upstairs is an exhibition on the theme of "There's An Old Spinning Wheel in the Parlor," with the spinning wheel, organ, love seat, and music box. There are also other exhibits, such as a fur-

nished bedroom, church, kitchen, doctor's office, and blacksmith shop. Outside is an antique tractor display.

Open Monday through Saturday from 9 to 11 A.M., 2 to 5 P.M., Sunday from 2 to 5 P.M. Donation requested for admission.

ORANGE
Map 4

Heritage House Museum
905 W. Division Street   Orange 77630
409/886-5385   H, T, N
The Jimmy Ochiltree Sims House, moved from its original location, now contains material relating to the history of Orange County, which was created out of Jefferson County in 1852.

Open Tuesday through Friday from 10 A.M. to 2 P.M., Sunday from 1 to 5 P.M. Closed January and August. Admission, adults $1, senior citizens and students, $.50, students on school tour, $.25. Members free.

Stark Museum of Art
712 Green Avenue   Orange 77630
409/883-6661   H, B
Opened in 1978, the Stark Museum of Art houses one of the country's most significant collections relating to the American West. The works of such artist-explorers as George Catlin, Alfred Jacob Miller, Paul Kane, John Mix Stanley, and John James Audubon are on display, as are works by later artists Albert Bierstadt, Thomas Moran, Frederic Remington, Charles M. Russell, and others. The museum owns an outstanding collection of the work of Taos and Santa Fe founders such as W. Herbert Dunton, Walter Ufer, Bert Greer Phillips, and Ernest Leonard Blumenschein.

There are also important collections of American Indian materials, including Plains Indian clothing, body ornaments, and beadwork; baskets, Pueblo pottery, Zuñi and Hopi kachina dolls, and a good collection of Navajo rugs and blankets. Steuben's The United States in Crystal collection is on display, as are Dorothy Doughty's porcelain models of American birds.

The building, designed by Page Southerland Page, won the Tucker Award from the Building Stone Institute for excellence of concept, design, and construction in the use of natural stone.

Open Wednesday through Saturday from 10 A.M. to 5 P.M., Sunday from 1 to 5 P.M. Closed Monday, Tuesday, New Year's Day, Easter, Independence Day, Thanksgiving, and Christmas. Admission, free.

John James Audubon, **Whooping Crane,** *1834. Engraving with aquatint (hand-colored), 35¼ × 24 (comp.). Courtesy Stark Museum of Art, Orange.*

Stark Museum of Art, Orange.

W. H. Stark House

610 W. Main   Orange 77630
409/883-0871   T, N, HABS

The William H. Stark House was constructed in 1894 by Stark, a successful businessman with interests in lumber, oil, rice, insurance, and banking, and Miriam Lutcher, his wife, who had come to Orange in the 1870s with her family from Williamsport, Pennsylvania. The fifteen-room, three-story structure was built of longleaf yellow pine from the Lutcher and Moore Lumber Company of Orange, the largest manufacturer and exporter of longleaf yellow pine in the country. Today the house stands much as it did at the turn of the century with its original furniture, rugs, family portraits, lace curtains, silver, ceramics, glass, lighting, and detailed woodwork that exemplifies the height of craftsmanship in Queen Anne–Eastlake style in Texas.

Open Tuesday through Saturday from 10 A.M. to 3:30 P.M. Reservations requested. Admission limited to adults and children age 14 or older if accompanied by an adult. Admission, $2.

John Mix Stanley, Gambling for the Buck, *1867. Oil on canvas, 20 × 15⅞ in. Courtesy Stark Museum of Art, Orange.*

OZONA
Map 7

Crockett County Museum

Courthouse Annex on U.S. 290   Ozona 76943
915/392-2837   B

Displays relate to the history of Crockett County from the prehistoric to the present. Rocks, minerals, and mastodon bones taken from various digs are on exhibit, as are various pieces of equipment and objects left by the Spaniards, soldiers, and explorers who traveled the Chihuahua Trail and the Old Government Road. Evidence of the early pioneer settlers include antique quilts, clothing, firearms, early Texas furniture, and a group of photographs.

Open daily from 2 to 5 P.M. except New Year's Day, Easter, Thanksgiving, and Christmas. A donation is requested for admission.

PADUCAH
Map 10

Bicentennial City-County Museum

Cottle County Courthouse Basement
Paducah 79248
806/492-2006   B

Exhibits relating to the history of Cottle County are changed frequently. Most exhibits are drawn from the small permanent collection of historical objects and artifacts, such as an old school desk, slate, and mementoes of early school days in the area. A collection of pioneer pictures and other historical photographs are being preserved and displayed, and local artists also display their work in the museum.

Open Monday and Wednesday from 1 to 5 P.M., Tuesday and Thursday from 10 to 11:30 A.M. and 1 to 5 P.M. Admission, free.

PALESTINE
Map 2

Howard House Museum

1007 N. Perry Street   Palestine 75801
No telephone

This historic house and museum relate to the history of the Palestine area. Palestine, located in the center of Anderson County, was named the county seat in 1846 because Houston, the original county seat, was two miles off-center.

Open by appointment. Admission, free.

PALO PINTO
Map 10

Palo Pinto County Pioneer Museum

Elm Street and 5th Avenue   Palo Pinto 76072
817/659-3751, 659-3781, or 659-3501
H (first floor only), T, HABS

The oldest public building in the county, the Palo Pinto Jail, a cubic structure of rugged masonry, today houses the Palo Pinto County Pioneer Museum. Exhibits recall the founding of the city in 1858 as well as later history of the area.

Open June through August on Saturday and Sunday from 1 to 4 P.M. Other times by appointment. Admission, free.

PAMPA
Map 9

White Deer Land Museum
116 S. Cuyler Street   Pampa 79065
806/665-5521   H, T

Housed in the White Deer Land Company building, constructed in 1916, the museum includes many items from early day settlers, such as artifacts from churches and schools, pioneer furniture, clothes, dolls, pictures, and a replica of the first oil well on White Deer Lands. Recent additions include the Arrowhead Room, the Sewing Room, Post Office, General Store, and several other exhibits. The museum also houses the records of the White Deer Land Company.

Open Tuesday through Sunday from 1:30 to 4 P.M.; anytime by special appointment. Admission, free.

PANHANDLE
Map 9

*Carson County Square House Museum
Fifth and Elsie Streets   Panhandle 79068
806/537-3118   H, B

The Square House Museum is part of a complex of restored buildings typical of the high plains. Containing exhibits showing the history of the area from the Indians through the Oil Boom, the museum also includes exhibitions on natural history and art. In addition, there is a restored dug-out home with furnishings used by Plains pioneers, farm and ranch buildings, a windmill, and a Santa Fe caboose, recalling the founding of Panhandle in 1887 as the terminus for the Panhandle and Santa Fe Railroad.

Open Monday through Saturday from 9 A.M. to 5:30 P.M., Sunday from 1 to 5:30 P.M. Admission, free.

PANNA MARIA
Map 4

Panna Maria Historical Museum
Panna Maria 78666   T, N

Located in Panna Maria in the St. Joseph School building behind St. Mary's Church on F.R. 81 one mile off S.H. 123, the Panna Maria Historical Museum exhibits artifacts and photographs relating to the Polish immigrants who settled the South Central Texas village in 1854 and named it after the Virgin Mary.

Open by appointment. Admission, free, but donations are accepted.

A. M. and Welma Aikin Regional Archives

Mike Rheudasil Learning Center
Paris Junior College   Paris 75460
214/785-7661

The A. M. and Welma Aikin Regional Archives contains material relating to the career of long-time Senator A. M. Aikin as well as a replica of his office in the State Capitol in Austin. First elected to the Texas House of Representatives in 1933 and to the Senate in 1937, Aikin was dean of the Texas Legislature when he retired in 1979. Perhaps he is most remembered for his co-sponsorship of the Gilmer-Aikin Law, which reorganized the State Board of Education and established the Texas Education Agency to assume state management of the public school system. The office he occupied in the Capitol was first used by the Texas Labor Department, then, from 1935 to 1946, by Senator Allan Shivers. Senator Aikin moved into the office in 1946. It was the only office in the Capitol that had not been renovated and updated from its original 1885 decor.

In addition, the archival center houses a gallery displaying Aikin memorabilia. Included is a bronze bust of the senator, a replica of the one commissioned by the Senate for the Senate Chamber.

Open during regular college hours. Admission, free.

Sam Bell Maxey House State Historic Structure

812 Church Street   Paris 75460
214/785-5716   H, T, N

Born in Kentucky in 1825, Samuel Bell Maxey was a graduate of West Point, a veteran of the Mexican War and the Civil War, and served as U.S. Senator from Texas for two terms. After a presidential pardon that permitted him to resume his law practice in Paris following the Civil War, Maxey completed construction in 1868 of this two-story frame structure in what has been called High Victorian Italianate style. His family occupied the house until 1967, when it was given to the Lamar County Historical Society for use as a county museum. The Society deeded it to the city, and the city gave it to the state for purposes of restoration and operation as a state historic structure. It has been restored to show how the generations of the Maxey family lived for almost 100 years. Guided tours are available.

Open Thursday through Monday from 10 A.M. to 5 P.M. Admission, adults $.50, children under 12 $.25.

Pasadena Historical Museum
Pasadena Memorial Park
Vince Street at S.H. 225   Pasadena 77506
713/477-7273   H

Located in a restored house typical of the turn-of-the-century farm houses in the Pasadena area, the Pasadena Historical Museum features exhibitions tracing local history from early pioneer days to the present, "from cattle to strawberry farming, to petrochemicals." The city was founded in the 1850s and named by surveyors of the Galveston, Harrisburg, and San Antonio Railroad that built through the area ten miles southeast of Houston. Of course, Pasadena is now completely engulfed in Houston.

Open Saturday and Sunday from 1 to 5 P.M. Admission, free.

Frio Pioneer Jail Museum
Corner of E. Medina and S. Pecan Streets
Pearsall 78061
512/334-3896   H, T, HABS

The museum, which is devoted to the history of the area, is located in the oldest building in town, the jail. Costing $11,000 in 1884, four years after Pearsall itself was founded, the jail is an outstanding example of Victorian public architecture and served as the jail and the jailer's residence until 1967. A small, one-room frame school and church are located on the grounds, having been moved from nearby Frio Town.

Open Saturday and Sunday from 1 to 5 P.M. Admission, free.

West of the Pecos Museum
Corner U.S. 285 and First Street   Pecos 79772
915/445-5076   T

Pecos was founded on the Pecos River in 1881, as the Texas and Pacific Railroad completed its western Texas route. The Orient Hotel opened for business fifteen years later, after the city had ridded itself of several notorious outlaws and settled down. The city bought the old hotel in 1962 and restored the lobby, dining room, and adjoining saloon to their turn-of-the-century beauty. It now houses rock and mineral exhibits, a rodeo room, general exhibits, and period rooms.

Open Monday through Saturday from 9:30
A.M. to 5 P.M., Sunday from 2 to 5:30 P.M. Admission, adults $1; children under 12 free.

PERRYTON
Map 9

Museum of the Plains

U.S. 83 North   Perryton 79070
806/435-6400   H

The Museum of the Plains consists of a Santa
Fe Railroad Depot (which has been moved from
its original site in Fargo, Oklahoma), a General
Store (from the site of old Ochiltree, Texas), and
an exhibits building which houses a number of
displays, including a wildlife exhibit. History of
the region is the subject. Perryton itself was
named the county seat of Ochiltree County in
1919.

Open Monday through Friday from 10 A.M. to
5:30 P.M. and Saturday and Sunday from 1 to 5
P.M. Admission, free.

PHARR
Map 5

Old Clock Museum

929 Preston Street   Pharr 78577
512/787-1923   H

Over 800 clocks from different countries tell
the history of early clock making and the different methods of telling time.

Open daily from 10 A.M. to midnight. Admission, free.

Pine Springs

See Guadalupe Mountains National Park

PLAINS
Map 9

Tsa Mo Ga Memorial Museum

1109 Avenue H   Plains 79355
806/456-3212   T

The museum is an original "Bonus Shack,"
built in 1905 for its occupant to qualify for land
under the Texas Homestead Act. It now contains items of early life on ranches in Yoakum
County, such as an old saddle, Indian artifacts,
an old piano, wood cook stove, and treadle sewing machine. The name is Indian for chief or
"the highest" and comes from the Tsa Mo Ga
Club (the local women's club) that owns and operates the museum.

Open by appointment. Admission, free.

PLAINVIEW
Map 9

Museum of the Llano Estacado

Wayland University   Plainview 79072
806/296-5521, Ext. 53   H, B

Exhibits relate to human cultural adapation to
the semiarid Llano Estacado (Staked Plains), including sections on Early Man, Historic Indians,
Military, and Settlement.

Open daily from 10 A.M. to 5 P.M. Admission, free.

Farmstead Museum

Heritage Center
1900 West 15th Street   Plano 75075
214/424-7874   H, B, T, N, HABS

A farmhouse, built in 1881, and twelve original outbuildings give an accurate picture of rural life at the turn-of-the-century in North Texas. Hunter T. Farrell acquired the property in the 1880s, soon after he had married Mary Alice Lanham Farrell. "Miss Ammie" Wilson, Mrs. Farrell's daughter, became a nationally known sheep breeder, and her colorful life and personal belongings draw attention to the house, which, along with its outbuildings, became the property of the Plano Heritage Association soon after Ammie's death in 1972. The farmstead is currently being developed into a living history museum representing a total working farm on the rich blackland prairie.

The house is closed for restoration work, but special tours can be arranged by request if work permits. The site should reopen in 1983.

Plano Cultural Arts Center

1076 Collin Creek Mall   Plano 75075
214/423-7809   H

Twelve arts groups have united to form the Plano Cultural Arts Council, which sponsors the Arts Center, unusual in that it is located in a retail space in a shopping center. Four major exhibitions are presented during the year, ranging across a wide variety of ethnic, historical, and visual arts. The Center also is an information center and ticket vendor for the members of the Council.

Open Monday, Tuesday, Wednesday, Friday, and Saturday from 10 A.M. to 5 P.M., Thursday from 12 to 9 P.M. Admission, free.

Longhorn Museum

U.S. 97 East   Pleasanton 78064
512/569-3219

Devoted to documenting the Atascosa County area as the "birthplace of the American cowboy," the Longhorn Museum features exhibits on area Indians, the Spaniards at San José Mission (where *vaqueros* first worked cattle in Texas), and the cattle industry itself. The museum exhibits also document several twentieth-century changes: uranium mines, oil fields, and strip mining for coal.

Open Tuesday through Saturday from 1 to 5
P.M. A donation is requested for admission.

Pompeiian Villa

1935 Lakeshore Drive   Port Arthur 77640
409/983-5977   N, HABS
Built by Isaac Ellwood in 1900, the Pompeiian
Villa is a symbol of the Port Arthur that never
was. After the Spindletop oil field blew in,
Arthur E. Stillwell, the railroad magnate who
had founded Port Arthur as the southern terminus of his Kansas City, Pittsburgh and Gulf Railroad five years earlier, interested a number of his
friends in building their summer homes on the
gulf coast, but few of the projects ever materi-
alized. Ellwood sold his villa to the St. Louis
industrialist James Hopkins, but Hopkins never
occupied the house because his wife refused to
live in the hot and humid climate on the gulf
coast. Port Arthur never became the summer retreat that Stillwell had planned, but the Pompeiian Villa remains, splendidly restored and
furnished by the Port Arthur Historical Society,
as a reminder of his dream.
Open Monday through Friday from 9 A.M. to 4
P.M. Admission, adults $2; children over five $1.

Port Arthur Historical Museum

Gates Memorial Library
Lamar University at Port Arthur
317 Stilwell Boulevard   Port Arthur 77640
409/938-4921, Ext. 337
Founded in 1964, the museum is dedicated to
telling the story of Port Arthur, which was
founded in 1895 when Arthur E. Stillwell purchased 53,000 acres of land in Jefferson County
to serve as the southern terminus and port for
his Kansas City, Pittsburg and Gulf Railroad.
Port Arthur was established on the site of an
1840 settlement that had been abandoned because of isolation and hurricanes in 1890. The
future of the city was assured in 1901 when
oil was discovered. Thousands of documents,
photographs, and objects have been assembled to
tell this story. On display are Indian points and
tools, recalling earlier cultures, as well as cannon balls from the Civil War Battle of Sabine
Pass, and other items relating to the history of
the area.
Open Monday through Friday from 10 A.M. to
2 P.M., other hours by appointment. Admission,
free.

Jail Museum

112 Bowie Street   Port Lavaca 77979
No telephone

The Old Port Lavaca jail contains several historical exhibits, including a miniature replica of the old port town of Indianola, which was destroyed by the hurricane of 1886. Port Lavaca was founded in 1840, and the historic furnishings, and personal belongings of many of the pioneer settlers in the area recall those early days. Portions of the old jail have also been restored for exhibition, including the living quarters of the jailors.

Open Tuesday and Thursday from 2 to 6 P.M. and Saturday from 9 A.M. to 1 P.M. Admission, free.

Garza County Historical Museum

117 N. Avenue N   Post 79356
806/495-2746   B, T, HABS

The Sanitarium was constructed by C. W. Post in 1912 as a part of his model city. Post City was intended to be home to farmers who owned their own land and homes. Constructed of native Garza County stone, the Sanitarium closed in 1918 when the doctors were called to service in World War I. It was used as an apartment house until it was given to the county for use as a museum, which today houses exhibits of artifacts and furnishings pertaining to local and pioneer history.

Open by appointment. Admission, free.

Fort Leaton State Historic Site

4 miles east of Presidio on F.R. 170
Presidio 79845
915/229-3613   H, T, N, HABS

Used as headquarters for rancher Ben Leaton in the late 1840s, this fortified adobe structure was a well-known point on the trade route between San Antonio and Chihuahua. The large, multi-roomed building has been restored, and guides unravel the history of Fort Leaton and the Presidio area on tours through the site. An audio-visual program and an interpretive exhibit describe the fort's Chihuahuan desert setting. A special exhibit feature is a full-scale reconstruction of a giant two-wheeled cart typical of the freight vehicles once used on the Chihuahua Trail.

Open daily from 8 A.M. to 5 P.M. Admission, adults $.50; children age 6 to 12 $.25.

Rattlesnake Bomber Base Museum

I-20 just outside Pyote   Pyote 79777
915/389-4921

The Rattlesnake Bomber Base Museum is located in the last remaining hangar of the Pyote Army Air Base, a World War II air base and prison camp. In addition to the material relating to pioneer history, the museum contains exhibitions and mementoes of World War II, when hundreds of B-17 and B-29 pilots trained here, and German prisoners of war were confined here. In fact, some of the museum display cases were built by the Germans.

The base was constructed in 1942 and closed in 1947. Because of the dry climate, the Air Force stored more than 2,000 airplanes, wrapped in plastic webbing and dehydrated for better preservation, on the two runways. But the weather that made Pyote such an ideal storage site turned vicious in 1948 and ninety percent of the planes were destroyed by a tornado and hailstorm. The remaining planes were smelted into aluminum ingots.

Each June the base comes alive again as the West Texas Wing of the Confederate Air Force stages an air show.

Open Saturday from 9 A.M. to 6 P.M. and Sunday from 2 to 6 P.M. Admission, free.

Copper Breaks State Park

12 miles south of Quanah on S.H. 6
Quanah 79252
817/839-4331   H

This park site is located near Medicine Mounds, on the Pease River, once within the range of the Comanche Indians. The visitor center contains a large exhibit which presents details of the Comanche culture and lifestyle and also tells about the development of the later ranching industry in the area.

Open daily from 8 A.M. to 5 P.M. September through May, 8 A.M. to 10 P.M. June through August. Admission, $2 for car park and entrance fee.

Hardeman County Historical Museum

Green Street   Quanah 79252
817/663-5902 or 663-5272   T

Located in the old stone jail built in 1891, the Hardeman County Historical Museum has two exhibits on the lower floor, one describing the history of Quanah and Hardeman County from the sale of the first town lots in 1886, the other a permanent loan from the National Aeronautics and Space Administration and the Smithsonian Institution that features the various missions of the astronauts. The upper floor is preserved as it was—cells for the inmates.

Open Saturday, Sunday, and Monday from 2 to 5 P.M. Admission, free.

QUITMAN
Map 2

Gov. Hogg Shrine State Park
518 S. Main Street
Route 3, Park Road 45   Quitman 75783
214/763-2701   H (Miss Ima Hogg Museum and restrooms), T

The Gov. Hogg Shrine State Park, established in 1941, contains the James A. Stinson home, the Honeymoon Cottage, and the Miss Ima Hogg Museum. James A. Stinson was the father of Sallie Ann Stinson, who married James Stephen Hogg, the first native Texan to be elected governor (1891–95). The house is virtually intact and was well-furnished by Miss Ima Hogg, the governor's daughter and a collector and authority on early furniture in her own right. The Honeymoon Cottage was the first home of Governor and Mrs. Hogg and was originally located about three quarters of a mile from the Wood County Courthouse on the Gilmer Highway. The existing structure is a replica.

The Miss Ima Hogg Museum was built in 1969 and named for the Governor's only daughter. On exhibit is the history of the area, natural history, and various personal items belonging to members of the Hogg family.

The park is open daily from 8 A.M. to 10 P.M. The museum is open Thursday through Monday from 9 A.M. to noon, 1 to 4 P.M. Admission, adults $.50; children over 6 $.25.

RALLS
Map 9

Ralls Historical Museum
801 Main Street   Ralls 79357
806/253-2425   H, T

Located in the historic John R. Ralls Building, the Ralls Historical Museum displays artifacts relating to early Indian cultures, first pioneers, and the history of Crosby County depicted in forty photographic panels. On the second floor is a series of period rooms depicting a pioneer home, town, ranch, and farm. Also on exhibit are collections of barbed wire, walking canes, glass, antique furniture, and nails from the first railroad.

Open Monday through Friday from 9 A.M. to noon, 2 to 5 P.M., Sunday from 2 to 5 P.M. Closed Saturday. Admission, free.

Rankin Museum

200 West 5th Street   Rankin 79778
915/693-2770   H, T

The lobby of the old Yates Hotel building has been restored to its original condition to house the Rankin Museum, which features the history of Rankin, which was founded on the Panhandle and Santa Fe Railroad, and Upton County. On exhibit are pieces of antique furniture that belonged to Upton County residents as well as old photographs of the region.

Open Thursday and Friday from 2 to 5 P.M., Saturday from 1 to 5 P.M. Admission, free.

Raymondville Historical and Community Center

Harris and 7th Streets   Raymondville 78580
512/689-3171   H

Exhibits relate to the history of Raymondville (founded 1904) and Willacy County and include a display of ranch artifacts from the La Parra (Kenedy) Ranch as well as artifacts discovered underwater at Port Mansfield. There are also natural history and art exhibitions.

Open Wednesday and Saturday from 1 to 5 P.M. Admission, free.

History of Aviation Collection

University of Texas at Dallas
Campbell Road at Floyd   Richardson 75080
214/690-2996

The History of Aviation Collection is one of the foremost aviation history research centers in the Western Hemisphere. It contains more than 2,500,000 library and archival items, spanning more than 5,000 years of progress in humans' desire to fly, from the earliest myths, legends, and Biblical references to today's space explorations. There are more than 800 hand-crafted models and hundreds of artifacts and hardware items, including such unusual items as huge propellers from the Convair B-36 and the dirigibles *Shenandoah* and *Los Angeles*, the radio operator's chair from the ill-fated *Hindenburg*, early aircraft engines, and a record-breaking soaring plane.

Open Monday through Friday from 9:30 A.M. to noon, 1 to 5 P.M., or by appointment. Closed on university holidays. Group tours and researchers welcome by appointment. Admission, free.

Fort Bend County Museum

500 Houston Street   Richmond 77469
713/342-6478   H, B

Museum exhibits depict 100 years in Fort Bend County history, from 1822 to 1922. Shown are artifacts and documents of Austin's "Old 300" settlers, Jane Long ("the mother of Texas"), and Mirabeau B. Lamar, president of Texas, and Carry Nation. The cotton, cattle, and sugar industries are represented and are complemented by numerous craftsmen's tools and farm implements. The museum also offers special six-month exhibits, guided walking and riding tours of Richmond, and spinning and weaving demonstrations.

The museum maintains the 1883 John M. Moore House, the 1896 County Jail, the Decker Historical Park, in which the 1850s-era McNabb House (home of Carry Nation's daughter) is located, the 1901 Southern Pacific Railroad Depot, and a log cabin similar to those built by the early settlers.

Open Tuesday through Friday from 10 A.M. to 4 P.M., Saturday and Sunday 1 to 5 P.M. Admission, free, except for the Moore House: open Sunday from 1 to 5 P.M. and by special appointment for groups; admission, $2 for adults.

Marine Laboratory and Museum

Texas Parks and Wildlife Department
Turning Basin   Rockport 78382
512/729-2328   H

Fishes and other denizens of the Gulf of Mexico are on display in the aquarium of the Marine Laboratory Museum. Red and black drum, spotted sea trout, southern flounder, sheepshead, and octupi are usually on view. Occasionally sharks and seahorses are added. The museum demonstrates the purpose of marine research through its exhibits of marine biology.

Open Monday through Friday from 8 A.M. to 5 P.M. Admission, free.

Central Texas Museum of Automotive History

12 miles south of Bastrop on S.H. 304
Rosanky 78953
512/237-2745   B

Located on the west side of Highway 304, the Central Texas Museum of Automotive History exhibits early automobiles and accessories in an effort to trace the development of the automobile as well as its social and economic impact. On display are such early automobiles as

the 1912 model T Open Tourabout; the 1914 T
model, which Henry Ford made available in any
color so long as it was black; the 1910 EMF 30
made by Studebaker; the 1927 La Salle, a handsome Roadster; and many more.

Open Wednesday through Saturday from 9
A.M. to 5 P.M., Sunday from 2:30 to 5 P.M.
Closed Monday and Tuesday. There is an admis-
sion charge.

ROUND ROCK
Map 3

Palm House Museum

212 E. Main   Round Rock 78664
512/255-5805   H, T

Palm Valley was the first Swedish settlement
in Texas. It is located in Williamson County and
was named for Mrs. Anders Palm and her six
sons, who settled there in 1853. Palm House was
the home of the patriarch of the colony. Two
rooms and a hall have been restored and furnished, including an elegant parlor and a pioneer
Swedish kitchen and slave cabins.

Open Monday through Friday from 8:30 A.M.
to 5 P.M. Admission, free.

Washington Anderson–Irvin House Museum

U.S. 79   Round Rock 78664
512/255-2605   H, T, HABS

The Anderson–Irvin House, also called El
Milagro, was built between 1854 and 1859 by
four black slaves and a Swedish foreman for
Washington Anderson, a Virginian who had
moved to Texas in 1835. Constructed of Texas
limestone, the historic house is Georgian in
style. It was restored by Colonel and Mrs. William Ross Irvin in 1950 and has always been a
private home. Various objects, including regimental and divisional insignia from the U.S.
Cavalry, are on display.

Open by appointment. Admission, $1.50. Call
for group reservations and prices.

ROUND TOP
Map 3

Henkel Square

Live Oak and First Streets   Round Top 78954
No telephone   HABS

Henkel Square includes a number of historic
houses that have been assembled and restored by
Mrs. Charles Bybee and is located in Round Top,
which probably got its name from a nearby
round top house built in 1847 by Alwin H.
Soergel, an early German settler and author of
an early emigrant guide. The Edward Henkel
House, a 2-story structure built c. 1851 by a German settler, is a part of that restoration, as is the
Zapp–Von Rosenberg House, a frame house with

clapboarding built c. 1875 by a German settler. Mrs. Bybee has also furnished the houses with authentic early Texas furniture.

Write for information on open hours and admission.

Winedale Historical Center
Four miles east on F.M. 1457
Round Top 78954
409/278-3530   H (parts of the complex), B, T, HABS

Administered by the University of Texas at Austin, this complex of historical buildings dates from c. 1834 when William S. Townsend, an Austin colonist who had received the land from the Mexican government in 1831, began building his house—now known as the Winedale Historical Center. The Townsend-Lewis house, completed when Samuel Lewis purchased the farm from Townsend, is a two-story frame house of eight rooms with a galleried porch and a dog-trot and is furnished with early Texas furniture and decorative arts. Other buildings in the complex include the Spies House Office and Visitor Center; Hazel's Lone Oak Cottage, a typical Texas frame farm dwelling with an open central passage; a log kitchen and smokehouse; a hay barn; the McGregor-Grimm

The Townsend-Lewis Farmstead, Winedale Historical Center, Round Top. Photograph by Ave Bonar.

House, a two-story Greek Revival farmhouse built in 1861 by a Washington County planter; and a restored barn used as a theater.

The Winedale Historical Center, which was donated to the University of Texas at Austin in 1965 by Miss Ima Hogg, is a superb historical restoration that houses early Texas furniture as well as other period furnishings. Tours of the complex begin at the visitor center.

Open Tuesday through Friday by appointment; Saturday from 10 A.M. to 5 P.M., Sunday from noon to 5 P.M. Admission, adults $2; children $.50.

RUNGE
Map 4

Runge Museum
Runge 78151
512/329-4372 or 329-4243

Housed in a turn-of-the-century building, the Runge Museum displays pictures, newspapers, clothes, dishes, and many other items associated with early settlers in the area. Runge was founded on the Texas and New Orleans Railroad by Polish settlers from nearby Panna Maria and was named for Henry Runge, one of the early residents.

Open by appointment. A donation is accepted for admission.

Runge Museum.

RUSK
Map 2

James S. Hogg Memorial Museum
Jim Hogg State Park
Two miles northeast of Rusk off U.S. 84
Rusk 75785
214/683-4850

Located in Jim Hogg State Park, the Hogg Memorial Museum contains material relating to the former governor of Texas. The "Mountain

Home" plantation, which Governor Hogg's father established in 1846 when he and his wife moved from Nacogdoches to Rusk, was the governor's birthplace. The Hogg family had moved to the new Republic of Texas from Tuscaloosa, Alabama in 1839. The Hogg family cemetery is located nearby.

Open daily from 10 A.M. to noon, 1 to 4 P.M. Admission, free.

SABINE PASS
Map 4

Sea Rim State Park Visitor Center

10 miles west of Sabine Pass on S.H. 87
Sabine Pass 77655
409/971-2559   H, B, R

Sea Rim State Park consists of more than 15,000 acres of coastal estuary and wetland where the marsh grasses extend into the surf zone of the Gulf shoreline. The visitor center features a large diorama depicting wildlife and plants of the different zones, from the beachfront across the dunes to the marshlands. Other exhibits discuss the archeology and fish life of the coast. A boardwalk nature trail acquaints the visitor with marsh ecology. Air-boat tours of Sea Rim Marsh are available from the concessioner.

Open daily from 8 A.M. to 5 P.M. Admission to the park, $2 per day per motor vehicle.

SAINT JO
Map 1

Stonewall Saloon Museum

Main and Howell Streets   Saint Jo 76265
817/995-2250   H, T

Saint Jo dates from an 1856 settlement on the headwaters of the Elm Fork of the Trinity River. It did not really develop into a town until cowboys began herding their Longhorns up the Chisholm Trail, which crossed the Red River nearby. The museum is housed in the oldest permanent building in the city, a saloon constructed for the cattle trade in 1873. It is a two-story building that now contains exhibits relating to the history of Montague County: early cattle brands, guns, household items, and farming and ranching equipment.

Open daily from 8 A.M. to 6 P.M. Admission, free.

SALADO
Map 3

Central Texas Area Museum

1 Main Street   Salado 76571
817/947-5232   B

Conveniently located across the street from the old Stage Coach Inn, the Central Texas Area Museum is housed in an early storefront that has recently been remodeled. Located in the heart of the early-day Robertson Colony, which settled most of Central Texas, the museum contains exhibitions that relate to the early history of the Salado area.

Call for information on open hours and admission.

SAN ANGELO
Map 7

E. H. Danner Museum of Telephony
2701 S. Johnson   San Angelo 76904
915/944-5306

The Danner Museum of Telephony, located in the General Telephone Building, contains a collection of over 100 antique telephones, including an original Gallows Frame Telephone designed by Alexander Graham Bell.

Open Monday through Friday from 8 A.M. to 5 P.M., except legal holidays. Admission, free.

Fort Concho National Historic Landmark
716 Burgess Street (between Avenues C and D)
San Angelo 76903
915/655-2121, Ext. 441   B, T, N, HABS

As an active military post from 1867–1889, Fort Concho was a center of personnel and supplies for the Red River Wars of the 1870s and the Victorio campaign of 1880. The first permanent sandstone structures were completed in 1868. Seventeen of the original buildings—the headquarters, two barracks, nine officers' quarters, schoolhouse/chapel, commissary, quartermaster storehouse, power magazine, and bakery—have survived and most are being restored. In addition, two barracks with adjoining mess halls have been reconstructed. Exhibits in the museum, which was founded in 1928, contain material relating to the settling of West Texas, the army's role on the frontier, and natural history.

Open Monday through Saturday from 9 A.M. to 5 P.M., Sunday from 1 to 5 P.M. Admission, adults $1; children $.50. Group rates by appointment.

SAN ANTONIO
Map 6

The Alamo
See Downtown Area, San Antonio de Valero

Brackenridge Park
Old Trail Drivers Association
3805 Broadway   San Antonio 78209
No telephone   B

The Pioneer, Trail Drivers, and Texas Ranger Building houses the collections of three organizations: The State Association of Texas Pioneers, the Old Trail Drivers Association of Texas, and the Former Texas Rangers Association. The building was constructed for the Texas

Centennial in 1936 and is referred to as Memorial Hall.

The Pioneer Museum contains books, historic furniture, treasury notes of the Republic of Texas, and some paintings. The Texas Ranger Museum displays the history of the Texas Rangers in pictures and memorabilia. The Old Trail Drivers have three cabinets of memorabilia including saddles, hats, pistols, rifles, and other archival material.

Open Wednesday through Sunday from 10 A.M. to 4 P.M. Admission, adults $1; children over 12 $.25.

Brackenridge Park
San Antonio Zoological Gardens and Aquarium
3903 N. St. Mary's   San Antonio 78212
512/734-7183   H, B, R

The San Antonio Zoo began in 1910 with a small group of animals in San Pedro Park. Today the zoo contains over 3,000 specimens, representing more than 700 species, one of the largest animal collections in the country. The setting is spectacular, with rock cliffs of an abandoned rock quarry surrounding the zoo and streams of clear, artesian water providing a habitat for waterfowl and animals from far-off places. The zoo's waterfowl collection is known worldwide, as is its antelope collection. The bear grottos and Monkey Island, with its colony of gelada baboons and its herd of Barbary sheep, have been a feature of the zoo since the 1930s. The latest

Polar bear at the San Antonio Zoological Gardens and Aquarium, Brackenridge Park.

renovations are the African Safari Walk and the Hixon Bird House. A $3 million children's zoo is under construction.

Open April through October from 9:30 A.M. to 6:30 P.M., November through March from 9:30 A.M. to 5 P.M. Admission, adults $3; children $1.

Brackenridge Park
*Witte Memorial Museum
3801 Broadway   San Antonio 78209
512/226-5544   H, B, HABS (Ruiz and Twohig houses)

The city art museum as well as the natural history museum when it opened in 1926, the Witte Memorial Museum, located in Brackenridge Park, is now devoted to history and natural history. Exhibitions deal with Texas wildlife and ecology, archaeology, and American Indians. In addition, there are other historic buildings on the grounds, including the home of Colonel Francisco Ruiz, one of the signers of the Texas Declaration of Independence, and the John Twohig house, home of a Texas patriot and successful San Antonio banker.

Among the permanent collections and exhibitions are Sounds of South Texas, a diorama of the birds and wildlife of this region. This exhibition features the bird and animal calls, followed by identification of the animal (while a spotlight shows the creature) and a brief explanation. Another semipermanent exhibition is "Whatsit?," which provides a guessing game with artifacts. Some of the more unusual items in the Witte's permanent collection are on display with a multiple-choice selection of names. The visitors attempt to reason the object's identification before lifting the label to find the correct answer.

Open Tuesday through Sunday, June 1 through August 31 from 10 A.M. to 6 P.M., September 1 to May 31, 10 A.M. to 5 P.M. Admission, adults $2; children under 12 $1. Group discount rates are available. Saturday and Sunday mornings are free.

Buckhorn Hall of Horns
See Lone Star Brewery

Carver Community Cultural Center
226 N. Hackberry   San Antonio 78202
512/299-7211   H

The Carver Community Cultural Center is a multi-cultural, multi-ethnic arts center which dates from 1929. Historically rooted in the San

The Witte Memorial Museum, San Antonio.

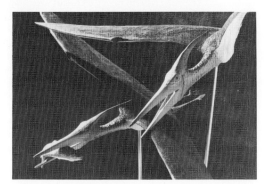

These life-sized Pteranodon reproductions are part of the "Dinosaurs: Vanished Texans" exhibition at the Witte Museum in San Antonio. Courtesy San Antonio Museum Association, San Antonio.

Antonio black community, the center is now considered a historic site. The center's program includes visual arts exhibits, performing arts events (with local, national, and internationally-known artists), and occasional Smithsonian Institution traveling exhibits.

Open daily from 7:45 A.M. to 4:30 P.M. There are frequent events during the evening hours.

Downtown Area
Hall of Texas History
HemisFair Plaza   San Antonio 78297
512/225-2266   H, B, R

The highlights of Texas history are displayed in this wax museum, including Cabeza de Vaca's

1528 shipwreck on Galveston Island, the Spanish Mission period, the Texas Revolution, the Republic, the Texas Navy, Statehood, the Civil War, and the Texas Rangers. A tapestry by Charles Beckendorf showing a Longhorn cattle drive is also on display.

Open daily from 10 A.M. to 5 P.M. Admission, adults $1.25; children 6 to 12 $.50.

Downtown Area
Hertzberg Circus Museum
210 W. Market Street   San Antonio 78205
512/299-7810

The Hertzberg Circus Museum, one of the most extensive circus collections in the country, was donated to the San Antonio Public Library in 1940 by San Antonio lawyer Harry Hertzberg. It includes one of the most extensive Tom Thumb collections in the world, featuring his mini-carriage, a piece of his wedding cake, and his mechanical piano; paintings, lithographs, woodcuts, and other rare printed material relating to the circus; one of the finest miniature circuses, with the sideshow tent, Big Top, menagerie, and various wagons; autographed photographs of circus stars; a collection of photographs and letters relating to the life of P. T. Barnum as well as his famous songstress, Jenny Lind; photographs and memorabilia from Buffalo Bill's Wild West Show; Clyde Beatty's white uniform and jungle hat; the mechanical clown Toto from Vienna, with his garish costume and grotesque makeup; and an old ticket wagon from the Gentry Bros. Circus. A research library contains many more circus items, including route books, programs, letters, pictures, and data.

Open Monday through Saturday from 9 A.M. to 5:30 P.M. May through October, open Sunday and holidays from 1 to 5 P.M. Closed New Year's Day, Thanksgiving, Christmas, and Battle of Flowers Day. Admission, free.

Downtown Area
La Villita Exhibit
Bolivar Hall, La Villita   San Antonio 78205
512/224-6163   H, B, N

The exhibition highlights the development of La Villita, from its earliest Spanish days through restoration by the W.P.A. in the 1930s. Artifacts, maps, and photographs portray this example of urban evolution in changing exhibitions. Bolivar

Hall is located in the La Villita National Register Historic District.

Open Tuesday through Sunday from 10 A.M. to 5 P.M. A donation is requested for admission.

Downtown Area
Navarro House
228 S. Laredo   San Antonio 78207
512/226-4801   H, T, N, HABS

A historic building, the Navarro house is the restored home of José Antonio Navarro (1795–1871), one of the two native-born Texans to sign the Texas Declaration of Independence. The site consists of the house, kitchen, and office of Navarro, who operated ranches around San Antonio, ran a general merchandise store, practiced law, and took an active part in the public affairs of San Antonio. He represented Texas in the legislature of the Mexican state of Coahuila y Texas, served in the congress of the Republic of Texas, was a member of the Convention of 1845 that voted to join the Union, and encouraged secession from the Union in 1861.

Open Tuesday through Saturday from 10 A.M. to 4 P.M. Admission, adults $.50; children $.25.

Downtown Area
Nuestra Señora de la Purísima Concepción de Acuña
807 Mission Road   San Antonio 78214
512/532-3158   T, HABS

Originally founded in 1716 in East Texas, Nuestra Señora de la Purísima Concepción fell upon hard times and was moved several times before it was finally located on the San Antonio River near San Antonio de Valero and San José in 1731. With its solid, 4-foot thick stone walls, Concepción is reportedly the oldest unrestored church structure in the United States.

Open daily from 9:30 A.M. to 5:30 P.M. Admission for Concepción only, adults $1; children $.50.

Downtown Area
San Antonio de Valero (the Alamo)
Alamo Plaza   San Antonio 78299
512/225-3853   H, B, T, HABS

Mission San Antonio de Valero, better known today as the Alamo, was the first of these missions established along the east bank of the San Antonio River in 1718. It was moved several times and even destroyed by a hurricane (in 1724) before finally being established in its pres-

Nuestra Señora de la Purísima Concepción de Acuña, San Antonio. National Park Service photograph.

The Alamo, San Antonio.

ent location. It gained its greatest fame after it had been abandoned by the padres. When Mexican General Antonio López de Santa Anna marched into Texas in 1836 to quell the uprising that ultimately won Texas its independence, Texans under the command of Colonel William B. Travis fortified the Alamo and refused to surrender to the vastly superior Mexican force. Santa Anna launched the final attack on March 6. All the defenders of the Alamo were killed in the battle or later put to death. A woman and child and fourteen other non-combatants were spared. "Remember the Alamo" became a rallying cry for the Texan army as they later defeated Santa Anna at the Battle of San Jacinto.

Today under the jurisdiction of the Daughters of the Republic of Texas, the Alamo is a museum displaying memorabilia of the Alamo and of the Republic of Texas, including maps, weapons, manuscripts, and portraits. Nearby, in a building formerly used as living quarters for the priests and a dining hall and kitchen, is the Long Barrack Museum, which contains two dioramas depicting the final hours of the siege of the Alamo, various historical artifacts, and an audiovisual presentation on the Battle of the Alamo. The Texas History Library of the Daughters of the Republic of Texas is located next door and also features small displays related to Texas history.

Open Monday through Saturday from 9 A.M. to 5:30 P.M. Sunday from 10 A.M. to 5:30 P.M. Closed Christmas Eve and Day. Admission, free.

Downtown Area
San Antonio Museum of Transportation
HemisFair Plaza   San Antonio 78209
512/226-5544   H, B

Founded in 1968, the museum has more than 100 vehicles on display, including a collection of rare antique, classic, and special-interest automobiles, bicycles, tricycles, and motorcycles, and a Herff miniature train. A highlight of the collection is a seven-passenger cream-and-black Model 338 Packard, built in 1915. A self-starter and progressive transmission complement its powerful engine. Also on display: a 1933 Dusenberg Model J, a 1917 Pierce-Arrow Model 66, a 1935 Packard Eight Sedan, and several models of Rolls Royce and Mercedes-Benz. The museum also owns a 1913 trolley (Old 300) that operates on a short run around the city. Each year vehicles from the museum are entered in the Battle of Flowers parade during Fiesta Week.

Open Tuesday through Sunday, June 1 through August 31 from 10 A.M. to 6 P.M., September 1 to May 31, 10 A.M. to 5 P.M. Admission, adults $2; children under 12 $1. Group discount rates are available. Saturday and Sunday mornings are free.

Downtown Area
Spanish Governor's Palace
105 Military Plaza   San Antonio 78205
512/224-0601   H, B, T, N, HABS

The Spanish Governor's Palace was constructed sometime after 1722 when the Marquis of San Miguel de Aguayo ordered the Presidio de San Antonio de Bejar reconstructed. The original thatch buildings where replaced with adobe. Ramparts, warehouses, officers' quarters, soldiers' barracks, and the *commandancia* were constructed. When San Antonio was made the seat of Texas government in 1722, the *commandancia* became the governor's palace. Construction probably was completed in 1749, the date engraved on the keystone above the front doors. The keystone also bears a Hapsburg Coat of Arms, honoring King Philip V of Spain. After 1822 the building was used as a second-hand clothing store, a tailor's shop, a barroom, a restaurant, and a schoolhouse. The City of San Antonio purchased it in 1929 and restored it. Antique items currently on display include a prayer bench, a desk for baptism records, and a seventeenth-century rosewood bed.

Open Monday through Saturday from 9 A.M. to 5 P.M., Sunday from 10 A.M. to 5 P.M. Admission, adults $.50; children $.25.

Downtown Area
Steves Homestead
509 King William Street   San Antonio 78204
512/225-5924   H (after the restoration), T, HABS

This elegant three-story mansion, thought to have been designed by San Antonio architect Alfred Giles, was built for Edward Steves in 1874–1876. Located on the banks of the San Antonio River, it is of Victorian symmetrical design with a mansard roof and Italianate detail, all blending rather harmoniously. It is one of the more graceful manifestations of elegance on what proved to be San Antonio's street of mansions and is furnished with authentic nineteenth-century pieces. The Steves Homestead is currently undergoing extensive restoration.

The 1906 Pungs Finch, the only roadster of its kind still in existence, at the San Antonio Museum of Transportation.

The Steves Homestead, 509 King William Street, San Antonio. Photograph courtesy San Antonio Conservation Society.

The Steves house, owned by the San Antonio Conservation Society, is part of the walking tour of King William Street. You may obtain a brochure for the tour by calling the Society at 512/224-6163. Other stops on the tour are the Yturria-Edmunds Home (1840–1860), 257 Yellowstone (see entry); Casa Villita (1850), 511 Paseo de la Villita; and the Spanish Aqueduct (1731), Acequia Park.

Open from 10 A.M. to 5 P.M. Wednesday through Sunday, from 1 to 5 P.M. Monday and Tuesday. Admission, adults $1; children $.50.

Downtown Area
The University of Texas Institute of Texan Cultures
801 South Bowie Street (HemisFair Plaza)
San Antonio 78205
512/226-7651   H, B, R

Founded in 1968 as the Texas Pavilion for the San Antonio World's Fair, the Institute of Texan Cultures exhibits the history of Texas, from prehistory to the present day, on a football field-sized exhibit floor. The exhibits are arranged by the more than thirty ethnic groups that settled the state. Interpreters use artifacts, historic photographs, furniture, tools, works of art, folk tales, and music to describe the contributions of the various ethnic groups. Highlight of the visit may well be the Dome Theater, where film and slide programs are presented daily on the thirty-six screens.

Special exhibitions are presented in the Lower Gallery and in the Hall of Mirrors. Visitors may

The rotunda movie-slide show is one of the most popular attractions at the Institute of Texan Cultures, San Antonio.

Fort Sam Houston Museum and the historic Quadrangle Tower, San Antonio. The Quadrangle photograph is by Todd Webb. Courtesy Amon Carter Museum, Fort Worth.

also stroll through the one-room school house and the frontier cavalry fort on the Institute's grounds.

Open Tuesday through Sunday from 9 A.M. to 5 P.M. Admission, free.

Downtown Area

Yturri–Edmunds Home

807 Mission Road   San Antonio 78214
No telephone

The Yturri–Edmunds Home, on the grounds of Mission Concepción, consists of three buildings that have been restored: an 1840 adobe house, a mill, and a carriage house. The house has historic furnishings and a colorful history associated with the missions.

Write for information on open hours and admission.

Fort Sam Houston

Fort Sam Houston Museum

Building 123   Fort Sam Houston 78234
512/221-6117   T, N, HABS

The Fort Sam Houston Museum tells the story of the military units and people who have been stationed in San Antonio, from 1845 to the present. The fort itself, which is located just northwest of the downtown area and is named after Sam Houston, the hero of the Battle of San Jacinto and later president of the Republic of Texas, U.S. senator, and governor of the state, was not established until 1879, when the Quadrangle was occupied. Other exhibitions relate to the U.S. Army in the Philippines, the Mounted Soldier (1845 to the present), the 5th U.S. Army (World War II to the present), the 2nd Infantry Division (both World Wars, and Korea), and Prisoners of War in Bataan and Corregidor.

The post is, of course, still active, but more than 500 acres of it have been designated a National Historic Landmark. The original Quartermaster Depot in the Quadrangle and the officer and NCO quarters and barracks, which date from 1876 to 1912, are still in use. The museum itself is located in a former troop mess hall which was built in 1905. A self-guided tour of the historic sites is available.

Open Wednesday through Sunday from 10 A.M. to 4 P.M. Closed Monday and Tuesday. Admission, free.

Fort Sam Houston
U.S. Army Medical Department Museum
Building 2264, Stanley Road
Fort Sam Houston 78208
512/221-2358

The approximately 8,000 square feet of exhibition space in the Medical Department Museum are devoted to telling the history and development of the U.S. Army Medical Department since its beginning in 1775. Various types of Army medical equipment, from the uniforms worn by medical personnel, to military insignia, to paintings depicting Army medical activities over the years, are exhibited. The museum also exhibits a number of captured medical items, including German and Japanese medical kits and instruments from World War II. A collection of scale-model medical evacuation vehicles includes Civil War, horse-drawn ambulances and hospital railway cars.

The museum was established in Washington, D.C., in 1862 and moved to Fort Sam Houston in 1955.

Open Monday through Friday from 8 A.M. to 4 P.M. Admission, free. Group tours may be arranged.

Hall of Texas History
See Downtown Area

Hangar 9—Edward H. White II Memorial Museum
See Missions Area
Hertzberg Circus Collection
See Downtown Area
History and Traditions Museum
See Lackland Air Force Base
Institute of Texan Cultures
See Downtown Area, University of Texas Institute of Texan Cultures

Jersey Lilly Saloon
312 Pearl Parkway   San Antonio 78215
512/226-0231   H, B

Housed in an 1894 stable for the horse teams that pulled the Pearl Beer wagons through the streets of San Antonio, this hospitality center and museum contains artifacts relating to Texas history. Among the exhibits are such items as an Apache squawbag, an oil painting of Pancho Villa, a collection of rare antique guns, and an assortment of beer steins. An added attraction is the dioramas depicting Judge Roy Bean. An exact replica of the Judge's saloon and courthouse is situated next to the hospitality center.

Open Monday through Friday from 10 A.M. to 4 P.M. Admission, free.

King William District
See Downtown Area, Steves Homestead

Lackland Air Force Base
History and Traditions Museum
Headquarters
Air Force Military Training Center
Orville Wright Drive, west of the main entrance to the base   Lackland Air Force Base 78236
512/671-3055   H

The History and Traditions Museum, which is located on Lackland Air Force Base in the southwest part of the city, consists of a collection of rare aeronautical equipment. The exhibits of aircraft, engines, instruments, and air weapons span the years of aviation development, from its origin to the aerospace age. More than 60 aircraft and missiles are displayed throughout the base.

Open Monday through Friday from 9 A.M. to 4 P.M., Saturday and Sunday and holidays from 9 A.M. to 6 P.M. Closed Thanksgiving and Christmas. Admission, free.

Lackland Air Force Base

U.S.A.F. Security Police Museum

Lackland Air Force Base 78236

512/671-2801 or 671-2802   H

Exhibits trace the history of the U.S.A.F. Security Police and include original paintings on loan from the U.S.A.F. art collection, photographs, and weapons used by the enemy in the Vietnam conflict. Also included are audio-visual presentations and a hall dedicated to educational exhibits as well as a Hall of Honor. The museum is located near the technical school for training Security Police, so concurrent tours can be accommodated.

Open Monday through Friday from 8 A.M. to 4 P.M., and on weekends and holidays by request. Admission, free.

U.S.A.F. Security Police Museum, Lackland Air Force Base.

History and Traditions Museum, Lackland Air Force Base. U.S.A.F. photograph by Donald D. Powell.

The Texas Hall in the Buckhorn Hall of Horns, San Antonio, features murals by Porfirio Salinas and the record 78-point white-tailed buck.

232

La Villita Exhibit
See Downtown Area

Lone Star Brewery
Buckhorn Hall of Horns
600 Lone Star Boulevard   San Antonio 78297
512/226-8301   H

When young Albert Friedrich opened his Buckhorn Saloon on Dolorosa Street in downtown San Antonio in 1881, he began collecting horns. By 1895 his horns and antlers had become something of a local attraction and grew steadily as cowboys, trappers, and traders brought in all kinds of horns to trade for drinks. The Lone Star Beer Company, which took over the collection in 1956, has continued to add to it.

Two large murals painted by Texas artist Porfirio Salinas provide a colorful backdrop for the exhibits. Also included in the exhibits are a Hall of Fins that displays rare and unusual marine specimens, and a Hall of Feathers where native and exotic birds are shown in natural habitat settings. Perhaps the most outstanding specimen in the Hall is a "stately 78 point world record non-typical whitetailed deer" that was found near San Antonio in 1892.

Open daily from 9:30 A.M. to 5 P.M. Closed Thanksgiving, Christmas, and New Year's Day. Admission, adults $1.25; children 6 to 12 $.50; under 6 free.

Lone Star Brewery
O. Henry House
600 Lone Star Boulevard   San Antonio 78297
512/226-8301   H, T, HABS

Although it was long thought that this modest house was the San Antonio residence of William Sidney Porter, better known by his pen name of O. Henry, it is now generally felt that Porter never lived there. Porter did frequent San Antonio and probably visited in the house with Henry Ryder Taylor, editor of a publication entitled *The Rolling Stone*, in which several of Porter's stories appeared. The Lone Star Brewing Company saved the house from destruction at its original site on South Presa Street and moved it to the Brewery grounds, where it is still known as the O. Henry House.

Open daily from 9:30 A.M. to 5 P.M. Closed Thanksgiving, Christmas Eve and Day, and New Year's Eve and Day. Admission, adults $1.25; children 6 to 12 $.50; under 6 free.

*Marion Koogler McNay Art Museum
6000 N. New Braunfels Avenue
San Antonio 78209
512/824-5368   H, B

One of the most tasteful and elegant museums in the state, the McNay Art Museum is located in a Mexican and Mediterranean-style mansion that Marion Koogler McNay began building in 1927. It houses the collection that she carefully assembled before her death in 1950 as well as important additions to it. When the museum opened in 1954, the McNay collection revealed strong holdings of French masterpieces by Cézanne, Gauguin, Redon, and Picasso as well as medieval and Mexican art. Mrs. McNay also had accumulated a large collection of watercolors by American artists such as Winslow Homer, Childe Hassam, and Maurice Prendergast, as well as a carefully selected collection of New Mexico folk art (rugs, *santos*, furniture, and paintings by contemporary Indian artists).

Paul Gauguin, Portrait of the Artist with the Idol, *c. 1893. Oil on canvas. 17 1/4 × 12 7/8 in. From the collection of the McNay Art Museum, San Antonio.*

Mary Cassatt, **Mother's Kiss,** *c. 1891. Color drypoint and soft-ground, 13⅜ × 9 in. Photograph by Michael Jay Smith. Courtesy McNay Art Museum, Gift of Mrs. Edgar Tobin.*

Front entrance to the McNay Art Museum, San Antonio. Photograph by Joe Lawrie.

235

Many fine works have been added to the collection since then. The distinguished Frederic Oppenheimer collection, consisting of some 130 sculptures, panel paintings, textiles, and decorative arts, such as medieval and gothic objects and Northern European and Italian panel paintings, was given to the museum in 1955. The Tom Slick collection, which the museum received in 1963, includes monumental sculptures by Barbara Hepworth and several major paintings by Georgia O'Keeffe and Picasso. Other paintings by Albert Gleizes and George Grosz have also been added to the collection.

The McNay also has an important print collection that began with a gift of Cézanne and Edvard Munch lithographs. It continued with the gifts of Jacques Villon and George Grosz prints and climaxed recently with the gift of Mary Cassatt's ten color prints, among the most beautiful ever executed by an American artist.

These works are beautifully exhibited in the house designed by San Antonio architect Atlee B. Ayres and his son Robert, with construction supervised by Mrs. McNay. The villa, lavishly trimmed with wrought iron and rare tiles, is built around a patio and pool, which is shaped like the famous rose window in San Antonio's San José Mission. Mrs. McNay had a hand in every detail of the house, including the handsome gardens. She was trained as an artist at the Art Institute of Chicago, and the painted ceilings are her own work. Several additions have been made since then, including a 1970 wing that includes a beautiful sculpture court, galleries to house the Lange collection, and the Frost wing in 1975, giving the museum spacious walls and high ceilings ideal for the exhibition of large, contemporary paintings.

Open Tuesday through Saturday from 9 A.M. to 5 P.M., Sunday from 2 to 5 P.M. A donation is requested for admission.

Missions Area
The Alamo
See Downtown Area, San Antonio de Valero

Missions Area
Hangar 9—Edward H. White II Memorial Museum
Brooks Air Force Base 78235
512/536-2203   T, HABS
Hangar 9, which is located on Brooks Air Force Base, across South Presa from the Mis-

sions National Historical Park, is the oldest aircraft hangar in the U.S. Air Force. It was built as a temporary structure in 1918 when Brooks Field was being constructed to serve as a training base for the Air Service of the Army Signal Corps. In 1969 it was restored and returned to the Air Force. It was subsequently dedicated as a memorial to astronaut Edward H. White II, a San Antonio native. It now houses the Museum of Flight Medicine and exhibitions concerning the history of the base and the development of manned flight.

Open Monday through Saturday from 8 A.M. to 4 P.M. Closed Sunday and holidays. Admission, free.

Hangar 9—Edward H. White II Memorial Museum, San Antonio.

Missions Area
Mission Concepción
See Downtown Area, Nuestra Señora de la Purísima Concepción de Acuña

Missions Area
San Antonio Missions National Historical Park
In 1978 Congress established the San Antonio Missions National Historic Park to help preserve and call attention to the unique frontier institution by which Spain tried to extend its influence and control and assimilate the Indians into Hispanic culture and Christianity. Mission Concepción is located just south of the downtown area, while the other missions are located on the San Antonio River south of Southeast Military Drive.

Admission to one mission, adults $1, children $.50. Admission to all missions, $2, available at any of the missions.

San Francisco de la Espada

Espada Road off U.S. 281   San Antonio 78221
512/627-2021   T, HABS

San Francisco de la Espada Mission was the
first mission established by the Spaniards in
East Texas in 1690 as San Francisco de los Tejas.
Following several moves, it, too, was relocated
to the San Antonio River, near San Antonio de
Valero and San José. The stone chapel, cloisters,
convent, and foundations of other dwellings still
survive. The Espada Dam, which is still func-
tioning today, can be seen on the San Antonio
River along Mission Parkway between San José
and San Juan. These dams supplied water for the
acequias, an extensive system of gravity-fed irri-
gation ditches. The Espada Aqueduct, which was
necessitated when one of these ditches needed
to cross over a natural stream, still stands today,
near San Juan on Espada Road, and still carries
water.

Open daily from 9:30 A.M. to 5:30 P.M. Admission to Espada only, adults $1; children $.50.

Missions Area
San José y San Miguel de Aguayo

6539 San José Drive   San Antonio 78214
512/922-2731   H, B, T, HABS

While staying at Mission San Antonio de Valero in 1719, Fray Antonio Margil de Jesús, a
remarkable priest and one of the greatest mis-
sionaries of his time, realized that he could begin a new work on the San Antonio River. He
moved down the river and began work on San

*San Francisco de la Espada, San Antonio. National Park
Service photograph.*

José. Called the "first Mission in America . . . in point of beauty, plan and strength" when it was finished in 1778, San José was the "Queen of the Missions" of Texas. Its Renaissance architecture with ornamental facade and sacristy window have been restored to much of their original beauty. Exhibits in the mission relate to its original use. It has been declared both a state and national historic site and is still in use as a church.

Open daily from 9:30 A.M. to 6 P.M. Admission for San José only, adults $.50; children under 12 $.25. Reservations for group tours may be made by calling in advance.

San José y San Miguel de Aguayo, San Antonio. National Park Service photograph.

San Juan Capistrano, San Antonio. National Park Service photograph.

San Juan Capistrano
9101 Graf Road   San Antonio 78221
512/532-3154   T, HABS

San Juan Capistrano was the third of the East Texas missions that was moved to the San Antonio River in 1731. A number of the buildings have been reconstructed, but some of the ruins are still visible. The two-tiered bell tower over the side entrance is somewhat unusual.

Open daily from 9:30 A.M. to 5:30 P.M. Admission to Capistrano only, adults $1; children $.50.

Museum of American Aviation
215 Blakeley Drive   San Antonio 78209
512/828-6862

Founded by the American Aviation Research Association, the museum contains examples of flight clothing, the home and research materials of the first man to fly an aircraft in San Antonio (Jacob Brodbeck in 1865), and the XC-99, the largest military aircraft ever built in the United States.

Open weekdays from 5 to 8 P.M. and afternoons on weekends. Admission, free.

The XC-99, the world's largest land-based aircraft, at the Museum of American Aviation, San Antonio. U.S.A.F. photograph.

Navarro House
See Downtown Area
Nuestra Señora de la Purísima Concepción de Acuña
See Downtown Area
O. Henry House
See Lone Star Brewery
Old Trail Drivers Association
See Brackenridge Park

San Antonio Museum of Art

200 West Jones Avenue   San Antonio 78209
512/226-5544   H, B, R, HABS

Located in a renovated Lone Star brewery on the San Antonio River, the San Antonio Museum of Art has won plaudits for its architectural splendor as well as for its exhibitions. The building is a castle-like brick complex with twin towers housing glass elevators that can be seen

Biernesa, **The Assumption of the Virgin,** *1737. Oil on canvas, 67½ × 55¼ (sight). Courtesy San Antonio Museum of Art.*

The San Antonio Museum of Art.

241

for miles. There are 66,000 square feet of exhibition space for contemporary and modern art, American photography since 1920, Texas furniture, paintings, and decorative arts, and pre-Columbian and Spanish colonial art.

The museum is one of a complex of eight historical buildings, which includes a sculpture garden of 2.5 acres. The first sculpture, installed in 1978, is David Deming's *Colorado Tri-Pod.* It is planned that riverboats will eventually be able to float from the downtown River Walk to a turn-around directly behind the museum.

Open Tuesday through Sunday, June 1 through August 31 from 10 A.M. to 6 P.M., September 1 to May 31, 10 A.M. to 5 P.M. Admission, adults $2; children under 12, $1. Group discount rates are available. Saturday and Sunday mornings are free.

San Antonio Museum of Transportation
See Downtown Area
San Antonio Zoological Gardens and Aquarium
See Brackenridge Park
San Francisco de la Espada
See Missions Area
San José y San Miguel de Aguayo
See Missions Area
San Juan Capistrano
See Missions Area
Spanish Governor's Palace
See Downtown Area
Steves Homestead
See Downtown Area
The University of Texas Institute of Texan Cultures
See Downtown Area
U.S.A.F. Security Police Museum
See Lackland Air Force Base
U.S. Army Medical Department Museum
See Fort Sam Houston
Witte Memorial Museum
See Brackenridge Park
Yturri-Edmunds Home
See Downtown Area
San Elizario
See El Paso, Los Portales

SAN MARCOS
Map 6

Aquarena Springs
Dr. Eli T. Merriman Home
Loop 82, Aquarena Springs   San Marcos 78666
512/392-2481   T

This original one-room log cabin was the first home in San Marcos. It was constructed by Dr.

Eli T. Merriman, who moved to the banks of the San Marcos River in 1847. As a part of Texana Village, it now contains antique furnishings and depicts the early history of the San Marcos area.

Open in the winter Monday through Friday from 8:30 A.M. to 6 P.M., Saturday and Sunday from 8:30 A.M. to 6:30 P.M.; in the summer Monday through Friday from 8 A.M. to 9 P.M., Saturday, Sunday, and holidays from 8 A.M. to 10 P.M. Closed Christmas. Admission, adults $1.20; combination ticket for all the village, $6.95.

Aquarena Springs
General Edward Burleson House
Loop 82, Aquarena Springs   San Marcos 78666
512/392-2481

This reproduction of the home of Edward Burleson, Texas frontiersman, Indian fighter, political leader, and one of the founders of San Marcos, contains personal documents, letters, and artifacts relating to his career. Burleson, along with Dr. Eli T. Merriman and William Lindsey, bought land near the headwaters of the San Marcos River and began to sell lots in 1851. Lindsey and Merriman continued the venture when Burleson died later that year.

Open in the winter Monday through Friday from 8:30 A.M. to 6 P.M., Saturday and Sunday from 8:30 A.M. to 6:30 P.M.; in the summer Monday through Friday from 8 A.M. to 9 P.M., Saturday, Sunday, and holidays from 8 A.M. to 10 P.M. Closed Christmas. Admission, $2.40.

SAN SABA
Map 6

San Saba County Historical Museum
Mill Pond Park (east of San Saba on U.S. 190)
San Saba 76877
915/372-5436, 372-3427, or 372-5276   T

The San Saba County Historical Museum is devoted to the history of the San Saba County area, from 1850 to the present. The city was founded on the river of the same name in 1854. Displays include objects and relics relating to early Indians, pioneer settlers, and industries of the area, including ranching, farming, hunting, and fishing. Within the museum is a log cabin built in 1850.

Open Sunday from 1:30 to 4:30 P.M. and weekdays by appointment. Admission, free.

Old Rock House

U.S. 84, one mile northwest of Santa Anna
Santa Anna 76878
915/348-3283

Santa Anna was named for the nearby mountain peak that was used as a lookout by Texas Rangers and Indians alike, rather than the Mexican president and general. This one-room pioneer cabin, built of limestone in 1873, is now furnished with frontier articles of the turn-of-the-century or earlier that recall the history of the settlement.

Open on request. Admission, free.

Big Thicket Museum

F.R. 770   Saratoga 77585
409/274-5000   H, B

The Big Thicket Museum features exhibitions and programs relating to the Big Thicket area. There is a local history room exhibiting glassware, an insulator collection, antique tools from the lumbering industry and from farming and ranching. The museum also has examples of snakes, fishes, insects, mushrooms, fungi, and birds, an exhibit of champion trees of Texas, and material relating to the lumbering, oil, and farming industries. Rosier Park, located about half a mile from the museum, has a half-hour walking trail for visitors. Saturday tours are available beginning at 9 A.M. and continuing throughout the day, and an annual three-day camping trip is sponsored each April. Big Thicket Day Festival is the first Saturday in June.

Open Tuesday through Saturday from 9 A.M. to 5 P.M., Sunday from 1 to 5 P.M., and by appointment. Closed Monday. Admission, $1. There is also a charge for the Saturday tour. Call for information and reservation.

Bay Area Museum

Clearlake Park Annex
Nasa Road I   Seabrook 77586
713/333-2015   B

The museum, which houses exhibitions related to the history of the Bay Area, particularly the period before NASA located there, is housed in the old Webster Church, which was built in 1900 after the Galveston hurricane destroyed the original church. It served three congregations, Methodist, Lutheran, and Presbyterian. In 1981 it was moved to its present location to house the museum. Two Indian mounds are located behind the church.

Open Tuesday, Thursday, and Saturday from 9 A.M. to 5 P.M., or special tours by appointment. Admission, free, but a donation is requested.

SEAGRAVES
Map 9

Gaines County Museum & Art Center, Seagraves-Loop Division

Main Street and Hill Avenue   Seagraves 79359
806/546-2810   H, T

A general museum featuring local history as well as arts and crafts, the Gaines County Museum & Art Center is located in a building constructed in 1926, the only building on Main Street to survive the March, 1928, fire that destroyed the town. The city was founded in 1915 by the Spearman Land Company.

Open Monday through Saturday from 2 to 5 P.M. Admission, free.

SEGUIN
Map 6

A. M. and Alma Fiedler Memorial Museum

Langner Hall
Texas Lutheran College   Seguin 78155
512/379-4161   H

With exhibits of rocks, minerals, fossils, and archaeology, as well as an outdoor rock garden, the museum provides a good introduction to the geology of Guadalupe County and surrounding area.

Open during college hours or by appointment. Admission, free.

Los Nogales Museum

S. River and E. Live Oak Streets   Seguin 78155
512/379-1567   T, HABS

The Los Nogales Museum, which is housed in an eighteenth-century building constructed by the Spanish government, contains historic exhibits relating to Texas. On display are memorabilia of Texas, pictures, and furniture.

The one-story structure was a station stop on El Camino Real in 1765, was used as a post office in 1823, and was occupied by Juan Seguin, for whom the town is named, in 1825. The building contains historic exhibits relating to Texas such as pictures and furniture.

Open Sunday from 2 to 4 P.M. A donation is requested for admission.

SEYMOUR
Map 10

Baylor County Historical Museum

200 W. McLain   Seymour 76380
No telephone

The Baylor County Historical Museum is located in the 1880s era home of Judge E. R. Morris, which is constructed of native limestone. The house was used as a boarding house and diner during the early years of the railroad in Seymour, but was turned into a museum during the Bicentennial. Collections on display date from Seymour's founding in the 1870s to the turn-of-the-century and beyond.

Open Tuesday and Thursday from 12:30 to 4:30 P.M. Admission, free, but a donation is requested.

SHALLOWATER
Map 9

Lubbock County Museum

10th and Avenue G   Shallowater 79363
806/741-8005

The Lubbock County Museum is a collection of outdoor exhibits of farm equipment typical of the equipment used by farmers in West Texas. The collection ranges from the horse drawn equipment of the late 1800s to steam tractors, combines, threshers, and other equipment necessary to plow, plant, cultivate, and harvest the crops grown in the area.

Open daily from daylight to dark. Admission, free.

SHAMROCK
Map 9

Pioneer West Museum

206 N. Madden   Shamrock 79079
806/256-3941

Devoted to the history of the Wheeler County Area, the museum includes displays that relate to pioneer settlers in the area as well as temporary exhibitions on the Texas Rangers and the manned space program.

Open Monday through Friday from 1 to 5 P.M., Saturday and Sunday by appointment.

SHEFFIELD
Map 7

Fort Lancaster Visitor Center

Fort Lancaster State Historic Site
U.S. 290, 33 miles west of Ozona
Sheffield 79781
915/836-4391   H, T, N

Fort Lancaster was established August 20, 1855, as a part of a frontier line of defense, on the east bank of Live Oak Creek, about half a mile above its confluence with the Pecos River. It was strategically located near an Indian crossing and situated on the El Paso–San Antonio Road. By 1860 Fort Lancaster was an impressive frontier post with 25 permanent buildings and an average complement of 72 men and four officers. The post was abandoned when the Civil War broke out in 1861. Confederate soldiers occupied it for a brief time, then, following the war, it was used as a bivouac for U.S. troops on at least two occasions, but no record of its use exists beyond 1871.

Exhibits in the visitor center include archeological specimens, historical items pertaining to frontier life, and photographs and maps.

Open daily from 8 A.M. to 5 P.M., except Christmas Day. Admission, free.

SHERMAN
Map 1

Sherman Historical Museum
301 S. Walnut   Sherman 75090
214/893-7623

The Sherman Historical Museum occupies the old Carnegie Library (1914) and presents exhibitions relating to the history of Sherman and the Grayson County area as well as state and national history. The Glen Eden exhibit recreates a room from the home of a well-known resident of nearby Lake Texoma. The Country Store shows something of the commercial life of Sherman at the turn-of-the century, and the Women's Work Area pays homage to the pioneer women who used the appliances of their day to make a home for their family.

Open Friday from 9 A.M. to noon and 1 to 5 P.M. and Saturday and Sunday from 2 to 5 P.M. Tours may be arranged at different times by reservation. Call for information on the current exhibition and admission.

SHINER
Map 4

Edwin Wolters Memorial Museum
306 S. Avenue I   Shiner 77984
No telephone

Items on display pertain to the Wolters family and to the history of Shiner, which was founded in 1887 and named for H. B. Shiner, who gave land for the townsite. Exhibits include natural history collections, weapons, and a period kitchen.

Open the second and fourth Sunday of each month from 2 to 5 P.M. A donation is requested for admission.

SIERRA BLANCA
Map 8

E. A. ("Dogie") Wright Collection
Hudspeth County Abstract and Title Company Building
East of the intersection of U.S. 80 and F.R.
1111   Sierra Blanca 79851
915/369-2011   H

Items on exhibit relate to the history of Sierra Blanca, which was established as a railroad town in 1881. There is a display of firearms, relics of former lawmen and desperados, and other material, collected by E. A. ("Dogie") Wright, son of a Texas Ranger and former Texas Ranger, U.S. Border Patrolman, and sheriff of Hudspeth County. There is also some material relating to the U.S. Cavalry along the Mexican border from the turn-of-the-century until 1969.

Open Monday through Friday from 10 A.M. to noon and 1 to 4 P.M. Admission, free.

SINTON
Map 5

Rob and Bessie Welder Wildlife Foundation

7.4 miles northeast of Sinton   Sinton 78387
512/364-2643   T

The Welder Wildlife Refuge was established in 1961 to provide the means and opportunity for research and education in wildlife, conservation, and the relationship of wildlife to other uses of the land. A small museum in the Spanish-style Administration Building houses the Quillan Memorial Egg Collection as well as changing exhibits.

The 7,800 acre refuge is a working ranch and research is on-going, so arrangements must be made in advance for a visit. Tour groups are admitted each Thursday afternoon, except on holidays, between 2:55 and 3 P.M. Gates are locked at all other times. (You should plan to arrive with the group and leave with the group insofar as possible.) Tours require approximately 2 1/2 hours and normally include inspection of the museum and other facilities, a discussion and slide program on the Foundation's objectives and research, and a tour of a portion of the refuge. You must provide your own transportation because the tour normally covers eight to ten miles. Because of locked gates, you should plan to remain for the complete tour. Tours are limited to age 14 and over and there should be 15 to 72 (the capacity of the lecture room) persons in the group. If the group is larger, or if you want to arrange a special time, please contact the Tour Director, P. O. Drawer 1400, Sinton, Texas 78387. No tours will be scheduled on Sunday. Admission, free.

SKIDMORE
Map 4

Skidmore Historical Society Museum

8th and Sullivan Streets (U.S. 181)
Skidmore 78389
512–287-3237   T

The restored house contains, among other items, a prayer room with an old pump organ and an upright piano that was shipped in pieces from the East coast to Texas. Antique farm machinery is displayed in the barn, and the turn-of-the-century jail has also been restored and placed on exhibit.

Open Sunday from 2 to 4 P.M. Admission, free.

Slaton Museum

155 N. 8th Street   Slaton 79364
806/828-6101   H

Located in an old store front, the Slaton Museum is dedicated to the history of Lubbock County, which was created out of Bexar County in 1876 and organized in 1891, and Slaton, which was founded on the Santa Fe Railroad in 1911.

Open Tuesday through Friday from 1 to 5 P.M. Admission, free.

Diamond M Foundation Museum

907 25th Street   Snyder 79549
915/573-6311   H

The Diamond M Foundation Museum in Snyder is an unlikely spot for twelve N. C. Wyeth paintings, as well as work by Peter Hurd, Andrew Wyeth, and other well-known American artists. Due to the generosity of the late C. T. and Claire McLaughlin, however, the museum exhibits these and more on a regular basis. The N. C. Wyeth gallery includes *Uncas*, *The Astrologer*, and *Courier of the Air*, among others. There are also works by Gerald Cassidy, Frederick C. Yohn, Harvey Dunn, W. H. D. Koerner, George Phippen, and Frank B. Hoffman. The collection contains bronze sculptures by George Phippen, Charles M. Russell, Frederic Remington, A. L. Bayre, and James Earle Fraser.

The museum's collection is decidedly Western, but there are also items such as Dresden china, Helena Rubenstein's jade collection, ivory carvings, Eskimo carvings, and a group of Currier & Ives prints. The museum also features changing exhibitions from its permanent collection as well as traveling shows.

Open Tuesday through Friday from 9 A.M. to noon and 1 to 4 P.M., Saturday and Sunday from 1 to 4 P.M. Admission, free.

*Scurry County Museum

Western Texas College   Snyder 79549
915/573-6107   H, B

The museum exhibits focus on the history of the Scurry County area, including material relating to the military and Indian trails, buffalo hunters, cattlemen, and farmers and oil men. The city traces its colorful history back to 1877, when W. H. ("Pete") Snyder established a trading post in central Scurry County and attracted so many desperadoes and fugitives from justice that it became known as Robbers' Roost. Sale of lots

N. C. Wyeth, **The Astrologer**. *Oil on canvas. 40 × 32 in.
From the collection of the Diamond M Museum, Snyder.*

began in 1882, and the county was organized in
1884. There are also special, traveling exhibitions that change monthly.

Open Monday through Thursday from 9 A.M.
to noon; Friday from 9 A.M. to noon and 1 to 4
P.M.; Sunday from 1 to 4 P.M. Admission, free.

SONORA
Map 7

Miers Home Museum
307 E. Oak Street (north of the Courthouse)
Sonora 76950
No telephone   H
The fifth home built in Sutton County, the
Miers home began as a two-room wood structure
that was enlarged to two stories over the years.
The house has been furnished in typical late-
nineteenth-century style and has turn-of-the-
century memorabilia on display. The old jail, located across the street, is also being restored to
display Western artifacts.

Open Tuesday from 2 to 4 P.M. Admission,
free.

Stationmaster's House Museum

30 South Townsend   Spearman 79081
806/659-3008   T, N

The Stationmaster's House is a historic building containing exhibits that relate to the history of Hansford County. The town dates from the 1920s, when the railroad was constructed through the area.

Open Tuesday through Saturday from 9 A.M. to 5 P.M. A donation is requested for admission.

Margaret A. Elliot Museum

Burlington Avenue   Spur 79370
915/271-3238 or 271-3350   H

The history of Dickens County is the subject of the displays in the Margaret A. Elliot Museum, from prehistory through the 1920s. Exhibits include pre-historic fossils, early Indian life, the military and early settlers, and farm and ranch equipment.

Open all day Monday and Wednesday, one-half day on Tuesday, Thursday, and Saturday. Admission, free.

Cowboy Country Museum

113 S. Wetherbee   Stamford 79553
915/773-2411   H, B

The Cowboy Country Museum was a bicentennial project of the Stamford Chamber of Commerce. The museum now houses exhibitions of farm and ranch artifacts of the early twentieth century, a period room displaying authentic furnishings from the turn-of-the-century, and antiques, books, and photographs from the region. The museum also includes an exhibit of Western American art as well as a gun collection. Special exhibitions are presented from time to time.

Open Monday through Friday from 8:30 A.M. to noon, 1 to 4:30 P.M., Saturday and Sunday by appointment. A donation is requested for admission.

Historic Jail Building

Courthouse Square   Stanton 79782
915/756-3336

Built in 1908, the old jail, sheriff's office, and cell block depict the history of law enforcement in Martin County.

Open by appointment at the sheriff's office. Admission, free.

Martin County Historical Museum

207 Broadway Street   Stanton 79782
915/756-2700   H, B

The history of Martin County and the surrounding region is the subject of this museum, which includes an old standard windmill as well as other outdoor exhibits. Stanton was established in 1881 as a section station on the Texas and Pacific Railroad. It was first called Grelton, but the German Catholic immigrants who arrived shortly after the railroad was built changed the name to Mariensfield. The name was changed to Stanton in 1890 after most of the German settlers had left and the new residents wanted to honor President Lincoln's Secretary of War, Edwin M. Stanton.

Open Tuesday through Saturday from 1 to 5 p.m. Admission, free.

STEPHENVILLE
Map 10

Stephenville Historical House Museum

525 East Washington   Stephenville 76401
No telephone   T, N

Several historic buildings are grouped to form the Stephenville Historical House Museum, including the J. D. Berry home, built in 1869, the carriage house, an 1899 gothic church, and two log cabins. The buildings are appropriately furnished for turn-of-the-century Stephenville, which was first settled in 1854.

Open Tuesday through Sunday from 2 to 5 p.m. Closed Monday. A donation is requested for admission.

Stonewall

See Johnson City

STRATFORD
Map 9

Sherman House Museum

213 N. Main Street   Stratford 79084
806/396-2494

This historic house museum is located in Stratford, which was named for Stratford-on-Avon, England, presumably because of its location on Coldwater Creek.

Open by appointment.

SULPHUR SPRINGS
Map 1

Hopkins County Museum and Heritage Park

416 N. Jackson Street   Sulphur Springs 75482
214/885-2387 or 885-5424

The house in which the museum is located was built in 1910 by George H. Wilson, a brick plant owner. On exhibit are items relating to the history of Hopkins County as well as carvings by a local artist. In the surrounding Heritage Park are a grist mill, syrup making machinery, a blacksmith shop, and a two-story log house. The museum also sponsors a tour of homes each year in April.

Open Saturday from 10 A.M. to 4 P.M., Sunday from 1 to 4 P.M. Admission, adults $1; children 12 and under $.50.

SUNSET
Map 1

Old West Museum
Sunset 76270
817/872-2027   H

Exhibits pertain to the Wells-Fargo Express, early ranching, and residents of the area, which was settled in 1881 and named by surveyors for the Fort Worth and Denver Railroad. Documents of the Republic of Texas, farm implements, artifacts and curios, and paintings by local artists are also displayed.

Open daily from 8 A.M. to 6 P.M. Admission, adults $.50, children under 12 free.

The Old West Museum, Sunset. Photograph by William Howze.

SWEETWATER
Map 10

City-County Pioneer Museum
610 E. Third Street   Sweetwater 79556
915/235-3627   H, T

Housed in the 1906 home of Judge and Mrs. R. A. Ragland, the City-County Pioneer Museum contains ten display rooms, including a pioneer kitchen, a collection of photographs of pioneers and early-day activities, antique furniture, an extensive Indian artifact collection, and a farm and ranch display. The Saddle Shop contains excellent examples of the craftsmanship of S. D. Myres, the famous saddle-maker.

Open Tuesday through Saturday from 2 to 5 P.M. Admission, free. Closed holidays.

Tahoka Pioneer Museum

1600 Lockwood (one block west of the traffic
light)   Tahoka 79373
806/998-5339   H

Relating to the history of Lynn County, the
displays of the Tahoka Pioneer Museum include
a blacksmith shop, a tack room, a bedroom,
kitchen, sheriff's office, dental office, school
room, and a church. Also on display are farm
implements, a windmill, a buggy, and several
hundred photographs of early days in Lynn
County, which was created out of Bexar County
in 1876 and organized in 1903. Adjacent to the
museum is the Pioneer Ranch Memorial Park,
developed by the Tahoka Garden Club in honor
of Cass O. Edwards, who established the first
permanent ranch on the lower South Plains in
1883.

Open Monday through Friday from 11 A.M. to
4 P.M. Closed Saturday and Sunday. Admission,
free.

Moody Museum

114 W. 9th Street   Taylor 76574
817/352-2485   H (downstairs only), T

The Moody Museum is the birthplace of Governor Daniel J. Moody, who served as Texas Attorney General (1925–1926) and Governor
(1927–1931). The governor's father purchased
the wood framehouse, which was constructed in
1887, when he moved his family to Taylor in
1890. Governor Moody was born there three
years later. He grew up in Taylor, eventually
serving as County Attorney of Williamson
County, then District Attorney of Williamson
and Travis counties. His sister, Mary, continued
to live in the house until 1970. The house with
its furnishings was presented to the city in 1978
to be used as a museum.

Open by appointment. Admission, free, but
donations are accepted.

Burlington–Rock Island Railroad Museum

208 S. Third Avenue   Teague 75860
817/739-2645   B, T, N, HABS

Housed in the old Trinity & Brazos Valley
Railroad Depot, the museum features history exhibits that include railroad memorabilia, the history of Teague schools, the Teague Volunteer
Fire Department (founded in 1907), an early
Texas room, a printing press room, and the Boyd
Room, which displays memorabilia relating to
Teague's first mayor. On the second floor are the

The Burlington–Rock Island Railroad Museum, Teague.

Military and Veterans Room, the local history rooms, the Boy Scouts Room, and the Teague Family Genealogical Research Center. The depot itself, a two-story Spanish Revival style structure, was designed by C. H. Page, Jr., and built in 1907.

Near the depot is the Colonel Benjamin A. Philpott log house, a two-room house constructed in the 1850s in nearby Freestone County near the community of Dew. It was moved to the museum and reassembled in 1975.

Open Saturday and Sunday from 1 to 5 P.M.; tours by appointment. Admission, adults $1, children $.50.

TEMPLE
Map 3

Railroad and Pioneer Museum
710 Jack Baskin Street (31st Street and Avenue H)   Temple 76501
817/778-6873   H

Housed in the old railroad depot from Moody, north of Temple on the Santa Fe line, the Railroad and Pioneer Museum recalls the history of the Central Texas area through exhibitions of objects, manuscripts, clippings, and artifacts, especially the significant role played by railroads as they built northward from Galveston through Central Texas during the 1880s. Also housed in the museum is an extensive collection of early tools, an authentic blacksmith shop, newspaper artifacts from the *Moody Courier,* and period clothing and memorabilia.

Open Tuesday through Saturday from 1 to 4 P.M. Admission, adults $.50; children $.25.

SPJST Museum
520 N. Main Street   Temple 76501
817/773-1575

The Slavonic Benevolent Order of the State of Texas founded this museum, which contains items brought from Czechoslovakia by immigrants who settled in America. Items on exhibit range from scarfs to plows. Other exhibits include a windmill, clothes, household utensils, a pioneer kitchen, a doctor's office, a blacksmith shop, a military display, and a replica of the first Czech home built in Texas.

Open 8 A.M. to noon, 1 to 5 P.M. daily. Admission, free.

TERRELL
Map 1

Silent Wings Museum
Municipal Airport   Terrell 75160
214/368-6097   B

The Silent Wings Museum contains gliders of World War II vintage, including a Waco CG4A combat glider. Also in the museum are various memorabilia of the war.

Open daily from 9 A.M. to 5 P.M. Admission, $5 for non-members.

Terrell Historical Museum
207 N. Frances Street   Terrell 75160
214/563-6463   T

In this general historical museum, exhibits relate to the pioneer and local history of Kaufman County. Settlement in the Terrell area began as early as 1848, but development of the town did not begin until after the arrival of the railroad in 1873.

Open Wednesday from 2 to 5 P.M. Group tours can be arranged by writing to P.O. Box 550, Terrell, 75160. Admission, free.

TEXARKANA
Map 2

Texarkana Historical Society and Museum
219 State Line Avenue   Texarkana 75504
214/793-4831   H, B, T, HABS

Located in the Offenhauser Building, the first brick building (1879) in Texarkana, the museum houses displays relating to archaeology and prehistory in the area as well as the history of the city and the region. The city was founded in 1873 as the builders of two railroads met on the state line between Arkansas and Texas. Many of the historic photographs in the library are used in the exhibitions. There is a small exhibit honoring Scott Joplin, the famous ragtime composer and performer, who was born near Texarkana. In addition, there are various room settings on the second floor, including a turn-of-the-century drugstore, doctor's office, and family rooms.

Open weekdays from 10 A.M. to 4 P.M., noon to 3 P.M. on Saturday and Sunday. Admission, free.

TEXAS CITY
Map 4

College of the Mainland Art Gallery
8001 Palmer Highway   Texas City 77591
409/762-7723, Ext. 348

The College of the Mainland Art Gallery features exhibitions of the work of regional as well as national artists. A regular series of lectures and workshops are also presented. Write or call for information.

Open Monday through Thursday from 10 A.M. to 4 P.M. and by appointment. Admission, free.

The Texarkana Historical Society, housed in the first brick structure in the city.

McMullen County Museum and Archives

S.H. 16   Tilden 78072
512/274-3305, 274-3341, or 784-3285   T
Located in the Old Rock Store on S.H. 16, the museum includes maps, books, pictures, a collection of family histories, and items used by Indians and early pioneers in McMullen County. The county was organized and the town founded in 1877.
Open Sunday from 2 to 5 P.M. and by appointment. Admission, free.

Charlton Museum

500 block of N. Pine   Tomball 77375
713/255-2148
The Charlton Museum, which includes farm equipment, a Texana library, a gun collection, and a horse-powered cotton press, deals with early Texas history. The museum, in a restored house with antique furnishings, also includes a replica of a church and a nineteenth-century doctor's office.
Open by appointment. Admission, adults $1; students $.50.

Swisher County Archives and Museum

Swisher Memorial Building
127 W. 2nd Street   Tulia 79088
806/995-2819   H
Exhibits relate to the history of Swisher County, which was organized in 1880. Of interest is the J. O. Bass workshop, a blacksmith shop containing its original turn-of-the-century equipment. Mr. Bass began making spurs and bits for the local cowboys in 1902. He ran a thriving business until his retirement in 1928.
Open Monday, Tuesday, Thursday, Friday, and Saturday from 1 to 4 P.M., Saturday from 9 A.M. to noon, Sunday by appointment. Admission, free.

Goodman Museum

624 North Broadway   Tyler 75701
214/597-5304   B, T, N, HABS
Constructed in the early 1860s and remodeled in 1880 and 1924, the Goodman House is an elegant reminder of the nineteenth- and early twentieth-century lifestyle in Tyler. The two front rooms and the central hall are the original structure, built by Samuel Gallatin Smith, a well-to-do young bachelor who called his house "Bonnie Castle." Dr. Samuel A. Goodman purchased the house from him, then sold it to his son, Dr. W. J. Goodman, whose name is still on

the brass name plate on the front door. On display in the museum are artifacts of East Texas Indians, Civil War flags, Dr. W. J. Goodman's instruments, various documents and weapons, antique furniture, and early photographs of Tyler and Smith County. Portraits of the Tyler Rose Festival queens line the wall of the circular stair leading to the second floor.

Open daily from 1 to 5 P.M. Closed Christmas and New Year's. Admission, free.

*Tyler Museum of Art

1300 S. Mahon Avenue   Tyler 75701
214/595-1001   H, B

Located in a handsome, contemporary building on the campus of Tyler Junior College, the Tyler Museum of Art features temporary exhibits, each focusing on an artist or collection of works. It is one of several small art museums in the state that frequently exhibit works by local and regional artists.

Open Tuesday through Saturday from 10 A.M. to 5 P.M., Sunday from 1 to 5 P.M. Admission, free.

UVALDE
Map 6

Garner Memorial Museum

333 N. Park Street   Uvalde 78801
512/278-5018   H, T

The large, two-story brick house was the home of Vice President and Mrs. John Nance Garner. When Mrs. Garner died in 1948, Mr. Garner, who served as Speaker of the U.S. House of Representatives and vice president under Franklin D. Roosevelt from 1932 to 1940, gave the house to the city of Uvalde as a memorial to his wife of fifty-three years and continued to live in the small cottage behind the house. When Mr. Garner died in 1967, just fifteen days short of his ninety-ninth birthday, he had served as congressman, speaker, and vice president for a total of thirty-eight years. On exhibit are Mr. Garner's collection of gavels as well as historical items pertaining to early Uvalde County settlement.

Open daily from 9 A.M. to noon, 1 to 5 P.M. Closed Sunday. Admission, free.

Uvalde's Grand Opera House Visitors Center

100 N. West Street, across from Fountain Plaza   Uvalde 78801
512/278-4082   B, T, N

The Briscoe Room, named in honor of Dolph Briscoe, Jr., who served as governor of Texas, is located in the Grand Opera House, which has

The Garner Memorial Museum, Uvalde.

The Briscoe Room is in the Grand Opera House, Uvalde.

recently been restored to its 1891 state. The exhibit traces the history of Uvalde from 1849 through 1920. The Opera House is also open to the public and shows a thirty-minute documentary film of "America's Biggest Train Robbery," the 1924 heist by the Newton brothers of Uvalde.

Call for hours. Admission, free.

Valley Mills Historical Museum
Santa Fe Park   Valley Mills 76689
No telephone   T

The history of the Valley Mills area is told here, beginning with exhibits concerning the Tonkawa Indians and continuing through the first settlers and the founding of the city, which was first settled in 1854 and incorporated in 1890. Also included are farming and ranching artifacts and the original mill stones that one of the pioneers brought from Arkansas.

Open the first and third Sunday of each month from 2 to 5 P.M. and by appointment. Admission, free.

Van Alstyne Museum
216 E. Jefferson Street   Van Alstyne 75095
214/482-5991

Van Alstyne grew out of nearby Mantua, which was established in nearby Collin County in 1854. This museum deals with the history of the area.

Open Monday through Friday from 1 to 4 P.M. Call for information on admission.

Lost Maples State Natural Area
Four miles north of Vanderpool on R.R. 187
Vanderpool 78885
512/966-3413   H, N

Lost Maples is an outstanding example of the Edwards Plateau flora and fauna. It features a large, isolated stand of the uncommon bigtooth maple, well-known for its splendid fall color. Rare species of birds, including the golden-cheeked warbler and the blackcapped vireo, have been seen in the park. An interpretive exhibit in the visitor center presents the natural history of the area. The self-guided trail is particularly popular in the fall.

Open daily from 8 A.M. to 5 P.M. Admission, $2 for car park and entrance fee.

Culbertson County Historical Museum
112 Commerce on U.S. 80   Van Horn 79855
915/283-2243   H, T, N

Located in the old Clark Hotel, the museum is dedicated to the history of Van Horn, which began as a water stop on the Texas and Pacific Railroad, and Culbertson County.

Open Sunday from 1 to 5 P.M., Monday from 9 A.M. to noon. Admission, free.

Bird Egg Collection of Robert L. More, Sr.

1907 Wilbarger Street   Vernon 76384
817/552-2506

More than 750 different kinds of eggs and bird species are on display in this private collection, which was started in 1888 by Robert L. More.

Open by appointment. Closed in the winter until Easter. Admission, free.

Red River Valley Museum

2030 Cumberland   Vernon 76384
817/553-4682 or 522-2936   H, T

On exhibit are items from the J. Henry Ray Collection of Indian Artifacts, sculpture by Electra Waggoner Biggs and others, a camera collection and photographs, and various other objects relating to the history of Vernon and Wilbarger County. Of special interest is an exhibit of antique barbed wire consisting of over 100 pieces. The museum, located in the old Vernon Clinic-Hospital Building, is also developing collections of historical and scientific interest to the area.

Open daily from 1 to 5 P.M. Admission, free.

McNamara House

502 North Liberty Street   Victoria 77901
512/575-8227   H (in the planning), T

This historic house contains period rooms, local history exhibits, and space for temporary exhibitions of history, design arts, and local artists' shows. The house itself is a beautiful example of a symmetrical Victorian frame house. An unusual feature is its construction in two separate sections connected by a long porch or gallery. The back wing contained the family dining room, kitchen, and Mr. McNamara's office, which had separate outside entrances.

Open Tuesday from 10 A.M. to noon, 1 to 5 P.M.; Wednesday and Thursday from 10 A.M. to noon, 3 to 5 P.M.; and Sunday from 3 to 5 P.M. Other times by appointment. Admission, free.

The Nave Museum

306 West Commercial   Victoria 77901
512/575-8227   H

The Nave Museum was constructed as a memorial to Texas artist Royston Nave, who specialized in portraits and Texas landscapes. A native of La Grange, Nave (b. 1886) studied with Pompeo Coppini in San Antonio and in New York with such well known artists as Walt Kuhn, Lawton Parker, and Robert Henri. Following his marriage to Emma McFaddin McCan, Nave moved to Victoria, where he continued his

The McNamara House, Victoria. Photograph by Todd Webb. Courtesy Amon Carter Museum, Fort Worth.

The Nave Museum, Victoria. Photograph by Phil Martin.

painting. He died unexpectedly at age 44 in 1930. The museum owns a collection of his work and presents eight other exhibitions each year.

Open Tuesday through Sunday from 1 to 5 P.M. Mornings by appointment. Admission, free.

The Texas Zoo
110 Memorial Drive (in Memorial Park)
Victoria 77901
512/573-7681   B, R

Located in a park and recreational setting, the Texas Zoo contains a number of animals native to Texas: javelina, prairie dogs, deer, and other indigenous creatures. The indoor and outdoor exhibits include more than 200 animals of 93 different native Texas species of mammals, reptiles, birds, amphibians, and fish.

Open September through May from 10 A.M. to 5 P.M. daily; May to August from 10 A.M. to 5 P.M. Monday through Friday; 10 A.M. to 7 P.M. Saturday and Sunday. Admission, adults $1.50; children age 6 to 12 $.50; under 6 and senior citizens free.

VIOLET
Map 5

Violet Museum

12 miles west of Corpus Christi on S.H. 44
Violet 78380
512/387-2273   T, N

The Violet Museum is housed in the old German Catholic Church built in 1910 and also used as the rural community's first school. The museum includes the original altar and the wooden pump organ, which was imported in 1916. Other exhibits include various memorabilia such as a mechanical ant killer and a funeral pickup basket.

The museum is open the first Sunday after Easter and the second Sunday in October from 11 A.M. to 4 P.M. Group tours may be arranged by appointment. Admission, adults $1; children $.75.

WACO
Map 3

The Art Center

1300 College Drive   Waco 76708
817/752-4371   H, B

The Art Center is located in the old William Waldo Cameron summer home, Valley View. Cameron, a lumber magnate, chose what he considered to be the most beautiful site in Waco, a high bluff overlooking the valleys of the Brazos and Bosque rivers, for his retreat that was planned as a simple summer cottage but that evolved into a Mediterranean style mansion with pergolas, pool, and cabana. The mansion, now a part of the campus of McLennon Community College and adjacent to the 500-acre Cameron Park, was adapted for museum use by the San Antonio architectural firm of Ford, Powell, & Carson.

The Art Center annually presents twelve to fourteen historic and contemporary exhibitions in the fields of folk art, graphic and industrial design, photography, crafts, and architecture in addition to the regularly featured paintings, drawings, prints, and sculpture. Plans have been made to turn the swimming pool into a sculp-

The Art Center, Waco.

ture garden, which has featured work by such
well-known Texas artists as Robert Wade, Herb
Rogalla, and James Surls. There are tours,
classes, and various other programs as well.

Open Tuesday through Saturday from 10 A.M.
to 5 P.M., Sunday from 1 to 5 P.M. Admission,
free.

Baylor University
Armstrong Browning Library
Eighth and Speight Streets   Waco 76706
817/755-3566

The Browning Library was founded in 1918
when Dr. A. Joseph Armstrong presented to Baylor University his private collection of Browning mementoes. The Library includes all first
editions of the works of English poets Robert
Browning and Elizabeth Barrett Browning, most
books about their lives and works, and most of
the major scholarly articles about them. Hundreds of other miscellaneous items are also included: the largest collection of original Browning letters as well as an extensive collection of
letters written to them, for example. On display
are hundreds of likenesses of the two poets as
well as the bronze cast of their clasped hands,
made from life in 1853 by the American sculptor
Harriet Hosmer.

The Library is housed in an imposing building
that was constructed from 1949 to 1951. Panels
of the bronze entrance doors illustrate ten of
Robert Brownings poems. The fifty-two stained-
glass windows of the library each depict a poem
of one of the Brownings. The Hankamer Trea-

sure Room is a museum and exhibit hall; the Jones Research Hall serves as the main library reading room; and the McLean Foyer of Meditation, the architectural highlight of the Library, is a forty-foot cube with a 23-karat gold dome that has three cathedral windows and eight Levanto columns from Italy. Furniture, jewelry, personal books, and other memorabilia of the Brownings can be seen and examined.

Open weekdays from 9 A.M. to noon, 2 to 4 P.M., Saturday from 9 A.M. to noon. Admission, free.

Baylor University
*Strecker Museum
Sid Richardson Science Building
South 4th Street   Waco 76798
817/755-1110   H (limited accessibility), B

Founded in 1893 and named for John Kern Strecker, who served as curator from 1903 until his death in 1933, the museum features natural science exhibitions on space, rocks, minerals, fossils, plants, invertebrate animals, fish, reptiles, amphibians, birds, mammals, and prehistoric and recent man in Central Texas. The museum exhibits the largest fossil marine turtle known. Based on the collections of the museum, which have been building since a teaching collection was formed in 1857 when Baylor University was located at Independence, Texas, the exhibitions are periodically changed and are often combined with loan collections from other museums. There is a "living museum" of amphibians and reptiles. The museum also serves as a research facility for the University and is heavily involved in educational programs, expeditions and field trips, and care of the large permanent collection.

Open Monday through Friday from 9 A.M. to 4 P.M., Saturday from 10 A.M. to 1 P.M., Sunday from 2 to 5 P.M. Call for holiday schedule. Admission, free.

Earle-Harrison House
1901 N. 5th Street   Waco 76708
No telephone   H, T

Built in 1858–59 by Dr. Baylis Wood Earle and his wife, Eliza Ann Harrison Earle, the house features period decorative arts and artifacts. Constructed in the popular Greek Revival style, it was later owned by Civil War veteran, General Thomas Harrison. It was restored in 1969 and contains displays relating to the Texas Cotton Palace (1894–1930) as well as costumes and other mementoes of Waco.

Open by appointment. Admission, $2.

Earle-Napier-Kinnard House

814 S. 4th Street   Waco 76706
817/756-0057   T, HABS

John Bayliss Earle built the original portion of this house in 1860; it was enlarged in 1868 by J. S. Napier. It is an outstanding example of classicism in architecture which swept the Deep South during the mid-nineteenth century. It has been restored and furnished primarily with Empire and early Victorian pieces.

Open Saturday and Sunday from 2 to 5 P.M. Admission, adults $2.00; children $1.50; children under 6 free.

East Terrace

100 Mill Street   Waco 76704
817/756-4101   T, HABS

Standing on the east bank of the Brazos River, East House was constructed by J. W. Mann in 1872. This architecturally adventurous house has now been restored and furnished with period furnishings.

Open Saturday and Sunday from 2 to 5 P.M. Admission, adults $2; children $1.50; children under 6 free.

Fort House Museum

503 S. Fourth Street   Waco 76706
817/756-4161   T, HABS

Fort House was constructed at the corner of Fourth and Webster in 1869 by Colonel William Aldredge Fort, who came to Waco from Alabama before the Civil War. Neo-classical in style, the mansion was restored in 1960.

Open Saturday and Sunday from 2 to 5 P.M. Admission, adults $2; children $1.50; children under 6 free.

Lee Lockwood Texas Scottish Rite Library and Museum

3801 W. Waco Drive   Waco 76707
817/754-3942

Exhibitions and collections relate to the history of Masonry and Texas.

Open Monday through Friday from 9 A.M. to 4 P.M. Admission, free.

The Earle-Napier-Kinnard House in Waco is a good example of the neo-classicism of the mid-nineteenth century. Photograph by Todd Webb. Courtesy Amon Carter Museum, Fort Worth.

The Fort House, Waco. Photograph by Todd Webb. Courtesy Amon Carter Museum, Fort Worth.

McCulloch House

407 Columbus Avenue   Waco 76701
817/753-5166   T, HABS

The McCulloch House was constructed by Josiah Caldwell and his wife, Maria, in 1866. The original one-story house consisted of two rooms (which are now the east wing) and a detached kitchen. In January, 1871, the property was sold to Champe Carter McCulloch and his wife, Emma Bassett. They built the present two-story Greek Revival residence, which remained the property of their family until 1971.

Open Saturday and Sunday from 2 to 5 P.M. Admission, adults $2; children $1.50; children under 6 free.

Masonic Grand Lodge Library and Museum of Texas

715 Columbus Avenue   Waco 76703
817/753-7395   H

Created to preserve the records, artifacts, and history of the Masons in Texas, the Masonic Grand Lodge Library and Museum of Texas includes various displays on Texas history.

Open weekdays from 9 A.M. to 4 P.M., except holidays. Admission, free.

Sims Log Cabin

1020 Sleepy Hollow   Waco 76710
817/772-3202   T

This Freestone County log cabin, built in 1851, has been restored and moved to Waco. A one-room house built of oak, it contains Indian relics as well as period furnishings and memorabilia.

Open by appointment. Admission, free.

Texas Ranger Hall of Fame and Museum

I-35 and the Brazos River   Waco 76703
817/754-1433   H, B, R

This reconstruction of Fort Fisher, located near the site of the 1837 Texas Ranger outpost, serves as headquarters of Company F of the Texas Rangers, Waco Tourist Information Center, and Homer Garrison, Jr., Memorial Museum. The Texas Ranger Hall of Fame depicts the more than 150 years of Ranger history through a multimedia presentation, exhibits, and life-sized wax figures in natural settings. The Homer Garrison, Jr., Memorial Museum

The Texas Ranger Hall of Fame and Museum, Waco.

honors the man who served as director of the Texas Department of Public Safety and Commander of the Texas Rangers for more than 36 years until his death in 1968.

Open daily from 9 A.M. to 5 P.M. from September 1 through May 31, until 6 P.M. from June 1 through August 31. Admission, adults $2.50, children $1.50. In groups of ten or more, admission, adults $2, children $1. Closed New Year's Day, Thanksgiving, and Christmas.

Texas Tennis Museum & Hall of Fame
Waco Drive at 14th   Waco 76707
817/756-2307

Sponsored by the Texas Tennis Association and the City of Waco, the Texas Tennis Museum is one of the newest museums of its kind in the country. Although the museum is not complete, there are several exhibits on view such as "Tennis Towns of Texas," featuring various cities and their outstanding tennis personalities, and the "Hall of Fame," which features portraits of the first six inductees.

In the same building are the Texas High School Football and Basketball Halls of Fame. The Paul Tyson Football Memorial also occupies one room.

Open Wednesday through Sunday from 2 to 5 P.M. Other hours by appointment. Admission, free.

Youth Cultural Center
815 Columbus Avenue   Waco 76703
817/752-9641, Ext. 36   H (to first floor only)

A children's museum, the Youth Cultural Center tells the story of civilization from prehistoric times to the space age. There are thirteen rooms and two halls of exhibition space.

The display halls are open from 9 A.M. to 4 P.M. Monday through Friday. The room tours are open Monday through Friday from 9 A.M. to noon and by appointment. Admission, free.

WASHINGTON
Map 3

Washington-on-the-Brazos State Historical Park
Anson Jones Home
Washington 77880
409/878-2214   H, T, HABS

Barrington, the plantation home of Dr. Anson Jones, medical doctor, prosperous planter, member of the first Congress of Texas, Secretary of State, Minister to the United States, and last President of the Republic, was built in 1844. Jones was president when Texas was annexed into the United States in 1845. The home was moved to the park from its original location in 1936. It was restored and refurnished in 1970.

Open daily from 10 A.M. to 5 P.M. from March 1 through Labor Day; Wednesday through Sunday 10 A.M. to 5 P.M. between Labor Day and March 1. Admission, adults $.50; children 6 to 12 $.25.

Washington-on-the-Brazos State Historical Park
Independence Hall
Washington 77880
409/878-2214   H, T

This building is a reconstruction of the building where Texas independence from Mexico was declared and where Sam Houston was appointed commander-in-chief of the Texas army. Exhibits pertain to the Republic of Texas. There is a thirteen-minute slide show on the Convention of 1836 that adopted the declaration of independence and wrote the constitution of the new republic.

Open daily from 10 A.M. to 5 P.M. from March 1 through Labor Day; Wednesday through Sunday from 10 A.M. to 5 P.M. between Labor Day and March 1. Admission, free.

Washington-on-the-Brazos State Historical Park
*Star of the Republic Museum
Washington 77880
409/878-2461   H, B, T

Located in Washington-on-the-Brazos State Historical Park, the Star of the Republic Museum, founded in 1970, honors the site of the signing of the Texas Declaration of Indepen-

Star of the Republic Museum, Washington-on-the-Brazos.

dence and the last capital of the Republic of Texas. The museum is dedicated to presenting the history of the Texas Republic through exhibits, publications, and media presentations. Exhibits depict all aspects of the Republic period, including social life, agriculture, transportation, politics, and military affairs. Special programs for groups are available by reservation. The Museum's research library, which includes a collection of rare books, maps, and manuscripts, is available to the public for research.

Open Wednesday through Sunday 10 A.M. to 5 P.M., September 1 through February 28; daily from 10 A.M. to 5 P.M. March 1 through August 31. Admission, free.

WAXAHACHIE
Map 1

Ellis County Museum

201 S. College (Courthouse Square)
Waxahachie 75165
214/937-9383   T, N, R

Housed in a former Masonic Hall and commercial building, the Ellis County Museum is in the process of restoring the building to its 1890s appearance. Exhibitions, including artifacts and photographs, pertain to the history of Waxahachie and Ellis County, which dates from the 1840s and '50s.

Open Monday and Wednesday from 9 A.M. to 5 P.M., Sunday from 1 to 5 P.M. Admission, free.

Mahoney-Thompson House

604 W. Main   Waxahachie 75165
214/937-1061   T

Designed and built by Dennis Mahoney in 1904, this elegant Greek Revival mansion was acquired by the Ellis County Museum in 1968. It features fine, exotic woods and Czechoslovakian beveled glass. It contains the Cheatham collection of antique fans, porcelains, and furniture.

Open Monday and Wednesday from 9 A.M. to 5 P.M., Sunday from 1 to 5 P.M. Admission, free.

WEATHERFORD
Map 1

Weatherford Depot Museum

410 Fort Worth Street   Weatherford 76086
817/594-3801
H (but a six-inch step at the entrance), T

The old Santa Fe depot, constructed in the traditional southwestern desert style by the Santa Fe Railroad in 1907, has been restored and turned into a historic museum. At that time, Weatherford was a metropolis, with six hotels, three national banks, seven saloons, and, of course, three railroads, which had turned the town into a city upon their arrival in the 1880s. Today the museum, resplendent in its copper, verde green, and salmon desert-color scheme, recalls the halcyon days of early Weatherford. The Jim Crow laws, which required segregation in public places, are evident in the restoration. The old Tappan "Frost Killer" wood stove is the centerpiece.

Call for open hours and admission.

WELLINGTON
Map 9

Collingsworth County Museum

1404 15th Street   Wellington 79095
806/447-5857

Most of the exhibits in the Collingsworth County Museum reflect rural life in West Texas. Included in the exhibits are displays of early dentistry, homes, farming, schools, and churches. Many of the items can be touched and explored by the visitor.

Open by appointment. Call in advance for tour.

WESLACO
Map 5

Weslaco Bicultural Museum

527 S. Kansas   Weslaco 78956
512/968-9142   B

The Weslaco Bicultural Museum examines the history of Weslaco through artifacts, furniture, photographs, and magazine clippings. Built in the late 1920s as a church and later converted to police headquarters, the building has been furnished with material from a variety of local families. Special exhibits include a display of old telephones, an early switchboard, and photographs of the mayors of the city. Changing exhibitions are also presented.

Open Wednesday and Thursday from 2 to 4 P.M. and Friday from 10 A.M. to noon and 2 to 4 P.M. Admission, free.

WEST COLUMBIA
Map 4

Varner-Hogg Plantation House

F.M. 2852 off S.H. 35, 2 miles northwest of town   West Columbia 77486
409/345-4656   T, HABS

Named for the first Anglo-American owner of the land, Martin Varner, and the last, former Governor James Stephen Hogg, the Varner-Hogg Plantation House was constructed c. 1835 by Columbus R. Patton and was known as "the Patton place" throughout much of the nineteenth century. Governor Hogg purchased the property in 1901 as a country and weekend home. After discovery of oil at Spindletop, he came to believe that equal quantities of oil lay beneath the surface of his plantation. He drilled several wells,

The Varner-Hogg Plantation House, outside West Columbia.

but oil was not discovered until 14 years later when the West Columbia field was brought in. His four children, Will, Ima, Mike, and Tom remodeled the home in 1920. Miss Hogg presented it to the state in 1958, furnished to show how an antebellum family of means might have lived.

Open Tuesday, Thursday, Friday, and Saturday from 10 to 11:30 A.M. and 1 to 4:30 P.M.; Sunday from 1 to 4:30 P.M. Admission, adults $.50; children under 13 $.25.

WHARTON
Map 4

Wharton County Historical Museum
231 Fulton   Wharton 77488
409/532-2600   H

The Wharton County Historical Museum features exhibitions that relate to the history of the county, including the "Shanghai" Pierce collection (he was a famous cattleman and rancher and importer of the first Brahman cattle), the Albert Clinton Horton exhibit (he was the first lieutenant governor of Texas), and artifacts from the period of the Republic. There are historical photographs on exhibit as well as other objects and artifacts. The first oil well "Christmas Tree" used on the Pierce Ranch is now mounted on the museum lawn. Special exhibits describe the world's largest sulphur dome, located in Wharton County, and Medal of Honor Recipient Master Sergeant Roy P. Benavidez, a member of the Green Berets and a hero of the Vietnam War.

The Kell House, Wichita Falls.

Open from 1 to 5 P.M. Tuesday through Saturday, 2 to 5 P.M. on Sunday. Admission, free.

WHEELER
Map 9

Old Mobeetie Museum
Old Mobeetie Jail   Wheeler 79096
806/826-3289   B, T
The Old Mobeetie Museum is located in the old rock jail, which was constructed in 1886, when Mobeetie was one of the only cities in the Texas Panhandle. There is a Hide Town display, a replica of a general store, and an antique barber shop. The original gallows is still in place. Also on display is a replica of old Fort Elliott, which was established nearby in 1875.

Open Monday and Wednesday through Saturday from 10 A.M. to 5 P.M., Sunday from 1 to 5 P.M. Admission, free. Camper hookups are available.

WICHITA FALLS
Map 10

Kell House
900 Bluff   Wichita Falls 76301
817/723-0623   T, N
The Kell House was built in 1909 by Frank Kell, a Wichita Falls pioneer. Restored, it now contains the original Kell family furnishings as well as textiles, photographs, and clothing from the 1909 to 1940 period. The architecture is distinctive with intricate woodwork and handsome design for this period.

275

Open Sunday from 2 to 4 P.M. for guided tours. Admission, nominal. Group tours at other times by reservation.

*Wichita Falls Museum and Art Center
Two Eureka Circle   Wichita Falls 78308
817/692-0923   H, B
    Begun in 1967, the Wichita Falls Museum and Art Center is a multi-purpose museum for art, science, and history. Art exhibitions encompassing a wide variety of periods and styles change approximately every six weeks. History and science exhibitions change approximately every three to six months. A special emphasis of the history program is the development of North Texas.
    The museum's permanent art collection consists of over 350 prints organized around the theme of "the history of American art through prints." The collection covers most major movements and themes in American art, from colonial days to the present. Beginning with a 1677 print of New England by John Foster, America's first printmaker, it includes works by such masters as Paul Revere, Rembrandt Peale, Fitz Hugh Lane, Asher Durand, Winslow Homer, Mary Cassatt, John Sloan, Jasper Johns, Jackson Pollack, and Leonard Baskin. The museum also houses a substantial collection of historical photographs and negatives primarily relating to the history of North Texas.
    Open from 9 A.M. to 4:30 P.M. Monday through Saturday, 1 to 5 P.M. on Sunday. Admission, free.

WIMBERLEY
Map 6

Pioneer Town
One mile south of Wimberley, 7A Ranch Resort   Wimberley 78676
512/847-2517   H, B, R, T
    This restored and reproduced nineteenth-century Texas village includes a cafe serving early day menus, a gunshop, a printing shop, barber shop, jail, ice cream parlor, emporium, hotel, arcade, opera house with melodrama and vaudeville shows, blacksmith shop, and a Western art gallery.
    Open June through August daily from 10 A.M. to 10 P.M.; September through May, weekends from 1 to 5:30 P.M. Closed December 10 to February 15. Admission: parking $.25.

Pioneer Town, Wimberley.

WINK
Map 7

Helmer Mercantile Lock & Tool Museum
123 N. Pyote Street   Wink 79789
915/527-3469   B

A private museum founded in 1980 and devoted to the "memory of the Craftsmen and Locksmiths, who forged the future of Amerca," the Helmer Mercantile Museum is located in the old Baker Sign Company building, constructed in 1928. There are displays of nineteenth-century tools as well as later tools related to the ranching and oil business in West Texas. Outdoor exhibits include an old ranch hand shack and an old Winkler County fire truck.

Open Sunday from 2 to 6 P.M. Special tours on weekdays by appointment. Admission, free.

WINTERS
Map 10

Z. I. Hale Museum
242 West Dale Street   Winters 79567
No telephone

This history museum contains antiques and other objects relating to community life, farming tools, early school items, antique doctor's office, a turn-of-the century bedroom and other displays from early settlement of the Winters area.

Open from 2 until 4 P.M. the second Sunday of each month and on special occasions.

Allan Shivers Museum

302 N. Charlton Street (two blocks north of the Courthouse)   Woodville 75979
409/283-3709

This Victorian dwelling was purchased by former Governor and Mrs. Allan Shivers to house the memorabilia of Shivers's term as governor. Displays include the Shivers's inaugural clothes and their daughter's festival gowns as well as an African Safari Room, a Freedom Shrine, a historical mural, and a number of original cartoons relating to the governor's public life.

Open weekdays from 9 A.M. to 5 P.M., Saturday from 10 A.M. to 2 P.M., and Sunday by appointment. Guided tours are available. Admission, adults $.50; children over 6 $.25. Groups of fifteen or more get a discount with advance reservations.

Heritage Garden Village

U.S. 190 West, just outside the city limits
Woodville 75979
409/283-2272   H (partially), B, R

More than thirty furnished buildings are on display at the Heritage Garden Village, including the Collier Store (stocked with materials from the original store), a railroad station made from materials from a station on the Texas and New Orleans line, and the Tolar log cabin, which was moved intact from its original site.

Open daily except New Year's Day, Thanksgiving, and Christmas. Admission, adults $1.50; children 6 to 12 $.75.

Yorktown Historical Museum

Corner of W. Main & Eckhardt Streets
Yorktown 78164
512/564-2661   T, HABS

Located in the Eckhardt Building, constructed in 1876, the Yorktown Historical Museum houses exhibits relating to the history of the area, such as the first fire pumper and uniforms of the Yorktown Volunteer Fire Department and quilts and china belonging to pioneer residents. The Eckhardt Building is an excellent example of commercial architecture during the latter part of the nineteenth century: a simple structure of plastered limestone built to house William Eckhardt's dry goods store.

Open Thursday and Sunday from 3 to 5 P.M., except during December, January, and February, when the museum is open on Sunday only from 2 to 5 P.M.

Heritage Garden Village, just outside Woodville.

The old Eckhardt Building houses the Yorktown Historical Museum. Photograph by Todd Webb. Courtesy Amon Carter Museum, Fort Worth.

APPENDIX

The museums are listed in the guide under the city in alphabetical order. If the entry in the Appendix contains a *see* reference, look under the name of the city, then under the *see* reference, then under the name of the museum.

ART MUSEUMS

Abilene Fine Arts Museum, Abilene
Amarillo Art Center, Amarillo
American National Insurance Tower, Galveston
Amon Carter Museum of Western Art, Fort Worth. *See Amon Carter Square*
Art Center, Waco
Art League of Houston Gallery, Houston
Art Museum of South Texas, Corpus Christi
Bayou Bend, Houston
Beaumont Art Museum, Beaumont
Biblical Arts Center, Dallas
Brown-Lupton Gallery, Fort Worth. *See Texas Christian University*
Brownsville Art League Museum, Brownsville
Carver Community Cultural Center, San Antonio
College of the Mainland Art Gallery, Texas City
Contemporary Arts Museum, Houston. *See Montrose Area*
Cowboy Artists of America Museum, Kerrville
Dallas Museum of Art, Dallas. *See Fair Park*
Diamond M Foundation Museum, Snyder
El Paso Museum of Art, El Paso
Elisabet Ney Studio, Austin
Fort Worth Art Museum, Fort Worth. *See Amon Carter Square*
Gaines County Museum and Art Center, Seagraves
Galveston Arts Center Gallery, Galveston. *See The Strand*
Hood County Museum, Granbury
Houston Center for Photography, Houston
Huntington Art Gallery, Austin. *See University of Texas at Austin*
Kimbell Art Museum, Fort Worth. *See Amon Carter Square*
La Lomita Farms Regional Museum, Mission
Laguna Gloria Art Museum, Austin
Leeds Gallery, Austin. *See University of Texas at Austin*
Longview Museum and Art Center, Longview
McAllen International Museum, McAllen
McNamara House, Victoria
Marion Koogler McNay Art Museum, San Antonio
Meadows Museum, Dallas. *See Southern Methodist University*
Memorial Student Center Gallery, College Station. *See Texas A&M University*
Moody Hall Atrium Gallery, Austin
Moudy Exhibition Space, Fort Worth. *See Texas Christian University*
Municipal Garden and Arts Center, Lubbock
Museo del Barrio de Austin, Austin
Museum of American Architecture and Decorative Arts, Houston
Museum of Fine Arts, Houston. *See Montrose Area*
Museum of Printing History, Houston
Museum of the Southwest, Midland
Nave Museum, Victoria
O'Kane Gallery, Houston
Old Jail Foundation, Inc., Albany

Plano Cultural Arts Center, Plano
Rice Museum, Houston. *See Rice University*
Rosenberg Library, Galveston
Rothko Chapel, Houston
Rudder Exhibit Hall, College Station. *See Texas A&M University*
San Antonio Museum of Art, San Antonio
Sarah Campbell Blaffer Gallery, Houston
Sewall Art Gallery, Houston. *See Rice University*
Sid Richardson Collection of Western Art, Fort Worth. *See Sundance Square*
Stark Museum of Art, Orange
Texas Tech Museum, Lubbock. *See Texas Tech University*
Texas Woman's University Art Museum, Denton. *See Texas Woman's University*
Tyler Museum of Art, Tyler
University Art Gallery, Arlington. *See University of Texas at Arlington*
University of Houston Gallery, Houston
Wichita Falls Museum and Art Center, Wichita Falls

COLLECTIONS

ACU Museum, Abilene
Aikin Regional Archives, Paris
Antique Dollhouse Museum, Galveston
Armstrong Browning Library, Waco. *See Baylor University*
Audie Murphy Room, Greenville
Babe Didrikson Zaharias Memorial, Beaumont
Barrow Foundation Museum, Eola
Bird Egg Collection of Robert L. More, Sr., Vernon
Bullfight Museum, El Paso
Church Heritage Center, El Paso
Confederate Research Center, Hillsboro
Danner Museum of Telephony, San Angelo
Dutch Windmill Museum, Nederland
Fields Museum of Fine Living, Haskell
Garner Memorial Museum, Uvalde
Helmer Mercantile Lock & Tool Museum, Wink
Heritage Garden Village, Woodville
Heritage Room, Hurst. *See Fort Worth*
Hertzberg Circus Museum, San Antonio. *See Downtown Area*
History of Aviation Collection, Richardson
Hogg Memorial Museum, Rusk
Houston Police Department Museum, Houston
Jersey Lilly Saloon, San Antonio
Layland Museum, Cleburne
McCord Theater Collection, Dallas. *See Southern Methodist University*
Moody Museum, Taylor
Museum of Oriental Cultures, Corpus Christi
Museum of Time, Granbury
National Cowgirl Hall of Fame, Hereford
Neiman-Marcus ArchiveShowcase, Dallas
Old Clock Museum, Pharr
Rangerette Showcase-Museum, Kilgore. *See Kilgore College*
Sam Rayburn Library, Bonham
Shivers Museum, Woodville
Sid Richardson Museum, Belton
Special Collections, Texas College of Osteopathic Medicine, Fort Worth. *See Amon Carter Square*
Texas Railroad Museum, Fort Worth
Texas Tennis Museum & Hall of Fame, Waco

Texas Woman's University Historical Collection, Denton. *See Texas Woman's University*
Texas' First Ladies Historic Costume Collection, Denton. *See Texas Woman's University*
Wright Collection, Sierra Blanca

GARDENS

Aboretum Inc., Arp
Dallas Arboretum & Botanical Society, Dallas. See *White Rock Lake Park*
Dallas Civic Garden Center, Dallas. *See Fair Park*
Fort Worth Botanic Garden, Fort Worth
Galveston Garden Center, Galveston
Lajitas Museum and Desert Garden, Lajitas
Mabel Davis Rose Garden, Austin
Municipal Garden and Arts Center, Lubbock

GENERAL MUSEUMS

Chamizal National Memorial Museum, El Paso
Corpus Christi Museum, Corpus Christi
El Campo Museum of Art, History, & Natural Science, El Campo
El Paso Centennial Museum, El Paso
Fort Worth Museum of Science and History, Fort Worth. *See Amon Carter Square*
Gaines County Museum and Art Center, Seagraves
Historical and Creative Arts Center, Lufkin
Houston Museum of Natural Science, Houston. *See Hermann Park*
Lajitas Museum and Desert Garden, Lajitas
McAllen International Museum, McAllen
Museum of the Southwest, Midland
Texas Memorial Museum, Austin. *See University of Texas at Austin*
Texas Tech Museum, Lubbock. *See Texas Tech University*
Witte Memorial Museum, San Antonio. *See Brackenridge Park*

HISTORICAL MUSEUMS

Admiral Nimitz State Historical Park, Fredericksburg
African-American Cultural Heritage Center, Dallas
Alabama-Coushatta Indian Reservation, Livingston
Asian-American Cultural Heritage Center, Dallas
Austin Memorial Center, Cleveland
Barker Texas History Center, Austin. *See University of Texas at Austin*
Burleson House, San Marcos. *See Aquarena Springs*
Cattlemen's Museum, Fort Worth
Chamizal National Memorial Museum, El Paso
Charles D. Tandy Archaeology Museum, Fort Worth
Corpus Christi Museum, Corpus Christi
Cowboy Country Museum, Stamford
Dallas Historical Society, Dallas. *See Fair Park*
Daughters of the Republic of Texas Museum, Austin. *See State Capitol Complex*
East Texas Oil Museum, Kilgore. *See Kilgore College*
El Campo Museum of Art, History, & Natural Science, El Campo
El Paso Centennial Museum, El Paso
El Paso Museum of History, El Paso
Fire Museum of Texas, Grand Prairie
Fort Leaton State Historic Site, Presidio
Franks Antique Shop and Doll Museum, Marshall
Frontier Times Museum, Bandera
George Washington Carver Museum, Austin
Gonzales Memorial Museum, Gonzales

Hall of Texas History, San Antonio. *See Downtown Area*
Historical Collection, Denton
Historical and Creative Arts Center, Lufkin
History of Aviation Collection, Richardson
Houston Museum of Natural Science, Houston. *See Hermann Park*
Houston Public Library, Houston
Hoya Memorial Library and Museum, Nacogdoches
Independence Hall, Washington. *See Washington-on-the-Brazos State Historical Park*
Institute of Texan Cultures, San Antonio. *See Downtown Area*
International Museum of Cultures, Dallas
Jefferson Historical Museum, Jefferson
John E. Connor Museum, Kingsville
Jourdan Bachman Pioneer Farm, Austin
La Maison des Acadiens, Nederland
Lee Lockwood Texas Scottish Rite Library and Museum, Waco
Los Nogales Museum, Seguin
Lyndon B. Johnson National Historical Park, Johnson City
Lyndon B. Johnson Space Center, Houston
Lyndon B. Johnson State Historical Park, Johnson City
Lyndon Baines Johnson Library and Museum, Austin. *See University of Texas at Austin*
McAllen International Museum, McAllen
Mark Withers Trail Driver Museum, Lockhart
Masonic Grand Lodge Library and Museum of Texas, Waco
Mexican-American Cultural Heritage Center, Dallas
Museum of African-American Life and Culture, Dallas
Museum of Printing History, Houston
National Broadcast Museum, Dallas
Native American Cultural Heritage Center, Dallas
Nita Stewart Haley Memorial Library, Midland
Old Trail Drivers Association, San Antonio. *See Brackenridge Park*
Panhandle-Plains Historical Museum, Canyon
Permian Basin Petroleum Museum, Midland
Presidential Museum, Odessa
Red Horse Museum, Mercedes
Rosenberg Library, Galveston
Sam Houston Memorial Museum, Huntsville
Sam Houston Regional Library, Liberty
San Jacinto Museum of History, Houston. *See San Jacinto Battleground*
Sophienburg Memorial Museum, New Braunfels
Special Collections Department, Arlington. *See University of Texas at Arlington*
Star of the Republic Museum, Washington. *See Washington-on-the-Brazos State Historical Park*
Stone Fort Museum, Nacogdoches
Texas American Indian Museum, Granbury
Texas Confederate Museum, Austin. *See State Capitol Complex*
Texas Forestry Museum, Lufkin
Texas Memorial Museum, Austin. *See University of Texas at Austin*
Texas Ranger Hall of Fame and Museum, Waco
Texas Sports Hall of Fame, Grand Prairie
Texas State Library, Austin. *See State Capitol Complex*
Texas Tech Museum, Lubbock. *See Texas Tech University*
Wax Museum, Grand Prairie
Western Company Museum, Fort Worth
Wichita Falls Museum and Art Center, Wichita Falls
Witte Memorial Museum, San Antonio. *See Brackenridge Park*
Youth Cultural Center, Waco

HISTORIC BUILDING MUSEUMS

Annie Riggs Memorial Museum, Fort Stockton
Archer County Historical Museum, Archer City
Burlington–Rock Island Railroad Museum, Teague
Callahan County Pioneer Museum, Baird
Carson County Square House Museum, Panhandle
Center for Transportation and Commerce, Galveston. *See The Strand*
Coupland Museum, Coupland
Courthouse-on-the-Square Museum, Denton
Daughters of the Republic of Texas Museum, Austin. *See State Capitol Complex*
Fire Hall Museum, Crowell
Foard County Courthouse Museum, Crowell
Fort Belknap Museum, Newcastle
Fort Bliss Replica Museum, El Paso. *See Fort Bliss*
Fort Concho National Historic Landmark, San Angelo
Fort Duncan Museum, Eagle Pass
Fort Griffin State Historical Park, Albany
Fort Lancaster Visitor Center, Sheffield
Fort Mason Officers Quarters, Mason
Fort McKavett State Historic Site, Fort McKavett
Fort Richardson State Park, Jacksboro
Fort Sam Houston Museum, San Antonio. *See Fort Sam Houston*
Freestone County Historical Museum, Fairfield
Frio Pioneer Jail Museum, Pearsall
Galveston Arts Center Gallery, Galveston. *See The Strand*
Galveston County Historical Museum, Galveston
Garza County Historical Museum, Post
Governor's Mansion, Austin. *See State Capitol Complex*
Grayson County Frontier Village, Denison
Gregg County Historical Museum, Longview
Hangar 9—Edward H. White II Memorial Museum, San Antonio. *See Missions Area*
Hardeman County Historical Museum, Quanah
Harlingen Hospital Museum, Harlingen. *See Industrial Air Park*
Harris County Heritage Society, Houston
Harrison County Historical Museum, Marshall
Heart of Texas Museum, Brady
Historic Jail Building, Stanton
Jail Museum, Port Lavaca
Jay Gould Private Railroad Car & Excelsior House, Jefferson
Jefferson Historical Museum, Jefferson
John Jay French Trading Post Museum, Beaumont
Karnes County Museum, Helena
Landmark Inn State Historic Site, Castroville
Landmark Museum, Garland
Layland Museum, Cleburne
Los Nogales Museum, Seguin
Los Portales, El Paso
Lyon Museum, Dublin
Medina County Museum, Hondo
Menardville Museum, Menard
Milam County Historical Museum, Cameron
Millard's Crossing Antiques, Nacogdoches
Mission Concepción, San Antonio. *See Missions Area*
Mission Espíritu Santo, Goliad
Mission Nuestra Señora de la Purísima Concepción de Acuña, San Antonio. *See Missions Area*
Mission San Antonio de Valero, San Antonio. *See Downtown Area*

Mission San Francisco de la Espada, San Antonio. *See Missions Area*
Mission San José y San Miguel de Aguayo, San Antonio. *See Missions Area*
Mission San Juan Capistrano, San Antonio. *See Missions Area*
Moran Historical Museum, Moran
Museum of the Plains, Perryton
Old City Park, Dallas
Old Jail Foundation, Albany
Old Jail Museum, Gonzales
Old Market House Museum, Goliad
Old Mobeetie Museum, Wheeler
Old Nacogdoches University Building, Nacogdoches
Old Post Office Museum, McKinney
Palo Pinto County Pioneer Museum, Palo Pinto
Pioneer Memorial Museum, Fredericksburg
Pioneer Town, Wimberley
Pioneer Village Museum, Lexington
Pioneer Village, Corsicana
Presidio La Bahía Museum, Goliad
Railroad and Pioneer Museum, Temple
Ralls Historical Museum, Ralls
Ranching Heritage Center, Lubbock. *See Texas Tech University*
Rankin Museum, Rankin
Roberts County Museum, Miami
San Antonio Museum of Art, San Antonio
Sherman Historical Museum, Sherman
Skidmore Historical Society Museum, Skidmore
Spanish Governor's Palace, San Antonio. *See Downtown Area*
State Capitol Building, Austin. *See State Capitol Complex*
Strand, Galveston. *See The Strand*
Texarkana Historical Society and Museum, Texarkana
Texas Confederate Museum, Austin. *See State Capitol Complex*
Uvalde's Grand Opera House, Uvalde
Weatherford Depot Museum, Weatherford
Winedale Historical Center, Round Top
XIT Museum, Dalhart
Yorktown Historical Museum, Yorktown

HISTORIC HOUSE MUSEUMS

Alley Log Cabin, Columbus
Anderson-Irvin House Museum, Round Rock
Anson Jones Home, Washington
Antique Dollhouse Museum, Galveston
Art Center, Waco
Ashton Villa, Galveston
Bastrop County Historical Museum, Bastrop
Bayou Bend, Houston
Beaumont Art Museum, Beaumont
Bishop's Palace, Galveston
Black Historical House, Hereford
Brown-Dorsey Medallion Home, Midland
Carson County Square House Museum, Panhandle
Cauthen House, Lampasas
City-County Pioneer Museum, Sweetwater
Copeland Historic Home, Grand Prairie
DeGolyer Estate, Dallas. *See White Rock Lake Park*
DeWitt County Historical Museum, Cuero
Earle-Harrison House, Waco

Neill-Cochran House, Austin
O. Henry Home Museum, Austin
O. Henry House, San Antonio. *See Lone Star Brewery*
Old City Park, Dallas
Old Rock House, Santa Anna
Overland Trail Museum, Fort Davis
Palm House Museum, Round Rock
Perry Homestead Museum, Carrollton
Pioneer Memorial Log House Museum, Houston. *See Hermann Park*
Pioneer Village Museum, Lexington
Pompeiian Villa, Port Arthur
Ranching Heritage Center, Lubbock. *See Texas Tech University*
Sam Rayburn House, Bonham
Samuel May Williams Interpretative Center, Galveston
Schandua House, Fredericksburg
Schilling's Medical Office Museum, Anahuac
Senftenberg-Brandon House, Columbus
Sherman House Museum, Stratford
Sims Log Cabin, Waco
Stark House, Orange
Stationmaster's House Museum, Spearman
Stephenville Historical House Museum, Stephenville
Steves Homestead, San Antonio. *See Downtown Area*
Stillman House Museum, Brownsville
Sturdy's Prairie Box House Museum, Cresson
Terry County Heritage Museum, Brownfield
Theis House, Boerne
Thistle Hill, Fort Worth
Trube House, Galveston
Tsa Mo Ga Memorial Museum, Plains
United Daughters of the Confederacy Museum, Columbus
Varner-Hogg Plantation House, West Columbia
Waller County Historical Museum, Brookshire
White-Pool Historic House, Odessa
Winedale Historical Center, Round Top
Ysleta del Sur Pueblo Museum, El Paso

HISTORIC SITE MUSEUMS

Alabates Flint Quarries, Fritch
Caddo Lake State Park, Karnack
Caddoan Mounds State Historic Site, Alto
Dinosaur Valley State Park, Glen Rose
Eisenhower Birthplace State Park, Denison
Fannin Battleground State Historic Site, Fannin
Fort Belknap Museum, Newcastle
Fort Bliss Replica Museum, El Paso. *See Fort Bliss*
Fort Concho National Historic Landmark, San Angelo
Fort Croghan Museum, Burnet
Fort Duncan Museum, Eagle Pass
Fort Griffin State Historical Park, Albany
Fort Lancaster Visitor Center, Sheffield
Fort Mason Officers Quarters, Mason
Fort McKavett State Historic Site, Fort McKavett
Fort Richardson State Park, Jacksboro
Fort Sam Houston Museum, San Antonio. *See Fort Sam Houston*
Hangar 9—Edward H. White II Memorial Museum, San Antonio. *See Missions Area*
Landmark Inn State Historic Site, Castroville

Magoffin Home State Historic Site, El Paso
Palo Duro Canyon State Park, Canyon
Seminole Canyon State Historical Park, Comstock
Zaragoza Birthplace, Goliad

LOCAL HISTORY MUSEUMS

Alanreed–McLean Area Museum, McLean
Alvin Museum, Alvin
American National Insurance Tower, Galveston
Annie Riggs Memorial Museum, Fort Stockton
Archer County Historical Museum, Archer City
Azle Historical Museum, Azle
Bastrop County Historical Society Museum, Bastrop
Bay Area Museum, Seabrook
Baylor County Historical Museum, Seymour
Baytown Historical Museum, Baytown
Benton Museum, Nacona
Bicentennial City-County Museum, Paducah
Big Bend National Park
Borden County Historical Museum, Gail
Bosque Memorial Museum, Clifton
Brazoria County Historical Museum, Angleton
Burleson County Historical Museum, Caldwell
Burlington–Rock Island Railroad Museum, Teague
Cactus Park and Museum, George West
Caddo Indian Museum, Longview
Callahan County Pioneer Museum, Baird
Carson County Square House Museum, Panhandle
Castro County Historical Museum, Dimmitt
Central Texas Area Museum, Salado
Chambers County Historical Museum, Anahuac
Chappell Hill Historical Society Museum, Chappell Hill
Charlton Museum, Tomball
Childress County Heritage Museum, Childress
City-County Pioneer Museum, Sweetwater
Coleman Museum, Coleman
Collingsworth County Museum, Wellington
Colorado City Museum, Colorado City
Comanche County Historical Museum, Comanche
Copper Breaks State Park, Quanah
Coupland Museum, Coupland
Courthouse-on-the-Square Museum, Denton
Crockett County Museum, Ozona
Crosby County Pioneer Memorial Museum, Crosbyton
Culbertson County Historical Museum, Van Horn
Dallas Historical Society, Dallas. *See Fair Park*
DeWitt County Historical Museum, Cuero
Deaf Smith County Historical Museum, Hereford
Deer Park Independent School District Historical School Museum, Deer Park
East Texas Oil Museum, Kilgore. *See Kilgore College*
Edgewood Heritage Center, Edgewood
Elliot Museum, Spur
Ellis County Museum, Waxahachie
Falls County Historical Museum, Marlin
Fannin County Museum, Bonham
Fayette Heritage Museum, La Grange
Fielder Museum, Arlington

Floyd County Historical Museum, Floydada
Foard County Courthouse Museum, Crowell
Fort Belknap Museum, Newcastle
Fort Bend County Museum, Richmond
Fort Bliss Replica Museum, El Paso. *See Fort Bliss*
Fort Concho National Historic Landmark, San Angelo
Fort Davis National Historic Site, Fort Davis
Fort Duncan Museum, Eagle Pass
Fort Griffin State Historical Park, Albany
Fort Lancaster Visitor Center, Sheffield
Fort Mason Officers Quarters, Mason
Fort McKavett State Historic Site, Fort McKavett
Fort Richardson State Park, Jacksboro
Fort Sam Houston Museum, San Antonio. *See Fort Sam Houston*
Fort Worth Interpretative Center, Fort Worth. *See Sundance Square*
Freestone County Historical Museum, Fairfield
Frio Pioneer Jail Museum, Pearsall
Galveston County Historical Museum, Galveston
Garza County Historical Museum, Post
Geraldine Humphreys Cultural Center, Liberty
Gladys City Boomtown, Beaumont
Grand Saline Public Library and Museum, Grand Saline
Grapevine Historical Museum, Grapevine
Gregg County Historical Museum, Longview
Hale Museum, Winters
Hall County Heritage Hall, Memphis
Hamilton County Museum, Hamilton
Hardeman County Historical Museum, Quanah
Harlingen Hospital Museum, Harlingen
Harrison County Historical Museum, Marshall
Heart of Texas Historical Museum, Brady
Heritage Garden Village, Woodville
Heritage Museum, Big Spring
Heritage Museum, Falfurrias
Heritage Room, Hurst. *See Fort Worth*
Hidalgo County Historical Museum, Edinburg
Hopkins County Museum, Sulphur Springs
Humble Historical Museum, Humble
Hutchinson County Historical Museum, Borger
Iraan Museum, Iraan
Irion County Museum, Mertzon
Itasca Historical Museum, Itasca
Jail Museum, Port Lavaca
Jefferson Historical Museum, Jefferson
John E. Connor Museum, Kingsville
Judge Roy Bean Visitor Center, Langtry
Karnes County Museum, Helena
Kenedy Museum, Kenedy
Kimble Historical Museum, Junction
Knox County Museum, Benjamin
Lamesa–Dawson County Museum, Lamesa
Landmark Museum, Garland
Layland Museum, Cleburne
Limestone County Historical Museum, Groesbeck
Llano County Historical Museum, Llano
Longhorn Museum, Pleasanton
Lubbock County Museum, Shallowater
Lyon Museum, Dublin

McDade Museum, McDade
McMullen County Museum, Tilden
McNamara House, Victoria
Marfa–Presidio County Museum, Marfa
Martin County Historical Museum, Stanton
Mason County Museum, Mason
Matagorda County Historical Museum, Bay City
Medina County Museum, Hondo
Menardville Museum, Menard
Midland County Historical Museum, Midland
Milam County Historical Museum, Cameron
Mills County Historical Museum, Goldthwaite
Mood Heritage Museum, Georgetown
Moore County Historical Museum, Dumas
Moran Historical Museum, Moran
Morris County Historical Museum, Daingerfield
Morton Museum of Cooke County, Gainesville
Museum of the Big Bend, Alpine
Museum of the Llano Estacado, Plainview
Museum of the Plains, Perryton
Neill Museum, Fort Davis
Nordheim Historical Museum, Nordheim
Nuevo Santander Museum, Laredo
O'Donnell Museum, O'Donnell
Old Fort Inglish Replica, Bonham
Old Fort Parker State Historic Site, Groesbeck
Old Jail Museum, Gonzales
Old Mobeetie Museum, Wheeler
Old Post Office Museum, McKinney
Old West Museum, Sunset
Overland Trail Museum, Fort Davis
Palo Pinto County Pioneer Museum, Palo Pinto
Panna Maria Historical Museum, Panna Maria
Pasadena Historical Museum, Pasadena
Patterson Memorial County Library and Museum, Cooper
Pioneer Memorial Museum, Fredericksburg
Pioneer West Museum, Shamrock
Polk County Memorial Museum, Livingston
Port Arthur Historical Museum, Port Arthur
Railroad and Pioneer Museum, Temple
Ralls Historical Museum, Ralls
Rankin Museum, Rankin
Rattlesnake Bomber Base Museum, Pyote
Raymondville Historical and Community Center, Raymondville
Red River Valley Museum, Vernon
Rio Grande Valley Museum, Harlingen
Roberts County Museum, Miami
Runge Museum, Runge
San Saba County Historical Museum, San Saba
Schilling's Medical Office Museum, Anahuac
Schleicher County Museum, Eldorado
Scurry County Museum, Snyder
Shelby County Museum, Center
Sherman Historical Museum, Sherman
Skidmore Historical Society Museum, Skidmore
Slaton Museum, Slaton
Somervell County Museum, Glen Rose
South Plains Museum, Levelland

South Texas Museum, Alice
SPJST Museum, Temple
Stationmaster's House Museum, Spearman
Stonewall Saloon Museum, Saint Jo
Swenson Memorial Museum, Breckenridge
Swisher County Archives and Museum, Tulia
Tahoka Pioneer Museum, Tahoka
Terrell Historical Museum, Terrell
Terry County Heritage Museum, Brownfield
Texana Museum and Library, Edna
Texarkana Historical Society and Museum, Texarkana
Texas Baptist Historical Center Museum, Independence
Tsa Mo Ga Memorial Museum, Plains
Valley Mills Historical Museum, Valley Mills
Van Alstyne Museum, Van Alstyne
Vanishing Texana Museum, Jacksonville
Violet Museum, Violet
Voyer Regional Museum, Honey Grove
Waller County Historical Museum, Brookshire
Weatherford Depot Museum, Weatherford
Weslaco Bicultural Museum, Weslaco
West of the Pecos Museum, Pecos
Wharton County Historical Museum, Wharton
White Deer Land Museum, Pampa
Whitehead Memorial Museum, Del Rio
Wise County Heritage Museum, Decatur
Wolters Memorial Museum, Shiner
XIT Museum, Dalhart
Yorktown Historical Museum, Yorktown
Ysleta del Sur Pueblo Museum, El Paso

MILITARY MUSEUMS

Battleship *Texas*, Houston. *See San Jacinto Battleground*
First Cavalry Museum, Fort Hood. *See Killeen*
Fort Belknap Museum, Newcastle
Fort Bliss Replica Museum, El Paso. *See Fort Bliss*
Fort Concho National Historic Landmark, San Angelo
Fort Davis National Historic Site, Fort Davis
Fort Duncan Museum, Eagle Pass
Fort Griffin State Historical Park, Albany
Fort Lancaster Visitor Center, Sheffield
Fort Mason Officers Quarters, Mason
Fort McKavett State Historic Site, Fort McKavett
Fort Richardson State Park, Jacksboro
Fort Sam Houston Museum, San Antonio. *See Fort Sam Houston*
Hangar 9—Edward H. White II Memorial Museum, San Antonio. *See Missions Area*
History and Traditions Museum, San Antonio. *See Lackland Air Force Base*
Second Armored Division Museum, Fort Hood. *See Killeen*
Third U.S. Cavalry Regimental Museum, El Paso. *See Fort Bliss*
U.S. Army Air Defense Artillery Museum, El Paso. *See Fort Bliss*
U.S. Army Medical Department Museum, San Antonio. *See Fort Sam Houston*
U.S. Army Museum of the Noncommissioned Officer, El Paso. *See Fort Bliss*
U.S.A.F. Security Police Museum, San Antonio. *See Lackland Air Force Base*

NATURAL HISTORY MUSEUMS

Big Bend National Park
Big Thicket Museum, Saratoga
Brazos Valley Museum of Natural Science, Bryan
Brazosport Museum of Natural Science, Brazosport
Buckhorn Hall of Horns, San Antonio. *See Lone Star Brewery*
Dallas Museum of Natural History, Dallas. *See Fair Park*
Davis Mountains State Park, Fort Davis
Guadalupe Mountains National Park
Heard Natural Science Museum, McKinney
Houston Museum of Natural Science, Houston. *See Hermann Park*
Lajitas Museum and Desert Garden, Terlingua
Lake Meredith Aquatic & Wildlife Museum, Fritch
Longhorn Cavern Museum, Burnet
Lost Maples State Natural Area, Vanderpool
Malaquite Beach Visitor Center, Corpus Christi
Monahans Sandhills State Park, Monahans
Moore Nature Sanctuary, Houston
Sea Rim State Park, Sabine Pass
Strecker Museum, Waco. *See Baylor University*
Vines Environmental Science Center, Houston
Welder Wildlife Foundation, Sinton
Wilderness Park Museum, El Paso
Witte Memorial Museum, San Antonio. *See Brackenridge Park*

SCIENCE MUSEUMS

Dallas Aquarium, Dallas. *See Fair Park*
Fiedler Memorial Museum, Seguin
Fort Worth Museum of Science and History, Fort Worth. *See Amon Carter Square*
Harrington Discovery Center, Amarillo
Insights: El Paso Science Center, Inc., El Paso
Lyndon B. Johnson Space Center, Houston
McAllen International Museum, McAllen
McDonald Observatory, Fort Davis
Marine Laboratory and Museum, Rockport
Museum of Medical Science, Houston. *See Hermann Park*
Natural Science Center, Austin
Science Place, Dallas. *See Fair Park*
Texas Tech Museum, Lubbock. *See Texas Tech University*
Western Company Museum, Fort Worth
Wichita Falls Museum and Art Center, Wichita Falls

TRANSPORTATION MUSEUMS

Age of Steam Museum, Dallas. *See Fair Park*
Breckenridge Aviation Museum, Breckenridge
Center for Transportation & Commerce, Galveston. *See The Strand*
Classic Showcase, Kerrville
Confederate Air Force Flying Museum, Harlingen
Elissa, Galveston. *See The Strand*
McAllen Hudson Museum, McAllen
Museum of Aviation Group, Fort Worth
Pate Museum of Transportation, Fort Worth
San Antonio Museum of Transportation, San Antonio. *See Downtown Area*
Silent Wings Museum, Terrell

ZOOS

Abilene Zoological Gardens, Abilene
Dallas Zoo, Dallas
Fort Worth Zoological Park, Fort Worth. *See Forest Park*
Gladys Porter Zoo, Brownsville
Houston Zoological Gardens, Houston
San Antonio Zoological Gardens and Aquarium, San Antonio. *See Brackenridge Park*
Texas Zoo, Victoria

MAPS

MAP I

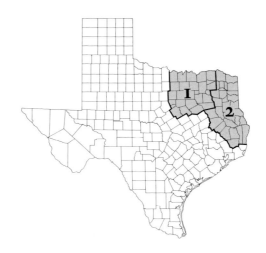

Nocona

Saint Jo

Sunset

Gainesville

Decatur

Denton

Azle

Weatherford

Fort
Worth ⊙

Granbury

Cresson

Glen Rose

Clifton

Itasca

Denison
Sherman

Van Alstyne

McKinney

Plano
Grapevine
Carrollton

Arlington

Cleburne

Waxahachie

Hillsboro

Valley Mills

Bonham

Richardson
Garland
⊙ Dallas
Grand Prairie

Terrell

Corsicana

Honey
Grove

Greenville

Paris

Cooper

Sulphur
Springs

Edgewood

Grand
Saline

MAP 2

Texarkana •

• Daingerfield

Quitman

Jefferson

Karnack •

Longview • Marshall •

Tyler • • Kilgore
• Arp

Henderson •

• Jacksonville

Center •

Rusk •

Palestine Alto • Nacogdoches

• Lufkin

• Livingston Woodville

• Saratoga

MAP 3

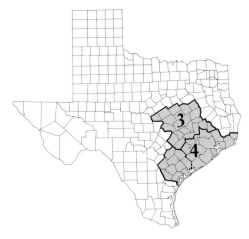

MAP 4

MAP 5

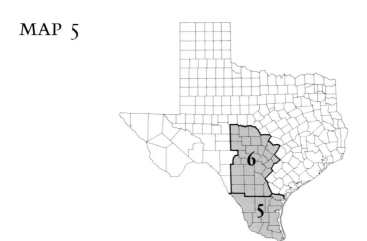

Sinton •

Alice •

Violet •
Corpus Christi •

• Laredo

• Kingsville

Falfurrias •

Raymondville •

Edinburg •
Mission • • Pharr
McAllen • • Weslaco
Mercedes • • Harlingen

Brownsville •

MAP 6

MAP 7

Colorado City

Big Spring

Stanton

Midland

Kermit   Odessa

Wink

Pyote   Monahans

Rankin

Fort Stockton   Iraan

Sheffield   Ozona

San Angelo

Mertzon

Eldorado

Sonora

Langtry

Comstock

Del Rio

Eagle Pass

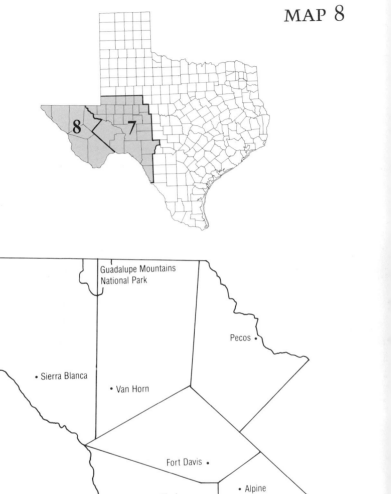

MAP 8

El Paso

Guadalupe Mountains
National Park

Pecos

Sierra Blanca

Van Horn

Fort Davis

Alpine

Marfa

Presidio

Lajitas

Big Bend
National Park

MAP 9

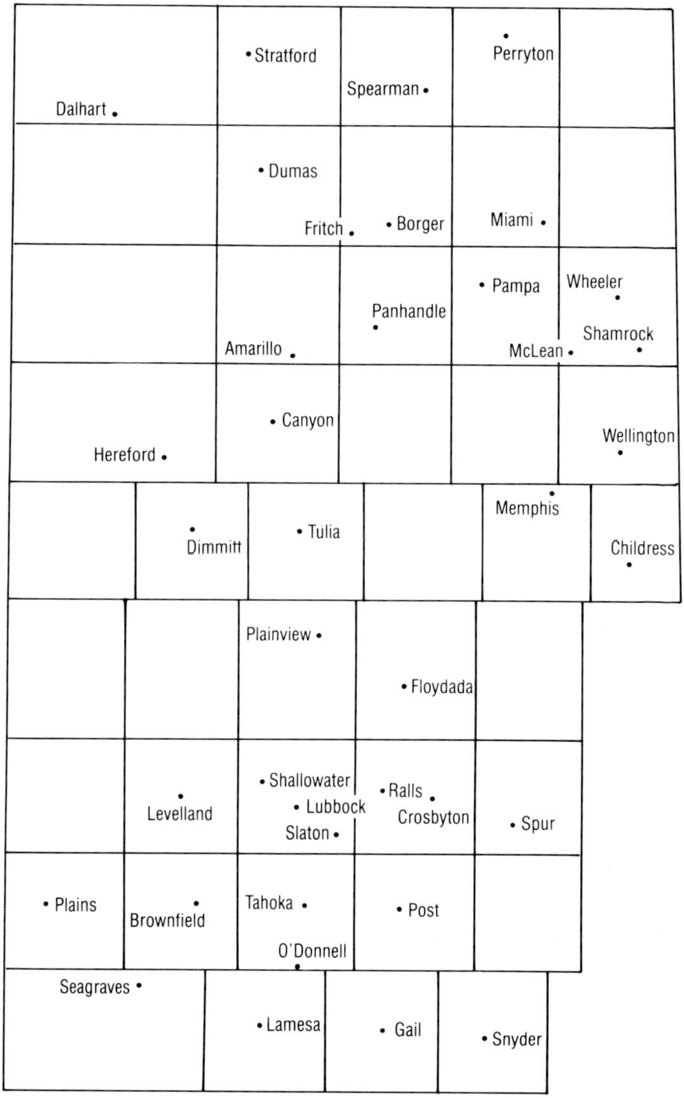

Dalhart •

• Stratford

Spearman •

Perryton

• Dumas

Fritch •   • Borger

Miami •

Amarillo •

Panhandle •

• Pampa

McLean •

Wheeler •

Shamrock •

Hereford •

• Canyon

Wellington •

Dimmitt •

• Tulia

Memphis •

Childress •

Plainview •

• Floydada

Levelland •

• Shallowater

• Lubbock

Slaton •

• Ralls

Crosbyton •

• Spur

• Plains

Brownfield •

Tahoka •

O'Donnell •

• Post

Seagraves •

• Lamesa

• Gail

• Snyder

MAP 10

9

10

• Quanah

• Vernon

Paducah
•

• Crowell

Wichita Falls
•

• Benjamin

• Seymour

Archer City
•

• Haskell

Newcastle
•

Jacksboro
•

Stamford
•

Albany •

Breckenridge
•

Palo Pinto
•

Moran •

Sweetwater
•

Abilene •

• Baird

Stephenville
•
• Dublin

Winters •

Coleman •
Santa Anna

Comanche
•

• Hamilton

Goldthwaite
•

INDEX

porary, 158; Currier & Ives, 249;
Eskimo, 249; historic, 66; Mexican, 158
Proctor, A. Phiminster (sculptor): *The Mus-
tangs,* 23

railroad car: antique, 126; locomotives, 3
Ralls: history of, 211
ranching: history of, 159, 172, 181; in the
Big Bend, 4; in South Texas, 3
Rankin: history of, 212
Ranney, William T. (artist): works by, 94
Rauschenberg, Robert (artist): work by, 98
Ray, J. Henry, Collection, 262
Rayburn, Congressman Sam, 31, 32
Raymondville: history of, 212
Reagan, John H.: papers of, 19
Reaugh, Frank (artist): work by, x
Red River: 163, 197; mentioned, 196;
Prairie Dog Town Fork of, 38
Red River Valley: history of, 142, 262
Red River Wars: mentioned, 218
Redon, Odilon (artist): *The Birth of Venus,*
101; work by, viii; 99, 234
Rembrandt van Rijn (artist): *Portrait of a
Young Jew,* 99
Remington, Frederic (artist): x, 80, 108;
work by, viii, 94, 154, 199, 249
Reno, Jim (sculptor): *The Brand Inspector,*
103
Renoir, Pierre Auguste (artist): work by, 154
Revere, Paul (printmaker): work by, 276
Ribera, Jusepe de (artist): works by, x, 80,
101
Richardson, Sid (collector), viii, 108
Rio Grande: 85, mentioned, 196
Rio Grande Valley: history of, 75, 138, 174,
182; mentioned, 29
Rivera, Diego (artist): work by, 67
Roberts County: history of, 189
Robertson, Sterling C., Colony, 217–218
Roche, Kevin (architect): work by, 110
Rogalla, Herb (artist): work by, 265
Rogers, Peter (artist): mural by, 19
Rothko, Mark (artist): work by, 60, 156
Runge: history of, 216
Rusk County: mentioned, 139; oil in, 170
Russell, Charles M. (artist): work by, viii,
24, 94, 108, 199, 249

Sabine Pass, Battle of, 208
St. Cyprian's Episcopal Church, Lufkin, 181
St. Peter's Novitiate, 191
Salinas, Porfirio (artist): murals by, 233
Salt Creek Massacre, 161
San Antonio: art galleries in, vii; as mu-
seum, xi; Brackenridge Park, 218–220;
museums in, vii, viii

San Antonio River, xi, 223, 226, 238, 240,
241
San Jacinto, Battle of: 18; mentioned, 159,
176, 225, 230
San Marcos River, 243
San Saba County: history of, 244
San Saba River, 188
Santa Anna: history of, 244
Santa Fe and Taos: artists in, 199
Santa Fe Railroad Depot: 126; Perryton,
206; Weatherford, 272; Galveston, 122
Schiwetz, E. M. ("Buck") (artist): works by,
44
Schleicher County: history of, 78
science: botany, 22; geology, 99; marine bi-
ology, 213; zoology, 22
sculpture: American, ix, 94, 154; European,
104, 154; Japanese Buddhist, x; pre-Co-
lumbian, 158
Scurry County: history of, 249
Shahn, Ben (artist): work by, 96
Sheeler, Charles (artist): works by, 94
Shelby County: history of, 41
Shiner: history of, 247
shrunken head, South American, 24
silver: American, ix
slave cabin, 51
Slavonic Benevolent Order of the State of
Texas, 256
Slick, Tom, Collection, 236
Sloan, John (artist): print by, 276
Smith, C. R. (collector), x
Smith, Erwin E. (photographer): work by,
23, 190
Solms-Braunfels, Prince Carl of, 194, 196
Somervell County: history of, 127
South Texas: history of, 172; natural his-
tory of, 49
Southern Pacific Railroad: depot, 213;
Hondo depot, 141; mentioned, 168; 174
Southwest: natural history of, 79, 86
Southwestern Exposition and Fat Stock
Show and Rodeo, Fort Worth, 96, 103
Spaniards in Texas: 7, 33, 75, 129, 157, 179,
193, 207; artifacts, 197; Spanish Fort,
197
Spindletop: 273; Oil Field, 208; Museum,
mentioned, 26
spurmaker, 258
Stamford, history of, 251
Stanley, John Mix (artist): works by, 94, 199
Stark, H. J. Lutcher (collector), ix
Staub, John F. (architect): work by, ix, 25,
142
Stella, Frank (artist): exhibition, x; men-
tioned, 98
Stephens County: airport, 34; history of, 34